Dangerous Obsessions

Dangerous Obsessions

Teenagers and the Occult

ANDREW BOYD

Foreword by David Alton

Marshall Pickering
An Imprint of HarperCollins*Publishers*

Marshall Pickering is an Imprint of
HarperCollins*Religious*
Part of HarperCollins*Publishers*
77–85 Fulham Palace Road, London W6 8JB

First published in Great Britain
in 1996 by Marshall Pickering

1   3   5   7   9   10   8   6   4   2

A catalogue record for this book is
available from the British Library

ISBN 0 00 627811-6

Printed and bound in Great Britain by
HarperCollinsManufacturing Glasgow

Contents

Foreword by David Alton   vi
Introduction   1

1   Through a glass darkly   9
2   In the stars   20
3   On the cards   27
4   Spirit of the glass   35
5   Beyond the veil   57
6   Alternative realities   73
7   Teenage dabblers   86
8   The sorcerer's apprentice   109
9   Pied pipers   127
10 Fade to black   151
11 Dangerous obsessions   169
12 Images of death   180
13 To parents and teachers . . .   193
14 Breaking out   210

Appendix I: Religion and the supernatural today survey   221
Appendix II: Analysis of key data   231
Further material   240
Notes   241

Foreword

Some years ago, Andrew Boyd wrote an excellent and well-researched book on the issue of ritual abuse, entitled *Blasphemous Rumours*. I read it from cover to cover, astounded by its findings and concerned at the lack of action being taken to deal with this very disturbing issue. Unfortunately, since then, the government has only contributed to the general atmosphere of denial on the subject of ritual abuse despite the fact that in a number of criminal trials where convictions were secured, evidence of ritual abuse has surfaced.

Like *Blasphemous Rumours*, *Dangerous Obsessions: Teenagers and the Occult* is prophetic and points to a growing problem that our society ignores at its peril. The increasing interest in the occult, especially by young people, is a disturbing symptom of the spiritual malaise which British society is suffering from. The occult is making insidious advances on many fronts, through some rock music, video nasties, books, comics and even games. It is all too easy to acquire occult paraphernalia and Andrew Boyd is right to point out the dangers for young people which this poses.

It is high time our government and society faced up to the dangers which the occult poses to the spiritual and moral health of this country. It is not simply the concern of 'raving Christian fundamentalists' as the vociferous pro-occult lobby would like to have us believe. This book will be a valuable contribution to the raising of awareness on this issue.

David Alton

Introduction

Into the Shadowlands

I'm Chucky ... wanna play?

A single character from a horror movie has been linked with the appalling murders of a two-year-old boy and a 16-year-old girl.

The accused have included teenagers and two ten-year-old boys. Their common connection has been the seeming obsession with small screen images of death.

The murders of James Bulger and Suzanne Capper have spurred MPs to call for a clampdown on horror films. And the killings have prompted further, welcome, research into the effects of saturation viewing of violence, horror and the occult.

Within weeks of those cases, during the closing stages of writing this book, three teenage members of a German satanic cult were jailed for strangling a 15-year-old classmate; four Greek satanists, including an 18-year-old woman, confessed to murdering a 14-year-old girl and planning human sacrifices; three self-confessed British satanists were jailed for slaughtering animals, and a paedophile trial at Swansea was hearing evidence of children being abused in a ritualistic context.

For the young especially, fascination with the occult can become a dangerous obsession. This book is about its effects. The occult has been defined as that which is 'hidden, secret, sinister, dark or mysterious'.[1] One clergyman has remarked:

People seem to want to know more and more about it. They can never read enough occult books, or get enough occult material. They start moving up towards the harder end of the occult and start believing it all. Then there is a real danger. Depression and fear are often the most common results.[2]

Follow my leader?

Satanism, table-tapping and the spirit of the glass – the staple diet of the horror movie – are exerting a new fascination as a world in political, social and economic upheaval lurches into a new millennium.

And world leaders are showing the way. In Britain, the Royal Family's interest in healing pyramids and the New Age is well documented. According to *Newsweek* magazine the trend is global: US negotiators employed psychic Uri Geller to try to read the minds of their Russian counterparts; in Hong Kong, palm readers and diviners charge 15% commission for giving advance notice about share prices; former Indian prime minister Rajiv Gandhi blamed political setbacks on a curse and staged a ritual to lift it, and when Indonesian President Suharto was told by a spiritist that he should forge closer links with socialist countries, the nation's trading policies shifted as a result.

In an age of uncertainty, a Babel of voices is calling out with often conflicting answers to the age-old question of identity. The cry 'Who am I?' is never more acute than during adolescence – the ripest age for religious conversion.

The occult may excite us, appal us, or stir us to scorn. But whether we regard the subject as an exploration of ultimate reality or superstitious stumblings in the dark, our reaction to the irrational is seldom one of indifference.

Inklings of belief

Whether you have Christian beliefs, like myself, or regard yourself as a sceptic, this book demands no religious convictions and no suspension of incredulity on your part. It simply calls for a shared concern about the effect upon young people of an unhealthy preoccupation with dark and morbid material.

Most of us, it seems, have at least an inkling of belief in psychic and occult phenomena. A survey conducted for Channel 4 TV found that 90% of British citizens accepted as fact some aspect of the paranormal.[3] When that sober newspaper, *The Times*, invited responses from its readers, 64% who wrote in said they were believers. Only 2% declared their open scepticism.[4]

A similar picture was painted in America. A national opinion poll conducted by the University of Chicago reported that 67% believed in the supernatural. Almost half of those claimed to have been in contact with somebody who had died.[5] In another survey more than a third of Americans said they believed astrology had some scientific basis.[6]

Even academics appear to have suspended their scepticism. A poll of US college professors revealed that half considered extra-sensory perception a likely possibility, and almost one in seven took it for a fact.

Teen beliefs

If that's what adults believe, then common sense suggests that children are likely to follow their example. And one might expect to find children less inhibited than their elders when it comes to putting their curiousity to the test.

A survey of schoolchildren was carried out especially for this book in conjunction with leading statistician Dr Leslie Francis of Trinity College, Carmarthen. Of 509 pupils aged 14 to 15 at state secondary schools in England and Northern Ireland, 42% said they were fascinated with the supernatural, and up to 88% said they had been involved in one or more occult practices.

That finding confirms a questionnaire conducted by author and Anglican minister Kevin Logan of almost 300 14- to 15-year-old pupils in Lancashire. Up to 87% said they had experimented with the occult. For most, that involved the ouija board.[7]

A much larger survey was carried out of schoolchildren in Bayern, Germany. It found that occult involvement at some level extended to a third of the 4,000 12- to 16-year-olds questioned. Psychologist Jergen Hilse put it down to curiosity and boredom as well as 'fear of the future, an identity crisis and a desire to rebel'.[8]

Warnings

Warnings about the dangers arising from children's wide-eyed excursions into the occult are being raised by a strange assortment of commentators. These include religious objectors, and even some occult practitioners.

It is evangelical Christians whose voices are most often raised in warning, since they regard the occult as a reality. Religious warnings presuppose some spiritual realm of darkness where individuals who venture into the shadows may be drawn into the night, with its attendant terrors.

But warnings are also being raised by doctors and psychiatrists who say they have identified psychological rather than spiritual dangers, and to whom it has fallen to pick up the pieces. These warnings are rational, rather than religious.

They question the wisdom of conducting a mystery tour into uncharted inner space that can leave the subject lost, frightened and disoriented. They argue that children are becoming disturbed as a result of confronting subconscious elements within themselves that they are emotionally ill-equipped to handle.

The harmful effects described in both waves of warnings – psychological, emotional, spiritual perhaps – may be similar, but different causes are held to blame.

How readily we accept the so-called dangers of the occult will hinge upon our own perception of its reality. Is the power of the occult real? Does it work? If so, how? Or is the occult only as powerful as our belief in its reality? And what takes place in the mind of a young person when curiosity becomes fascination and fascination explodes into obsession?

This book is not concerned with proving the unprovable – that the occult has some objective reality. In a rational world there can be no satisfactory way of measuring a mystery. The occult – if it exists at all – is by definition hidden from our five senses.

It is the subjective reality that occupies us: the potent reality that exists inside a believer's mind. Although we may never witness the cause, we can measure the effects of depression and fear, especially among the young who have plunged into the murky waters of the occult and found themselves out of their depth.

From Britain, doctors and therapists are treating children and young people who are disturbed, depressed, even suffering from mental illness, where an occult connection is claimed. In North America and elsewhere, some teenage suicides are being linked with an obsession with the paranormal.

Court cases

Just how far that curiosity and rebellion can be pushed is now being recorded in the courts. A growing body of evidence is emerging linking occult involvement and drugs with cases of teenage crime. The pathway from one to the other is, it seems, obsession. Young people have been involved in occult-related murders in the United States, Germany, Hungary and the United Kingdom. Teenagers have also taken part in related acts of church and graveyard desecration and animal mutilation.

A small but increasing number of young Americans are now awaiting the death penalty for murder in cases where jurors have been told that the ultimate trip into the dark unknown – satanism – was a feature.

In some states law enforcement officers are being trained specifically to combat occult crime. They say satanism has become a fashion fad, the latest expression of teenage rebellion. They have their own crime category for the perpetrators – the Dabbler – and say the factors behind occult involvement include family breakdown, disillusionment and the ready availability of drugs. American police officer Bill Keahon observed:

> You take a mixture of some very disturbed young people with anti-social behaviour in their background, and you have a daily dose of drugs: angel dust, mescaline and the like. From there you go to kids who sacrifice animals . . . and the next step is murder.[9]

One young man named Stephen Newberry was bludgeoned to death by friends who had become jaded with 'sacrificing' animals and wanted to move on to something bigger. Tommy Sullivan, aged 14, mutilated and murdered his mother with a boy scout knife after making a pact with the devil. That was before he committed suicide by attempting to decapitate himself. Sean Sellers murdered a shop assistant in cold blood, and then went on to kill his mother and stepfather as they slept. He became the youngest inmate on Oklahoma's death row. 'There's such an attraction to satanism,' he explained; 'in power, curiosity, and more importantly, a place to fit in; a need to feel wanted by your peers, to fit in where you don't fit in anywhere else'.[10]

And in eastern and western Europe, too, satanic or occult-related crimes committed mainly by young men have been recorded, albeit on a lesser scale.

Paul Bostock was only 19 when he was convicted of double murder. He left a black magic circle near the mutilated body of his first victim. After returning to her grave to relive his fantasies, he turned on a passer-by and killed again. In his home were dozens of demonic and sadistic drawings. The prosecution drew the court's attention to his interest in 'horror, the occult and black magic' and said Bostock had 'worshipped the devil'. That was in Britain.

And there are other cases. The examples are so extreme, so numbing, that we can find ourselves forgetting to question whether the occult was the cause of the disturbance in these young lives, or merely a symptom. It certainly provides a convenient scapegoat for those who would wish to exonerate society from bearing any blame.

A spiritual vacuum?

Rachel Storm, writing in *The Independent*, comments:

> Many attribute this increased interest to the spiritual needs of a materialist and power-obsessed age: rather than to turn to a low-image religion, the spiritually hungry . . . turn to the occult which promises power and excitement.[11]

Mike Morris, Secretary for Social Affairs with the British-based Evangelical Alliance says:

> I think we've got a great spiritual vacuum. The Church has largely lost its role in offering spiritual direction. Materialism has taken hold and many people have found that unsatisfying. So in a search for spiritual answers to their lives and spiritual experience, the Church is seen as outdated, outmoded and irrelevant. Other forms of spiritual experience are being investigated and the occult with all the excitement attached to it draws people into a growing interest in the darker side.

There's certainly plenty of material around to stimulate that interest. If there's a vacuum, then occult material is rushing in to fill it. Readership for horror and the occult doubled in the eighties. By the turn of the decade demand was put at some 20 to 30 million volumes. By 1993, 20% of all books dealt with the esoteric or occultic. The following year, a survey of teenage readers found that 65% of boys and 70% of girls read horror books, while 58% of girls said it was their preferred reading.

For the growing number who would rather watch than read, roughly one in every 16 videos for hire in high street stores features an occult-related theme. A tally of tapes on offer in a small family video outlet found 109 such movies, including *Child's Play* 2 and 3, prominently displayed only a fortnight after being linked with the killing of two-year-old James Bulger.

In the film *Rosemary's Baby* the role of the devil was played by Anton Szandor LaVey, founder of the San Francisco-based First Church of Satan, and author of the bestseller *The Satanic Bible*. His book advocates extreme self-indulgence, but draws the line at criminality. Even so, some US law enforcement officers cite *The Satanic Bible* as a prized possession of teenagers involved in occult-related crime.

Ritual abuse

In 1994, a British Health Department inquiry acknowledged that it had found three substantial cases involving the ritual abuse of children, which it put down to the work of paedophiles. But other reports suggest that children are being ritually abused in two distinct settings. Firstly, that children and young people are being enticed by paedophiles using the lure of drugs, drink, or a roof for the night, or by convincing demonstrations of so-called occult powers. Secondly, that some children are growing up in abusing households where a perverted and criminal form of religion has been the family practice for generations.

Any rational person of a sound and healthy mind will find such claims outlandish, unbelievable, and probably offensive. But in the light of recent court cases, parents and teachers equally cannot afford to ignore them.

Our personal beliefs about the occult, and even the beliefs of the perpetrators, are irrelevant if abusers are cynically manipulating children's own beliefs in the supernatural to frighten and control them in order to molest them. Jan van Wagtendonk, a consultant in child sexual abuse for the National Children's Home, has admitted:

> Children are telling us about seeing babies killed, of killing animals, drinking urine and eating human flesh. I have been a social worker for seventeen years. It was hard enough to deal with physical abuse and then sexual abuse. When I heard at first about ritual abuse I just did not want to know. It was unimaginable.

The unimaginable and the unthinkable. Fears of ritual abuse and warnings of a witchhunt, talk of the devil, demons and the paranormal make for a hubble bubble of heady material. And here we have a problem. The very subject carries a potent emotional charge: there is a reluctance to believe that young people are being abused in such a bizarre manner.

The occult has an uncanny way of stirring up our curiosity while threatening to exhume our innermost fears. It confronts our basic religious and rational convictions and tilts at our concept of reality.

It is a subject that we would prefer to ignore. But where children are involved we can afford no such luxury. We have no other option but to face the issue and brace ourselves against overreaction. It's a tall order, but let's see how we get on . . .

1

Through a glass darkly

Understanding the occult

> It's basically a thirst for power and more importance. People get
> hooked on it.
>
> Canon Dominic Walker

So why do some teenagers wade out of their depths into the treach-
erous currents of destructive occultism? If we're to understand them,
we have to venture to understand what it is that is exerting such a
powerful fascination – the nature of the occult itself. As voyages of
discovery go, there's none more bizarre . . .

The *Encyclopaedia Britannica* defines the occult as 'theories,
practices and rituals based on esoteric knowledge, especially alleged
knowledge about the world of spirits and unknown forces of the
universe'.[1]

Dr Ron Enroth, Professor of Sociology at Westmont College,
Santa Barbara, California, says the occult 'may be said to have the
following distinct characteristics: (1) the disclosure and communication of information unavailable to humans through normal means
(beyond the five senses); (2) the placing of persons in contact with
supernatural powers, paranormal energies or demonic forces; (3) the
acquisition and mastery of power in order to manipulate or influence other people in certain actions.'[2]

Revealing the hidden

The occult may chill us or thrill us, but whatever our personal beliefs
about it, our concern here is for those who *do* believe, for whom
occult practices do have some meaning because they appear to work
for *them*.

No book could provide definitive proof that occult practices do or
do not work. It's a matter of belief. What matters to us is whether the
attempt to find out can be harmful to young, impressionable people.

For some, the occult must forever retain its magic and remain
mysterious, defying each and any attempt to explain away its

secrets. For others, who feel ill at ease with the supernatural, the word 'unexplained' may have a more comfortable ring. With a word, the emphasis has shifted us away from the unsettlingly irrational towards the reassuringly empirical, towards observable effects for which science may eventually discover a cause.

Each approach to the occult, be it rational or irrational, explores the suggestion that a source of power exists to effect change to ourselves, our environment or others, in a way that has yet to be explained by conventional wisdom. Where those approaches differ is in their view of where the source of that power lies. That difference is crucial. The famous spoonbender Uri Geller has said, 'We all have some kind of paranormal ability within us . . . some kind of energy; some kind of a power inside our mind.' On the other hand, the medium Doris Collins claims, 'There's a great deal of energy in this world and very few people know how to use it. I'm just a channel for the use of it.'³

Is the so-called power of the occult simply the power of personal conviction? Or does the ability to effect change go beyond the dynamic of positive thinking? If so, where is the seat of that power? What is its source? Is it a psychological, scientific, or a spiritual reality?

Whether we are inclined to view occult phenomena as fact or fantasy, our attitude towards it will probably fall somewhere within the following three categories: *rational, quasi-scientific* or *supernatural*.

Rational explanations

1. *Fraud*. This is the view of the sceptic, who holds that demonstrations of occult powers are fake. He sees them as nothing more than clever conjuring tricks to entertain and impress the gullible, to gain power, respect, or financial reward. Sometimes the intention can be well-meaning. Dr Kurt Koch cites one such example:

> A doctor living in a town just south of Hanover had the following way of successfully removing warts. He would stroke the warts of the patients at the same time murmuring the first few lines of the Odyssey . . . since the patients were unable to understand the meaning of the quotation it worked like a magic spell and the warts would disappear.⁴

2. *Chance.* The do-it-yourself tarot card reader may achieve success through a combination of coincidence and self-delusion. Failures are forgotten while every success is marvelled at and shared around. Hazard enough guesses and sooner or later some predictions must come true.
3. *Wish-fulfilment or fear-fulfilment.* This is where we subconsciously bring to pass the hopes and fears that fill our minds and so make some predictions come true. It is nothing more than self-delusion taken to extremes.

Quasi-scientific explanations

Those who believe the occult has some quasi-scientific basis argue that there are some occurrences for which science and psychology have yet to provide explanations.

4. *Paranormal.* There are natural forces at work that scientists have yet to define and laws that have yet to be formulated. An example would be the occult practice of dowsing, the theory that a diviner can detect the presence of water or minerals with a forked twig, which will twitch or dip when passed over the correct location. Some believe the presence of water is exerting an as yet unexplained influence, like the tug of a magnetic field. This quasi-scientific explanation cannot be applied to extensions of that practice, such as map dowsing, where an object such as a pendulum is swung over a map to locate a missing object.
5. *Psychological.* This explanation argues that psychic powers are not supernatural but operate by a process of super-intuition. Information is processed and deductions made at an unconscious level, pretty much like the charlatan's inspired guesswork.

   Psychologist Carl Jung theorized that what people described as spirits could be exteriorizations of the unconscious: outward projections of our powerful inner fears, conflicts and desires.

   Some say Jung moved closer towards accepting an external spiritual reality in his later years. He wrote: 'Those who are not convinced should beware of naively assuming that the whole question of spirits and ghosts has been settled and that all manifestations of this kind are meaningless swindles.'[5]
6. *Parapsychological.* The word *psyche* is from the Greek for breath, life or soul. It is the essence of the individual. Some who believe in psychic powers acknowledge their source as

the hidden potential of the human mind. Jung described the conscious mind, the part that breaks surface, as merely the tip of the iceberg. Little is known about what lies unseen below.

What is usually described as psychic phenomena includes telepathy, telekinesis (the ability to move material objects), healing, premonitions, etc. Some refer to these as abilities or powers, others as gifts. The distinction is important, as the word 'gift' implies a giver, and suggests psychic powers may be divine in origin rather than latent within the individual.

Some see poltergeist activity as a manifestation of the inner energy of a susceptible individual who is going through a period of disturbance. This is often associated with anxious, pre-pubescent children and is said to disappear when the reason for the stress is removed.

Quasi-religious explanations

The quasi-religious view is based upon belief in a separate spirit dimension. There are three distinct streams of thought on this. Firstly, that the spirits who are called on for help and information are human beings who have 'departed'. Secondly, that there are intelligent, non-human spirit entities who may be asked to provide power as well as knowledge. Thirdly, that the power comes from an impersonal spirit-force or forces.

7. *Spiritistic.* This view believes that contact can be made with the spirits of the dead via channelling and mediumship. At its most mundane this claims to offer reassurance and guidance to relatives through contact with the spirits of their loved ones. At its most advanced it is claimed that spirit guides who had insight in this life and who now possess some loftier understanding are willing to impart their knowledge through the channeller for the benefit of humanity.
8. Non-human spirit beings. These are said to be gods, spirits, demons or elementals. Practices include the conjuring of demons to do the magician's bidding, the casting of spells in the name of these spirits, or, more commonly, consulting the spirit of the glass via the ouija board.

    The practice of appealing to intelligent non-human spirit beings extends to some branches of witchcraft and satanism, though different systems of ritual invocation are used and different deities are called upon.

9. *Life-force*. There are three views: either belief that occult powers are attained by attuning to a god-force which indwells all creation; or by realizing that man himself is a deity and therefore the possessor of divine powers; or that occult powers are a gift from God himself.

These are just attempts to rationalize what occultists see as a hidden, mysterious world which is only capable of comprehension by the adept. In other words, if you want to find out more you have to take the plunge.

And if you already feel you are floundering, spare a thought for the 14-year-old who's trying to get his head round these ideas! I said it would be a strange voyage . . . and the most bizarre is yet to come.

Not every explanation of occult phenomena can be fitted neatly under a single heading. A degree of overlap is inevitable. Take, for example, the *magical* viewpoint, as described by Peter Ackroyd:

> The central beliefs of modern magic are that thought can affect matter and that the trained imagination can alter the physical world, that all aspects of the universe are interdependent, that the trained observer will be able to discover correspondencies and connections between hitherto disparate phenomena.[6]

This view is not so much mind over matter, as mind *with* matter. The magician acknowledges an essential unity of all things, spiritual and material. He then exercises his will in a way that is in sympathy with the life force in order to bring about the change he desires. The seat of power is said to be both within and without, because all things are one.

The religious dimension

Occult practices take on a recognizably religious dimension where the source of power is thought to be external to the believer. This is where the energy to make things happen (to make spells work or to see into the future) is believed to come from some spirit or force which has to be summoned through the use of rituals.

The Pagan Federation, for example, both personalizes and deifies Nature. Members hold to the following: 'Acceptance of the polarity of deity, the reality of both Goddess and God. Active participation in the cosmic dance of Goddess and God, female and male.'

Witchcraft, with its appeals to the Goddess and Horned God is clearly a religion. On the other hand, exponents of ESP and telepathy – and some satanists – argue that the power to make things happen comes not from *someone out there*, but from the human mind, will or psyche. Rational satanists see Satan not as a spiritual being but a projection of the satanist's own ego and desires. So not all occultists believe in a god, nor would they regard themselves as observing a system of faith or worship, which is how religion is usually defined.

So we can draw a line between religious and non-religious occultists. But the distinction between the occult religions and the mainstream religions can be tricky. After all, Judaism, Christianity, Islam and others all appeal to a deity in the hope of achieving much the same as the magician: to effect change in the material world and the life of the believer.

One clue is implicit in the word 'occult', which carries the sense of something hidden, secret and mysterious. The suggestion is of esoteric practices to be penetrated only by the initiate and performed only by the adept. The feel is of activities that take place after nightfall or behind closed doors.

Some religious occultists would argue that prejudice forces the concealment of their faith. Proponents of the mainstream religions are likely to counter by saying that God is light and in him is no darkness at all, so their practices are, and should be, open to public view.

Religions which worship a single supreme God are unanimous in their condemnation of many occult practices, which they regard as drawing upon the powers of darkness. Where there is less agreement is over precisely what constitutes occult activity. This is a theme to which we will return later.

Still confused? So are occultists. There is no single, unified view of the occult even amongst its practitioners. The occult has many branches, stemming from a variety of traditions. Each has its own notion of ultimate reality, and its own way of explaining the force that is said to power occult practices.

Even religious satanists, who believe in a devil, are divided as to his nature and even his name. Some see Satan as good, and claim he has been misrepresented. Others acknowledge that his character is unrelentingly evil and exercise a conscious choice to celebrate that fact.

So what actually powers the occult has been put down to charlatanism; fearful or wishful thinking; the power of the unconscious mind; natural laws that have yet to be defined or understood by science; communication with the spirits of departed human beings; communication with intelligent non-human spirit beings; or the actualization of life force, which some regard as impersonal and others personalize as one or many deities.

By now, the image in our crystal ball is either becoming clearer or we may find ourselves swirling in a vortex of relative and divergent views and no nearer to understanding!

But does it work?

If we cannot say with certainty what the occult is, then can we say that it works? Perhaps like electricity, what we cannot see can best be described by observing its effects.

There have been many attempts to test occult phenomena to try to demonstrate or disprove its reality, but the argument has yet to move decisively beyond doubt or belief and towards quantifiable, evidential proof. Peter Brookesmith remarks, 'The trouble is that most of the "evidence" concerning divination systems is . . . anecdotal, impressionistic and unsatisfactory, because it lacks all statistical validity.'[7] Susan Blackmore says, 'Psychical research has failed . . . We have no viable theory to account for the supposed phenomena . . . We cannot produce or control them. We are still asking more or less the same questions we were a hundred years ago . . . We have landed in a blind alley.'[8]

Four steps to heaven?

The practising occultist has to make a series of assumptions that amount to steps of faith. The first, and most crucial, is a belief in the possibility of an occult dimension, and a willingness to experiment to find it.

What happens next will determine whether the believer grows sceptical, or increasingly convinced of the reality of the occult. And this will determine whether he falls for the second assumption, that occult practices – from casting spells to fortune-telling – get results.

Once that step is taken, a third assumption has to be made, concerning the power that drives the occult and makes it 'work'. This is to do with the location of that power – whether it is to see into the future, levitate, or move the glass on the ouija board. The energy must come either from within the individual or from some source outside of him.

If the source of occult power is believed to be external, then a fourth assumption has to be made concerning its nature. With the exception of 'black' magic, which is worked only for the gain of the magician often at another's expense, practising occultists commonly believe that the source of their power is neutral, like electricity. Or they see it as benign and dedicated to the service of humanity. It's a final step of faith that could be a fatal assumption.

The problem is, no-one has yet found a way of proving any of it. So the argument is forced inexorably into a religious corner – any discussion about the occult inevitably falls back onto a question of *belief*.

All we can be certain of is conviction itself. So of one thing we can be clear: an individual's concept of reality will affect his view of himself and his place in the scheme of things. His beliefs and the self-image that results from them are likely to have a significant bearing on his well-being and behaviour – especially during his formative years. Consultant psychiatrist Dr Roger Moss writes, 'People's mental state can be seriously affected by contact with the occult, particularly among the vulnerable. This a factor we have to reckon with and study more closely.'

The *Daily Mail* reckons 'at least 50% of school children dabble in the occult at some stage or other'. That compares with a figure of 88% for our own survey and the 87% recorded among school-children in Lancashire. However you read it, fascination for the occult – and the next step of experimentation – runs like a river through childhood.

While it would be absurd to suggest that paddling at the edges of the supernatural always results in a headlong plunge into satanism, some children can still find themselves floundering in the shallows.

Doctors' warnings

Consultant psychologist Dr Stuart Checkley has treated clients whose involvement in the occult has left them in need of psychiatric treatment. He says symptoms include depression, hallucinations and loss of control. At its most extreme the damage to the personality can resemble schizophrenia.

Another psychiatrist, Dr Michael David, has treated a number of patients for depressive symptoms which he says have arisen as a result of occult involvement. 'Such people are very often vague, generally miserable, anxious and discouraged without knowing why.' In some cases he has been able to trace the symptoms back to direct involvement with spiritualism, the tarot or black magic.[10]

Psychiatrists' warnings are nothing new. Twenty years ago, Dr Richard Mackarness, then assistant psychiatrist at Park Prewitt Hospital, Basingstoke, wrote in *The Practitioner*: 'Just as psychiatrists are seeing more patients for drug abuse, so a number of patients involved with occult practices are coming into mental hospitals. Some . . . are severely disturbed and do not respond well to orthodox psychiatric treatment.'[11]

Gordon Wright has been counselling occult victims for more than 20 years, including many who have attempted suicide:

> There's a preoccupation with death. The words spelt out by the ouija board are often concerned with death and blood. There is a morbid curiousity, a drawing towards the idea that death has some kind of lure or enticement.
>
> I've spoken to many adults and children who have attempted suicide or have mutilated themselves. They have described not an impulsive act but something they feel almost drawn to like a magnet. It becomes obsessional: something they almost have got to do. And this has been linked with the occult.
>
> There could be other factors as well, but involvement in the occult might well be a precipitating factor that triggers off behavioural change.

The occult up-ends conventional values, systems of belief and concepts of our own identity. That in itself cannot be wholly to blame for related cases of mental disorder, but some doctors liken experimenting with the occult to opening a floodgate, which can allow mental illness to overcome the potentially unstable.

And they suggest that those most prone to depression, introspection or instability are most at risk. Why and how occult involvement may trigger instability has yet to be adequately explained by psychiatry, but in wrestling to understand it, we need to consider the important role played by the ego.

Ego trip

The ego is the part of me that *is* me. It contains my concept of reality and the sense of my own individuality. It is who I am and how I fit in to the world around me. The ego is sometimes described as the adult within whose job is to keep under control the child within. This inner child is the id, the instinctive, impulsive, irrational element of my personality, which cavorts through a fantasy realm of desires, dreams and terrors. It follows that if we take the lid off our perception of reality and our concept of identity, then the darker stuff deep within may bubble up and spill over. Dr Stuart Checkley writes:

> The ego is the intelligent adult part of the mind. It keeps the child within from running wild all over the house. In exposing oneself to the occult, the ego is actually giving up its responsibility for screening out what comes in: the fantasies, free associations, dreams and nightmares. The major difficulty would be madness, and the product of insanity could drive one to kill oneself.

So it would seem that some individuals who step into the occult, with its ill-defined, confusing and often contradictory concepts of reality, may lose themselves within a supernatural shadowland of myth, magic and morbidity. They may be working to actively undermine their own psychological well-being.

Dr Checkley would extend his warning to any pursuit that involves bypassing the ego to open up another layer of the mind. And that would include the practice of transcendental meditation, which is often promoted as therapeutic. He claims that one of his clients suffered serious mental disorder as a result of TM, which required her to empty her mind of everything.

In Dr Checkley's estimate, 3–5% of his many outpatients had suffered from problems associated in some way with occult practices: 'I have seen patients whose involvement with relatively minor forms of the occult has caused them to suffer mental illness.'

As a Christian, Dr Checkley has a religious objection to the occult. But no accusation of bias could be levelled against Nottingham psychotherapist Norman Vaughton. He professes no religious belief, yet has had to glue back together a number of personalities that have come unstuck through occult involvement. In his experience, fascination with the occult has taken those who may be already teetering and tipped them over the edge. They include 'adults who may be already borderline in their own grip on reality, and children whose idea of reality is not strong in any case. If they get drawn into fortune-telling, clairvoyancy, ouija boards – any of those sort of things that may blur their perceptions of what is real and unreal – it is going to be confusing and potentially damaging to them.'

Psychologist Dr Dale Griffith of Tifflin, Ohio, regularly lectures health care and law enforcement officials in the United States. His own research lends support to what is now being said in the United

Kingdom, as he explained to the magazine *Illinois Medicine*: 'In my experience, over 60 per cent of adolescents in drug and alcohol treatment programs have been involved in some aspect of the occult.'[12]

Occultists' warnings

Even among practitioners of the occult who are convinced of its authenticity and power and who advocate its use, there are those who raise their voices in caution. One of them has warned: 'Anything that raises power can attract people who feel unstable in themselves. The power is very powerful and needs to be treated with respect.'[13] Another has said: 'We realize that handling the occult and occult matters is like handling volatile chemicals.'[14]

Bristol clairvoyant John Starkey spent two years researching what he described as 'the dark side of the occult'. His principal concern was witchcraft and satanism, but his warning extended to other occult practices. His conclusion: 'Do not be tempted to dabble in the occult . . . or any practice that you may not be certain about. They will rot your mind.'[15]

Divination or fortune-telling is the soft end of the occult. It is where most people begin, and where most are likely to stop. But the thirst for knowledge of what the future may hold could have driven some to pick up a poisoned chalice.

2

In the stars

Astrology

> A woman appeared at a police station and stated that she had just shot and killed her son. An astrologer had told her in a written horoscope that her son would never regain his full mental health. Wanting to save this boy from a terrible future, she had killed him. The woman was arrested and finally sentenced after a long trial.
>
> Kurt Koch[1]

No magazine would be complete without its page of horoscopes, it seems. The widespread popularity of 'your stars' means astrology is most people's first point of contact with the occult. What holds true about attitudes to this system of divination also applies to many other occult beliefs.

This book aims neither to vindicate nor debunk belief in the occult, but to point out the possible dangers to young people of becoming involved in occult practices. If we're to understand the dangers, then we must understand how some of these practices work. And that could mean slaying a few sacred cows.

If debunking were the intention, then astrology, everybody's favourite 'dabble', would seem a soft target. In the words of British astronomer Patrick Moore, 'Astrology proves one scientific fact only – that there is a fool born every minute.'[2] Or, as America's self-styled psychic investigator, James Randi, puts it: 'Astrology is the oldest form of claptrap to be foisted on the civilized world.' And with tongue in cheek this seasoned debunker adds: 'but of course the main reason I don't believe in astrology is that I'm a Sagittarius, and we're known to be very hard to convince of such things.'[3]

It's the boast of astrologers that their particular superstition is the priestly science of the ancient world. And today's technology has done nothing to diminish its popularity. The Babylonians, Egyptians, Greeks, Romans, Indians and Mayans were among the ancient races who believed their fates rested with the gods who ruled in the heavens.

The precedent established by the Babylonian King

Nebuchadnezzar in the 6th century BC has been pursued throughout history and across the globe. Elizabeth I and Edward VII are said to have turned to astrologers for guidance, as did Napoleon. Indian politician Indira Gandhi staged her parliamentary elections at the advice of her astrologers – and blamed them when she lost power in 1977. And US President Reagan's wife Nancy made sure her husband stuck to the schedule shown in the stars – especially when it came to venturing onto an aeroplane.

They would appear to be in good company. *Time* magazine reckoned there were at least 185,000 practising astrologers in the USA, while Britain, according to *The Independent*, has some 250 full-time astrologers and thousands of part-timers.

Many are harnessing high technology. One company produces 10,000 computerized horoscopes per month and there's a growing market for astrological financial newsletters.[4] In 1987 a group of businessmen using astrology predicted the stockmarket crash, switched shares into gold and saved a fortune. Yet when astrology is subjected to scientific scrutiny it usually fails dismally.

In San Francisco, 118 subjects were asked to identify their own horoscopes from a batch cast by experts. Dr John Maddox, Editor of *Nature*, wrote: 'they couldn't recognize their own charts any more accurately than by chance . . .' Later the experts were given the opportunity to redeem themselves. Thirty top astrologers were invited to pick out the personality profiles of people for whom they had full astrological information. They still did no better than you or I could achieve at random.

Authors Bob and Gretchen Passantino offer a psychological, rather than a scientific explanation for astrology's enduring popularity:

1. Predictions are usually so general or so vague as to be untestable ('Something bad will happen'); 2. The forecast predicted is a safe bet ('You will pay more taxes this year'); 3. The prediction is common sense ('Don't make rash decisions'); 4. The recipient makes the prediction self-fulfilling ('Don't leave home today'); 5. The prediction comes right by chance.[5]

What it boils down to is wishful thinking or wish-fulfilment. Anyone determined to believe in astrology will remember the successes but filter out the failures. The few predictions that 'come true' will prove the point, while the majority of unfulfilled predictions will be screwed up with yesterday's paper and forgotten. On the basis of coincidence alone just enough predictions are likely to come true to permanently whet the appetite.

Alternatively, if a reader is convinced of the power of the prediction, then simply reading it and keeping it in mind, coupled with her fears or hopes about what she believes might happen, could work powerfully to bring those words to pass. Kurt Koch says, 'The person who seeks advice from the astrologer comes with a certain readiness to believe the horoscope. This predisposition leads to an autosuggestion to order his life according to the horoscope and thus contribute to its fulfilment.'[6]

So what happens, then, when a serious believer in such stuff visits a professional practitioner in whom she also has faith and is told that she is going to die or become seriously ill? At a darker level are those who may find their lives clouded by fear as a result of someone's potent prediction.

Two examples of this are cited by Christian counsellor Audrey Harper. The stars told one woman that it could be dangerous to go out. She ignored the warning and had a minor accident. Coincidence? Almost certainly, but an unnerving one. She was badly shaken. To be on the safe side, she decided not to go out of the house unless her horoscope said it was clear to do so. Few horoscopes are that specific. As a result she developed agorophobia and became housebound. Absurd? Of course. Unreal? Not to her.

A recently widowed woman was trying to sell her house, to make a fresh start somewhere smaller. Feeling vulnerable and in need of guidance, she went for an astrology reading. Under no circumstances, she was told, should she sell her house for three years. Dutifully, she took it off the market and resigned herself to waiting it out in her painfully familiar surroundings. After three years had elapsed, the market had slumped, the house was worth less than it had been bought for and the delay had cost her thousands of pounds. The stress of remaining in this unhappy place and losing part of her life savings also cost her her peace of mind. She ended up under psychiatric treatment.[7]

But tales of casualties who fall by the wayside are unlikely to deter died-in-the-wool stargazers who continue to insist that this occultic technique delivers the goods – and does so consistently.

Those who refute astrology will argue that predictions can only be effective if you want them – or fear them – badly enough to make them happen. But if, as some argue, astrology works by some other means, then what could that be? Are astrological predictions powered by some psychic or intuitive ability, or does the source of the astrologer's knowledge lie elsewhere?

Some believe that divination operates through conscious or unconscious contact with spirit forces. These relay information only they could know to a person who is sensitive to them. Some believe astrology, when results go beyond mere guesswork, works in such a way – the astrologer is acting as a medium. Like a radio set, he or she must be sensitive enough to pick up what is being sent and have the ability to tune in to receive the message. And for every message there has to be a messenger.

Charles Strohmer, an expert astrologer who renounced his craft, claims the receiver's mind is drawn to a part of the astrological chart that relates to a detail in the client's life. The agency that is doing the drawing, he claims, is actually a familiar spirit: 'This is a detail that a familiar spirit is privy to. It is the spirit that is somehow doing the "focusing". The focusing is influenced not by a planet . . . but by a deceptive invisible being.'

Strohmer is now a practising Christian and sees his successful past predictions in a new light. Today he has radically different ideas about the source of the information he received.

Conventional Christian teaching acknowledges a spiritual reality. Man is seen as a creature with body, personality and spirit. A spirit realm exists beyond the material world of our five senses. This realm is inhabited by spirit beings and is divided unequally into light and darkness. On the one hand are God's superior and ultimately triumphant forces of light, and on the other, a lesser hierarchy of dark spiritual powers. These have turned against their Creator and, left to their own devices, grow increasingly corrupt.

These siren spirits seek to seduce man away from God to follow them in spiritual rebellion. They do so by grasping any open hand that reaches into their own sphere of influence. So those who ignore or who are in ignorance of the clear biblical injunctions against occult practices, and who persist in trying to draw back the veil that separates the hidden realm from ours, may find themselves making contact with malevolent spirits.

But any would-be seducer who delivered his come-on line stark naked and leering would be doomed to frustration. So these spiritual predators avoid being too obvious about their intentions. They put on a smiling face and operate by deception, masquerading as benevolent guides and helpers. Those who take the first faltering steps towards them are lured deeper with offers of insight, knowledge and power.

The aim of these seducing spirits, according to standard Judaeo/Christian teaching, is to enslave those who have themselves sought mastery of the occult. Their ultimate intention is to turn aspirant adepts into spiritual pimps; people who will draw others into the same process of seduction, leading to their ultimate spiritual destruction.

This concept of spiritual seduction is one reason for the concern of church ministers such as Kevin Logan, author of *Paganism and the Occult*. He believes the risks run right through the whole gamut of occult practice:

> People like us Christian ministers are having to counsel young people time and time again. The soft stuff, the horoscope, the tarot cards . . . draws them into this power that they don't understand that they can't control. They go from bad to worse, and they lose the ability to be people in their own right and to make choices. I would like to say to youngsters today: don't start on that path, because it is a very slippery slope that ends in disaster.[8]

Ian Thain developed an interest in astrology in his teens. He went on to become the director of a computer software business in Oxfordshire. In his adolescence, he learnt what he could about the subject from books that were readily available – though in smaller quantities than today – and found that the horoscopes he was drawing up were becoming increasingly accurate. Eventually, he says, he achieved an 80% success rate.

Like Charles Strohmer, he is persuaded from experience that astrology works, and has grown equally convinced that it is dangerous and should be avoided. He explains:

> There are two sides to horoscopes. There's the character analysis side and there's the predictive side. It's not difficult to be right about character analysis because you know the people and you can selectively tune and filter what you tell them. Even when you don't know them you can guess by looking at them. But on the predictive side you have to be right, and I used to be able to predict things which would happen in my own life and in the lives of others.

Quite a claim, but how does he say it worked? He continues:

> The underlying theory of astrology is that the universe is evolving as a whole and that human affairs evolve as part of it. By looking at the motions of the sun, the moon and the planets with respect to one another we can see a corresponding trend in affairs among people. One is an indicator of the other.
>
> But astrology is not just a matter of drawing charts, measuring angles and taking inferences from positions. The practice involves drawing upon psychic powers in order to produce an interpretation of a horoscope.

This is where the real success comes, because you're not just looking at figures in a book [to make predictions] any more than somebody using a crystal ball is actually using the ball to produce images. They're simply a way of tapping psychic power, and it's the psychic powers that you develop that give you your success rate.

Ian holds the view that psychic abilities are latent in everyone, but draws the line at developing them. He has become convinced that to do so would be highly dangerous. Since becoming a Christian he has felt it necessary to renounce occult practices and lay aside his psychic abilities.

Ask him why and he will quote the Bible off by heart: 'Let no one be found among you . . . who practises divination or sorcery, interprets omens, engages in witchcraft, or casts spells, or who is a medium or spiritist or who consults the dead. Anyone who does these things is detestable to the Lord' (Deuteronomy 18:10–12). Ian explains:

The reason we are forbidden in Scripture to use psychic powers is not because they are in themselves wrong but because they are an open door into spiritual powers from which the real energy comes to produce the effects.

Latent abilities are open to being hijacked by demonic forces. When a man or a woman develops psychic powers they think they are in control of what they are doing. They believe the powers they are using are their own and are not open to influence. That is not in fact the case.

The moment you begin to develop latent psychic powers you will find that the demonic world latches on to the fact and will take them over. You will find that you are yourself caught and can't get off them.

Although these powers resided in me, the energy that's channelled through them to make them work did not. It came from outside me and the source was demonic. It's rather like an electric fire that needs to be plugged into a power source before it will actually work.

For Ian, adolescent occult involvement began with astrology and ended with a terrifying experience which has haunted him ever since. He was in his late teens when he had a potent vision of evil. The effect upon him was profound:

I felt as though everything within me, my soul, my personality, everything, was being sucked out of me into this thing until I was left as just an empty husk. It devoured me into its eyes. I was left very shaken and remember to this day what I felt like. It was a most unnerving and appallingly frightening experience.

Not an experience one would wish upon an intelligent and sensitive teenager!

The ever-present horoscope is still the most common point of contact with the occult art of divination. Most teachers will tell you that when it comes to astrology, adolescents are positively starstruck.

Our own survey found that an astonishing 88% of the 14- to 15-year-olds questioned said they read their stars; almost a third consulted them on a daily basis, and 38% admitted to actually believing in them.

If mature adults can find themselves emotionally disturbed as a result of less than illuminating 'guidance' from their stars, then how much greater is the risk to those whose identities and attitudes are still being formed?

Most see it as innocent fun. For some the fun turns to fear. And for others, like Ian Thain, the undercurrent of fascination for the occult draws them in deeper.

As the physicist Anthony Garrett has written:

There exists no remotely plausible explanation of how astrology might work. Is astrology not just harmless fun? The answer is no: it fools people and is potentially dangerous.[9]

3

On the cards

Tarot cards

My favourite thing is my tarot deck. Tarot cards are used to tell fortunes, and they manage to do it quite precisely. There are 22 cards in the Greater Arcana. These range from good to bad . . . some not so good cards are the Devil of Death and the Moon. It is quite easy to read tarot cards once you have learnt. As well as the tarot I use a crystal ball, rune stones and playing cards to tell fortunes. The tarot are my favourite because they are mysterious.

'Julie', aged 13[1]

The tarot

Tarot cards are among the most popular methods of divination. Alluring, brightly coloured, intriguingly designed packs are readily available – even in some toy shops. The latest innovations are premium-rate tarot phone lines and multimedia tarot on the computer: 'with appropriate sound gear you'll hear the creaking of the hangman's rope, the thundering hooves beneath the charioteer . . .'

Some sources say the tarot has its origins in the 15th century, others that it originated in Egypt as a pictorial compendium of ancient lore.[2] Among the 78 cards in the pack are the 22 trumps of the Greater Arcana. Each has its own special significance. They include the Lovers, the Wheel of Fortune, the Hanged Man, the Devil, and Death. The Hanged Man, to take one, represents adaptability, the desire to learn, violent change and sacrifice.

Divination is carried out with the full pack or just the 22 trumps, which alone are said to offer a vast number of combinations of readings. The cards are laid according to a design and the diviner then interprets and applies their meanings. Books explaining how to use the tarot pack have made this means of fortune-telling widely accessible, to both the practised and the plain curious. The tarot has become part of popular culture.

The death card

Agony aunts Claire Rayner and Marjorie Proops are two gurus of our tabloid culture. Both have had to help people who have been distressed after the attentions of fortune tellers. One mother wrote to Claire Rayner on behalf of her daughter saying she is 'now distraught with worry as she was told she and her husband would be on the poverty line within ten weeks'. The tarot reading continued: 'shortly after she would be involved in a car accident and her passenger would be killed'. To add to her fears, the usual passenger in her car was her baby daughter.

Claire Rayner's comments were typically direct: 'If I had my way these charlatans who tell people cruel rubbish of this sort and take good cash for it would be hauled into court to be punished.'

Another worried reader contacted her colleague Marjorie Proops on behalf of a friend. A palm reader at a party had told the woman that she might never marry and would get involved with an unsavoury character who was a harmful influence. The woman wrote: 'My friend has been in a terrible state ever since.'

Those were both adults, but when credulity is combined with adolescence, the tarot's grim warnings can become all the more devastating. Dianne Core of Childwatch writes:

> I had a phone call from a mum whose daughter's friend had brought tarot cards onto the school playground. The death card came out and this little girl was convinced she was going to die. They had a terrible time with her.

Maureen Davies, a counsellor, asks:

> How would you feel if you were thirteen and somebody came and read your tarot cards and said you were going to be committing suicide in three months? That's happened. We've had calls from individuals who've been told they are going to die or commit suicide. The death card, the Hangman; all these sorts of things: they're not healthy.

Sixteen-year-old 'Alison' was into the occult and the bad feelings she had been getting recently had returned. Every time she had this feeling in her head and in her stomach, she was convinced that somebody she knew would die within a matter of weeks. So she asked a friend to read her tarot cards.

'Roger' would take the pack and shuffle it fast until a card dropped out. Whatever was on the card would be the message. He did that now, and the cards flew between his fingers until one of them just seemed to flip out. It was the death card. Before Roger could say a word Alison started screaming and crying: 'She went berserk', he recalls. Shortly afterwards a letter arrived from a friend to tell her she had cancer. Alison kept her distance from that time on.

At the age of 17 'Gary' decided to take one of his girlfriends to a medium he knew personally to have their tarot cards read. 'Mine came up quite rosy,' he says, 'with the usual generalizations. Then she read my girlfriend's cards and forecast that there was death and pregnancy in the reading. My girlfriend freaked out and instantly rejected it.'

Three months later she informed Gary that she was pregnant and was going to have an abortion. 'I had no say in it. My relationship with the lady who had given the reading collapsed.' His relationship with his girlfriend followed. 'It made me question the whole moral basis of the occult and what you can and can't sanction.'

Several years later he stumbled upon his former girlfriend in a pub. Slightly the worst for drink, her feelings flooded out, 'the bitterness, the anger and the regret'. Gary sometimes wonders how their lives would have turned out if that tarot card reading had never taken place.

Were the cards right or wrong? The first reading added greatly to a young girl's fear. The second offered the justification for an abortion a teenager lived to regret. The cards – or certainly their belief in them – added greatly to their unhappiness.

Potent symbols

Regardless of any disputed spiritual dimension to the tarot, the cards themselves represent potent symbols. They depict death and love, hope and fear, which some argue can give a jolt to the subconscious and can result in mental disturbance.

Canon Dominic Walker is Co-Chair of the Christian Deliverance Study Group. He is not a believer in the Devil or a personal power of evil, but has been sought out for counselling by many who have been troubled as a result of occult involvement.

In tracing the origins of their disturbance, he is inclined to search out psychological reasons. He will look for some subconscious psychological wellspring into which occult involvement has tapped, allowing dark and toxic matter to come hissing to the surface:

'Tarot cards have symbols on them which are deep and archetypal,' he says. 'A bad reading can have a profound psychological effect upon someone and can lead to psychiatric illness, violence or depression. A whole variety of things can happen as a result of a bad reading.'

Dr Kenneth McAll says he has dealt with more than 100 clients whose troubles can be traced back to occult involvement. He likens the occult activity to a trigger mechanism which can set off the disturbance:

> There are elements of the subconscious that are brought up into the conscious. This mental mechanism is known by the psychologists as the endo-psychic censor. It is there to prevent the infiltration of unacceptable id material from the deep unconscious into the conscious. Whether that is unleashed; whether the plugs are pulled out by occult involvement, I simply do not know. The existence of danger, my own experience and conviction shows, is very, very real.

Clients who have sought his help after becoming involved in the occult have, commonly, become 'cut off from any sense of aim or purpose in life. They've lost sleep; relationships within the families are affected; there are many divorces. They're the unhappy section of our psychiatric work.'

Among the worst cases, he says, are those who have ended up in 'padded cells, under electric shock therapy or certified. Some are just called schizophrenics, because there is no other label.'

In 1986, the tarot cards were cited in a murder trial at Glasgow High Court. A 23-year-old woman told the court that she had attempted to murder her baby under the instructions of her Tibetan spirit guide. After seeing faces in the clouds and being told that her baby must die, Sheena McLaughlin drove with her boyfriend to a deserted spot on the banks of Loch Lomond and tried to kill her three-month-old child. When she failed, her lover Alan Porter, a spiritualist and faith healer, took the baby from her and strangled her himself. The court heard that McLaughlin's 'life was ruled by the occult and tarot cards'.[3]

Jane

Jane was 14 and heavily into fortune-telling. She had been taught various forms of divination by her grandmother. As a plump and unattractive child she was bullied at school. Now she began to use her prowess at fortune-telling to even the score and earn respect. She made sure she didn't cheat by inventing messages, but if it was in the cards she told it straight, regardless of the consequences.

One little girl had come to her for a reading: 'I saw the death card but I knew that it wasn't a person. I didn't see any death around her or her family. Then the card of the beast came up. I told the child her dog was going to die. I knew she had a dog anyway, but I just felt an overwhelming thought that that was going to happen, so I told her.'

Jane was convinced that she had tuned in to the message of the cards. 'You interpret them mediumistically, though some of it is just guesswork. The cards themselves are just a front.'

The little girl was understandably distressed. 'She was crying and in a bit of a state. Her friends tried to console her and came up to me and asked me. "Is that right?" I said, "Well that's what the cards said. It's nothing to do with me."'

The next day the girl was missing from school. The following day she came in, crestfallen. 'Her dog had died. It had choked. She said she hated me, that it was all my fault, that I had made it happen.'

Thirty years later, Jane looks back: 'I think there was an element of truth in that; it was like a curse. These things are in the cards, but speaking it out makes them happen. I find it hard to forgive myself.' The girl was troubled and disturbed for six months – an unnaturally long time to grieve for a pet – until her parents bought her another dog.

'At the time I did it because it gave me a kick. It gave me power,' Jane reflects. 'The more I did it the more power I had. It's all to do with power.'

From early childhood her grandmother had taught Jane palmistry, the tarot, the crystal ball and other black arts. And as far as Jane was concerned these were neutral but effective tools. But by the age of fourteen she describes herself as 'hooked on the power'. It was an enormous struggle to let it go, even when she firmly made up her mind that she wanted to. Bouts of mental illness dogged her into adulthood.

Many of her so-called psychic gifts were used to hurt and manipulate others. 'There is always damage. Even if it doesn't come out till later. People become addicted. They find that they can't live without it, and there are some people who won't do anything without seeing their medium first.'

It was reading the Bible that convinced Jane that what she had been doing was wrong. 'I opened the Bible at great passages against it, but even so, the roots proved difficult to pull.'

Amanda

It was a school project that kindled 'Amanda's' interest in the occult. Like many ten-year-olds, Amanda imagined she had an invisible friend who would tell her secret things and give her special powers. The supernatural had always excited her. Now, encouraged by the teachers at her church school, she set out to investigate a project on the subject.

'From there my interest in the occult increased. I spent all of my time at the local library looking up books about ghosts, poltergeists and ESP. I became absolutely obsessed with it and started reading occult magazines.'

She gave herself to the project with such a will and invested so much time that she won a school commendation. Amanda was called in to see the headmistress who congratulated her for her fine work and suggested that she should continue to investigate the supernatural.

Her parents were so pleased with her achievement that on Christmas Day Amanda found a pack of Osiris cards in her stocking. These fortune-telling cards were like the tarot pack, only Egyptian in origin.

The explanatory leaflet which came with the cards was rudimentary. But Amanda, now 11, became fascinated with one of its suggestions. 'It said that you had to look inside yourself and peer inside the person in order to find the answers that you were looking for. Very soon I found that I was able to read them accurately for myself and for other people. I couldn't explain how I knew the answers, but I knew.'

Amanda's reputation for reading the cards grew, and soon she was discovered by the teachers at the church school. But far from frowning at what she was doing, they actively encouraged her. 'It became almost like a school trick,' she says. 'A lot of the teachers were very interested in that kind of thing, and when they saw me reading cards for a friend, before or after a lesson, they would ask me to read their own.'

Her parents lent her a book about divination, which explained many different ways of fortune-telling. It was palm reading which caught her imagination and then the rune stones. In the end she became so proficient at different methods of divination that she could dispense with the props and still get results. 'I didn't need them, but it was easier to get people to accept what I was saying by having the props there.'

The tools of divination had become irrelevant. Amanda was

working mediumistically. She just *knew*. 'By that time it really didn't matter what method I used at all. I had some kind of knowing power to predict or know situations.'

During youth weekends run by the Anglican Church she was even encouraged by her youth leader to read the tarot cards. Some people thought she was perceptive, others acknowledged the power which she was convinced she possessed. 'And that was great, because in a lot of ways I had a very poor self-image.'

Amanda's parents were well-off and had sent her to private school, but compared to the died-in-the-wool rich kids around her, she felt something of a misfit. They were in a different league and she felt the need to compete.

Some of her friends were popular because they were good-looking or brilliant in class. 'I gained popularity by being the kind of person who would sit and do readings. I solved my insecurities by feeling that perhaps there was something mysterious about me.'

Amanda admits to deliberately using the cards to manipulate her friends. 'When I was younger I used to manipulate whether people would go out with one another. If someone else had said to me, "Make sure that they are not interested," then I would just say it: "They're not interested in you – it says it clearly here."'

On other occasions the messages of the cards were unmistakable and she offered advice which deeply affected the believing teenagers who drank it in. 'I told one girl who was 16 and doing her 'A' levels that she would never pass her exams, so she left school.' Another time, she told a 19-year-old student nurse that he too would fail his exams. He also left.

At the time she was convinced the cards were saying those things, but now, with hindsight, she regrets giving that advice. 'If you predict anything like that over somebody it will box them in. If you said that they would never be any good at maths, then they never will be.'

She recalls other examples too, which had a damaging effect on those whose fortunes were being read. 'Things are said and predicted such as, "You will marry twice and your first husband will die." Obviously, that's not very helpful if you get married and always treat your husband as a temporary arrangement! Another was that you will never be accepted within your chosen field or career.' Years later, she fears that her ill-advised predictions are still shaping the lives of those who heard and believed: 'People are probably only now reaping the results of what they believed in: the things that were predicted which fed their insecurities and doubts. I didn't realize at the time that what I was saying was being harmful to people. I simply said the things which came to me without really considering the effect they would have.'

One in ten?

Amanda and Jane were to wade deeper and deeper into the occult until they were well out of their depth and in serious difficulties. We will come back to their stories later.

Meanwhile, in a school of a thousand young teenagers, there are likely to be 100 potential Amandas and Janes. According to our survey, 10% of year-ten pupils said they used the tarot. Fourteen will turn to the tarot on a monthly basis and a further twelve will consult the cards for explicit guidance and advice each week.

And as well as the tarot, another 190 pupils in our thousand-strong sample will strain to glimpse into their futures with other fortune-telling devices.

Thankfully, 36% of 14 to 15-year-olds sense the hidden dangers. But an equal number of undecided pupils could well be open to the idea, and more than one in four believe that trying to tell the future could have positive benefits.

So for adolescents what lies behind the lure of divination? The search for meaning in life and the reassurance of finding a pattern; the comforting sense that 'someone is watching over me' – those are part of the answer. A fascination for the supernatural and a quest for knowledge is another. As Amanda and Jane discovered all too early in life, knowledge is power, and when exercised over others it commands attention and respect and puts you firmly in control – for good or for ill.

The journey of discovery can be a dangerous one, turning the voyager either inwards and beyond the conscious self, or outwards into the void. With the tarot, the diviner seeks knowledge by consulting the cards; with the ouija board, knowledge is sought from the spirit of the glass: a reaching outwards, but to what? And when the ouija board was launched as a game and marketed in toyshops, it became a bargain basement trip into the unknown without a courier that was available to all, regardless of age, experience, or emotional maturity.

4

Spirit of the glass
Ouija

Pop singer Sinead O'Connor shook with fear after trying to contact her dead mother by using a ouija board. The sinister session ended with her three year old son Jake screaming in terror as frightened Sinead stopped the ouija session.
The Sun[1]

The ouija board

The yes-yes board – its name is a combination of French and German – has been around in different forms for thousands of years. But anyone who thinks it's just a fortune-telling game, be warned – ouija has been described as one of the most dangerous introductions to the occult ever devised. Adolescents have been driven to seek psychiatric help after its use. As far as parents and teachers are concerned the yes-yes board should be strictly a no-no. But why?

Ouija is a method of divination which uses a system of symbols, letters and numbers and a pointer to pick them out. A question is asked and the pointer is supposed to swing round to different letters to spell out the answer.

Sometimes an upturned tumbler is moved around a lexicon of cards to spell out its message. Participants rest their fingers lightly on the glass in the belief that it will glide around the board of its own volition. In 1853, a French spiritualist called Planchette experimented with a pencil mounted on castors as a device for spelling out messages from the 'spirits'.[2] This gave way to the modern ouija board, on which is printed the alphabet, numbers, and the words 'yes', 'no' and 'goodbye'. Its inventor, William Fuld of Baltimore, patented the design in 1939. Boards had been produced commercially beforehand during the First World War, and at the height of its popularity in 1920 3 million were sold.

The game manufacturers Parker Brothers acquired the ownership in 1966. In the following decade sales were said to top 7 million.[3] In the United Kingdom ouija was marketed as a family game by

Waddingtons House of Games. Protests followed and it was later withdrawn. In the last 40 years an estimated 20 million copies were purchased across Europe and America.[4]

A nationwide survey of the United States in 1983 found that 30% of those who used this 'fun game' did so to try to contact the dead. According to author Edmund Gruss an even higher proportion used it to try to develop psychic powers or receive guidance from the spirit world over major issues such as marriage, health and investments.[5] A British survey, which claimed to have questioned some 80,000 schoolchildren, found that 80% had been involved in ouija sessions or playground seances.[6]

Our own survey found that 1 in 50 14- to 15-year-olds claimed to have consulted 'the spirit of the glass' on a regular basis. A further 21% said they had experimented with ouija. So in a class of 25, five or more pupils are likely to have used the ouija board.

Disturbing answers

Part of ouija's fascination is that it sometimes appears to come up with right answers for which there can be no obvious explanation. Author John Richards offers the following baffling example:

> Bill Johnstone of South Shields lost contact with his father when his dad went away to sea. Relations thought he had either died or emigrated to Australia. Bill attended a ouija session and, like so many others, 'imagined they were pushing the glass from one letter to another.
>
> I asked the spirit if he knew where my father was. Back came the message – 'Dumfries, Scotland.' Enquiries of Dumfries Council revealed that a Mr Bryce Johnstone was there and living at Alderman Hill Road.
>
> When father and son met, father said, 'No-one in South Shields could have known where I was. Bill was a baby when I met him.'[7]

On occasions the board is said to reveal with alarming accuracy personal information known only by one person in the group – often to that individual's astonishment or embarrassment. That person may be adamant that whoever it is making the glass dictate their innermost secrets, it is certainly not *them*! Mike Morris from the British Evangelical Alliance says:

> Our experience is that children will often find that messages

actually do come back. As the glass moves round the cards, giving information which is private, privileged, and known only to one child, it scares them rigid. We find ourselves having to deal with very frightened teenagers where the ouija has provided information no-one else could know.

We return to the case of teenager 'Amanda'. One day she was conducting a ouija board session. Among the participants was her friend 'Liza'. Liza sat and listened and said nothing, though the board had plenty to tell her. The spirit of the board told her things about herself she believed no one else knew: her mother's first name, her address, the German name of her boyfriend's mother.

Amanda insists that no one else there knew the details, and what came out left Liza badly shaken. 'She couldn't deal with the idea that somebody knew about her. She became paranoid about people following her, and began to believe that people were watching her all the time.' It got to the state where she was afraid to step out of bed at night to go to the loo. A state of irrational fear persisted for the next two years.

Even more worrying is this account from a counsellor. 'Barry' was about 13. He and a group of friends were playing the ouija board. To begin with the glass appeared to move at random and unpredictably, spelling out gibberish. But then the ouija board spelt out one clearly discernible word: death.

Next it spelt out the name of one the friends who was playing. When this happened they were all afraid and stopped playing immediately. A week later the boy who had been named was walking beneath some scaffolding when a pole fell on his head and killed him.

Whether or not it was a coincidence, the group was terrified by what had happened. Barry became afraid for his own safety. His nights were filled with bad dreams. He remained disturbed by the event right into his adulthood, and even now the nightmares persist. The counsellor is convinced that a measure of his disturbance has rubbed off on his five-year-old son who screams abnormally, frequently wets the bed and has terrible nightmares.

So what moves the glass?

In his book *Paganism and the Occult*, author Kevin Logan cites four possible explanations for the way the board appears to yield its messages:

1. Fraud. A practical joke or a means of frightening the other participants.
2. Involuntary movement of the pointer by those taking part. This argument weakens where the pointer begins to spell out actual phrases.
3. Subconscious movement to express the deep, repressed, hopes, fears and fantasies of one of the participants.
4. Movement under the direction of an external guiding influence – a spirit.

Once again we find ourselves hung up on the imponderable and the unprovable: is the power that shifts the glass human, or non-human? John Allen thinks the power could be human in origin:

> It is possible to bypass the censor which normally filters the impulses deriving from our subconscious, and let out things which ought to be kept in. I think there is overwhelming evidence to show that at least some of the time a ouija board can be a device (like a crystal ball or pendulum) for releasing the forces of the subconscious in an irresponsible way, which can cause untold damage to the human personality.[8]

But others believe the power comes from a non-human source:

> Sir William Barrett, after testing the validity of the ouija board as far back as 1914 stated: 'Whatever may have been the source of the intelligence displayed, it was absolutely beyond the range of normal human faculty.'[9]

What caused Barrett to come to his surprising conclusion was the claimed accuracy of tests conducted by blindfolded operators. To make doubly sure that there was no way they could influence the results they worked with boards whose alphabets had been rearranged, or which were hidden beneath opaque screens. Barrett's tests were conducted for the American Society for Psychical Research.[10]

Canon Dominic Walker of the British-based Christian Deliverance Study Group has his own view on the workings of the ouija board:

> There seems to be three possible explanations for why the glass is moving:
> • Either it is an involuntary muscle action – although the glass will also sometimes move when no-one is touching it;

- Or it is a spirit of some sort that is moving the glass;
- Or it could be psychokinesis (the power of the mind to move objects), an energy that is being created by the people involved.

And he plumps for the third option:

I would say that the users are in touch with their own unconscious: the anger, aggression, fear, guilt and hatred that is inside of them. They are bringing that to the surface, and so creating the energy which makes the glass move. It can spell out all kinds of messages to them from their own unconscious which they cannot handle, and they believe it comes from evil spirits.

Human or non-human, fraud or involuntary movement, whatever it takes to make a moving glass produce a message, the effect can be disturbing, and sometimes fatal. On one memorable occasion, a clutch of heavy goods drivers descended on Dominic Walker:

While they were resting on the motorways they had started playing with a ouija board, and they began to feel that some power or spirit was getting into the cabs of their lorries to try to drive them off the road or into the oncoming traffic. I had to get them together and work out what was going on.

Playing with the ouija board was bringing to the surface all sorts of problems within themselves, and some of those were destructive. I had to get them to see that they weren't in fact in spiritual danger, but that they were dealing with something inside of themselves. They were playing a very dangerous game of psychodynamics. So it was a matter of trying to sort out the kind of fears and hatreds that were inside them. Only by dealing with that was it possible for those symptoms to go away.

To help banish the fear that had been generated by using the board, each sitter pledged to have nothing more to do with ouija, and the board was symbolically destroyed. This account is recorded in the book *Deliverance*, to which Dominic Walker was a contributor.

Whether such fears came from the inner world of the subconscious or some outer world of evil spirits, the fact that such dark and troubled material is believed to be messages from the spirit world can only add to the anxiety:

Sitters take them literally as communications from an outside entity, when they may be veiled and symbolic and arise from that part of the subconscious where repressed images, unacceptable to the conscious mind, are lurking. Such images may be of violence and death, and if taken literally may cause great fright and upset, and even lead to mental breakdown.[11]

But the Deliverance Study Group's findings do not rule out the other uncomfortable possibility that the power behind the board could come from contact with spiritual forces, and it adds this warning:

> Whether this activity is powered by the sitters' subconscious or by directing spirits is a moot point. If it is the work of spirits, then we have no means of telling whether they are well-meaning and truthful, or evil and intent on deceit . . .
> Ouija is often tried out by the emotionally and spiritually immature in an atmosphere of dare-devilry . . . The dabbler may well be on his way to bondage to occult powers before he knows what's happening to him. The only advice to offer is, 'Don't.'[12]

Self-fulfilling prophecies?

Pauline used to stage weekly ouija board sessions for a giggle. They continued for six months until the message came, 'You fool . . . you will regret laughing . . . you will be ill.'

Within a week she had had a nightmare about being confined to a wheelchair. Within a month she had developed stomach pains and doctors had diagnosed polio. She is now paralysed from the waist down and confined to a wheelchair.

'Nothing went right for me from that day on,' she told a newspaper. 'To this day, I constantly feel there is a cold, evil breeze around me. I've been driven out of the house by it before now.'[13]

Similar accounts are not uncommon, but explanations for them vary. The stock answer is 'coincidence', or as the psychologist Jung put it, synchronicity. Jung argued that meaningful coincidences occur when we come into contact with powerful primeval images deep within our unconscious.

There could be other psychological explanations. For example, wish-fulfilment – manipulating events, perhaps subconsciously, to get what we want. Likewise, there might also be fear-fulfilment. At its most extreme this can take the form of thanatomania, the death-wish.

A prime example would be the death curse of the witch doctor. If the hapless subject of that curse firmly believes in its power and considers himself doomed, then psychosomatic symptoms might follow; the will to live can evaporate and the witch-doctor's curse may prove to be effective through the basic but potent power of suggestion.

A European example is given by the German writer, Kurt Koch. A young girl visited a graphologist and was told that her handwriting revealed that she would be murdered in her 30th year. She decided to pack as much 'living' as she could into the years she had left. She became a prostitute, had several abortions, and died of ulcerated colitis. She was 24.

The doctor declared that her lifestyle had killed her. The graphologist had been wrong about the year but the 'curse' still proved effective, thanks to the girl's overriding belief in it.[14]

Most reported cases of ouija-related disturbance followed frequent use of the board. But there are examples where a single ouija session appears to have been one too many. What matters may not be how often one consults the board, but the intensity of that involvement and the level of fear that is raised by what takes place. Consultant Psychiatrist Stuart Checkley writes:

> I have seen someone who as a result of one experiment with a ouija board suffered frightening experiences outside his control, including automatic handwriting. He found himself writing frightening messages to himself.[15]

Messages from the spirits

Automatic writing is one step on from asking the spirit of the glass to spell out a message. The ouija board itself may be used, or the person may hold a pen or pencil over a blank page and invite a spirit to control the hand to produce its message. This is a solitary occupation, but even without fear and tension from others which could be conducive to group hysteria, the result can be every bit as disturbing, as counsellor Gordon Wright explains:

> I have come into contact with children and young people who have practised automatic writing. They have experimented with holding a pen or pencil very lightly, almost not expecting anything to happen. They are often surprised and scared stiff when something *does* happen.
> Some of it is illegible, almost scribbles. Some of it has used words like murder and blood, spelling out the darker side of life. Sometimes it has given answers to specific questions. One of the dangers is that these answers will be believed. Fear is the major

characteristic, bringing a loss of peace and confusion. Complete disorientation often occurs.

And in that case, and some of the others raised, the intensity of belief does not appear to have been a factor. It seems to matter little whether those who take part believe the process will actually produce results – that 'contact' will be made. Even some sceptics have been able to produce automatic writing.

One celebrated case is that of Mrs John Curran from Missouri, whose ouija board 'dictated' three historical novels set in Imperial Rome and medieval England. The historical details and the language used were said to be accurate, although the woman had left school at the age of 14 and was not widely travelled.

Occult author Jane Roberts claimed to have contacted a spirit known as Seth through the ouija board. Within a week, she said, she was able to receive messages from Seth without the use of the board. This is another example of ouija being a mediumistic prop, a means of 'tuning in' which may eventually be dispensed with as the subject's sensitivity increases.

The Rev. Donald Page, exorcist of the Christian Spiritualist Church, has stated that most of his 'possession' cases are 'people who have used the ouija board [and that] this is one of the easiest and quickest ways to become possessed'.[16]

The principle behind the ouija board means it cannot be classified as a simple fortune-telling device. Implicit in the practice of calling upon the 'spirit of the glass' is the assumption that the ouija board is a kind of spiritual telegraph for contacting the spirit world.

The view that the ouija board is a mediumistic hot-line for contacting spirits is not entirely without scientific support. As Sir William Barratt reported in his findings for the American Society for Psychical Research:

> Reviewing the results as a whole, I am convinced of their supernormal character, and that we have here an exhibition of some intelligent, discarnate agency, mingling with the personality of one or more of the sitters and guiding their muscular movements.[17]

But if spirits *are* involved – and it's a big *if* – then what exactly are they? Human or non-human, benign or malevolent? And how certain can the user be that his shout in the dark will be heard and answered by the kind of spirit he would be happy to bring home to mother?

If as rational outsiders we discount the activity of spirits in favour of some alternative explanation, then we must still reckon with the effect that the very suggestion of reaching out to spirits could have on an adolescent's fears. Is the 'game' worth the gamble with someone's psychological well-being?

The frame of mind that the board either induces or amplifies is characteristically dark, depressing, morbid, oppressive and obsessive. Whether this is the work of spirits, or simply commercial interests, then they would not always appear to have the best interests of the sitter at heart – as the workload of counsellors and therapists dealing with the aftermath of disturbance and suicide would suggest.

Ouija on trial

In 1994 the British Court of Appeal ordered a re-trial after a jury used a makeshift ouija board to ask a murder victim who had killed him. Four jurors made the ouija board 'for a laugh' after a drinking session. The board spelt out the dead man's name and accused the defendant of shooting him. It went on to instruct the jurors to 'vote guilty tomorrow'. They did. The judge ordered a re-trial at an estimated cost of half a million pounds.

But ouija was cited in the courts as long ago as 1933, when 15-year-old Mattie Turley shot and killed her father after allegedly receiving instructions to do so by a spirit. Her testimony in Juvenile Court was recorded by *The New York Times*: 'In a ouija board seance with her mother, the board told her to kill her father, so her mother . . . could marry a young cowboy.'[18]

In another American case a ouija board told a woman that her husband had taken a mistress and lavished a fortune on her. His wife then treated him so badly that he killed her.[19]

More recently there have been two serious court cases in Great Britain in which the ouija board has been cited in evidence:

A London woman was jailed for five years for torturing a runaway teenage girl with an electric carving knife during ouija board sessions. Hazel Paul took in the 15 year old girl after she had run away from a children's home. She punched her and beat her, hit her feet and hands with a hammer and cut her arm with a hacksaw. The girl's ordeal lasted six days. Assisting Paul were a 17 year old girl and a 15 year old boy who claimed she had used psychic powers to make them help her. The girl was sent to prison for 18 months and the boy was detained for two years.

Evidence about the ouija board emerged during the trial at the Old Bailey in 1988.[20] The board cropped up again in Gloucester Crown Court:

> A woman who had practised black magic and tried to summon spirits via a ouija board tried to kill her four year old son with a pair of scissors because she believed he was the Devil. Gloucester Crown Court head that Lyn Loughrey had a history of instability and had been involved with an apparently overzealous religious group. Her husband had rushed in when he heard the child screaming and pulled the scissors from his back. But his wife grabbed them from him and then tried to stab herself. She was put on probation for unlawful wounding and sent for psychiatric treatment. The boy later recovered in hospital. The case took place in 1986.[21]

In both cases children were the victims of demented attacks by individuals whose use of the ouija board was regarded as of sufficient relevance and significance to be raised by the crown prosecution in evidence.

The ouija board and mental disturbance appear to go hand in hand. Ouija was banned from use in an English psychiatric hospital after it was connected with outbreaks of disturbance among the patients. A number of staff at the hospital were involved in occultism and were using the board on the premises. According to one nurse there, whenever the board was in operation several of the patients would become uncontrollable.

The consultant psychiatrist established a pattern between the use of the board and the disturbed behaviour of the patients. A memo was sent to all staff saying that if they were going to be involved in the occult, they should not do it in the grounds of the hospital, because the evidence suggested that it was increasingly detrimental to the welfare of the patients.

Warnings echoed

As with the tarot, the loudest voices raised in warning are predictably those of Christians with a spiritual objection to the practice. But warnings against the ouija board are echoed by counsellors, doctors and carers, not all of whom are committed Christians.

And perhaps surprisingly, their warnings are reiterated by a number of practising occultists, who point out that the ouija board spells trouble; though they can't seem to agree as to exactly why. A practising witch has said:

> It is a powerful tool in the occult and we would warn anybody who does not know what they are doing to stay well clear of the ouija.[22]

Another has warned:

> Ouija is verging on the dangerous, because it will work with anyone, regardless of their intelligence, their maturity, how much training they have had.
> What ouija seems to be particularly good for is bringing out the rather dirty bits in people's minds; bringing out their fears and nightmares, so particularly if somebody's got a rather excited, spooky, attitude to what they are doing, those fears will come out in fantasy form, or poltergeist form, and will frighten them. I will not have a ouija board at my festivals. I would like to see them banned and not sold anywhere.[23]

Professional medium Sandy Thompson feels much the same, but for different reasons again:

> Ouija boards can be very dangerous in the wrong hands. You're likely to get in touch with bad or mischief-making spirits, and this can do more harm than good.[24]

Even magician Danny Korem, a hardened sceptic, and author of the book, *The Fakers*, takes ouija seriously enough to issue his own warning:

> I have never witnessed, read, or heard of a credible report of something of a supernatural nature taking place through the use of the ouija board. I have seen, heard and read, however, of many negative experiences that have entrapped people who have sought knowledge with a ouija board. If you own a board or similar diversion, my advice is to destroy it and never encourage others to tinker with such devices. You never know what emotional disturbances might be triggered in yourself or others through their use.[25]

A mediumistic tool for contacting the spirits, or simply a device for unleashing the dark subconscious and letting it run rampant? Either way, there would seem to be good reason why Danny Korem's suggestion may be the best advice for anyone with a ouija board.

Playground pastime?

Russ Parker writes:

> I have counselled a number of people, including children, who have been deeply disturbed at what happened when 'playing' this deadly game . . . In one case a local minister was called in to a school where some pupils were in a hysterical and suicidal state, frightened by their experience of this 'game'.[26]

In case after case, counsellors say school is often the place where teenagers are introduced to the ouija board. But on one occasion it wasn't only the pupils who were traumatized. At a military academy in Miami teachers and students alike 'went berserk' after 'a ouija board game had got out of control', reported *The New York Times*. The paper quoted police officer Harry Cunnill, who stated that teachers and students at the Miami Aerospace Academy 'were running around tearing up things'. The report said doors were ripped off their hinges and holes kicked in the walls. One youth was hospitalized after putting his hand through the window.

The class teacher, who later resigned, declared: 'Everybody just got carried away and it was a riot . . . There were girls screaming that there was a spirit inside the board.'[27]

In Essex, England, a headmaster had to deal with twelve frightened schoolchildren who had used their home-made board to try to contact spirits. Bizarre behaviour changes included: a 15-year-old boy who stood bolt upright in a geography lesson shouting at a spirit to get off his shoulder, before running out of the classroom and out of the school; a girl claiming to have woken in the night to see a person in her bedroom; a frightened child who said he had been barred by a spirit from leaving the toilet block where he had used the ouija board.[28]

Dianne Core of the charity Childwatch has been contacted on numerous occasions by parents and teachers whose children have been badly upset after using the ouija board:

> They've been very worried; they've had some very disturbed children on their hands for a few days afterwards.
> The children have become very frightened: things happened

while they were using the ouija board that they cannot explain, such as glasses moving, feelings of unexplained fear and terror. Children have talked about things flying across the room. Friends have suddenly become vacant and won't speak to anybody; and the children have become very distressed and have needed a lot of help.

Teachers are very worried about it as well. In some schools in the Humberside area ouija boards have been banned.

Death threats

The ouija board has an uncanny knack of unleashing some of our deepest fears. Time and again, its morbid message returns to the theme of death.

In 1989, two schoolgirls from Southampton, England, ran away from home after claiming to have contacted a spirit through the ouija board which had threatened to take their lives.[29]

At a school near Barnsley in South Yorkshire, teenage pupils became hysterical after a lunchtime session with the ouija board got out of hand. A vicar had to be called in to calm the class after a girl received a message from the board that she was going to die.[30]

'I can't go. I feel ill. One of us is going to die and I don't know who.' The 15-year-old schoolboy and his two friends poured out their story to school visitor Audrey Harper. They were pale, frightened and shaking.

Five friends had been meeting at the boy's house after school to use the ouija board. For the past few months they had been in deep communion with a 'friendly' spirit called Jim. But Jim, it seems, wanted to get even better acquainted with his new-found buddies.

The boy explained: 'Two weeks ago he said he was lonely and needed a companion. He said that one of us would die at a party, but he wouldn't say which one. It was as if he was laughing at us, but we didn't dare stop playing in case he got mad.'

When asked why they had used the ouija board, they replied: 'It's only a game – only this time it's gone wrong.'[31]

Teachers called for Audrey Harper when a boy was found running round the playing field, sweating, screaming and shivering violently. A group of fifth-formers had made their own ouija board and were trying it out – for a laugh. To the boy's surprise it began to spell out his name. 'I couldn't move. I was so scared. The board was talking to me. Then the marker spelled out the name of my best friend, followed by the words: "kill him". I just flipped.'

There are many possible explanations for that message, but the method used to manufacture the communication is irrelevant. What matters is that the boy swallowed the message in its entirety and was left deeply distressed and in a state of shock.[32]

Mental disturbance

A seventeen-year-old boy attempted to strangle his mother after a ouija session at a neighbour's home 'for fun.' It took a week to calm him down. He later recalled: 'afterwards I started shaking uncontrollably. I felt as though I'd changed and began to hear voices telling me to kill my parents. I couldn't eat or sleep, and didn't know how to find help. I'll never dabble with ouija boards again'.[33]

The Sun

Children seem particularly susceptible to psychological disturbance brought on by this so-called family game. And trouble may follow, irrespective of any history of mental illness.

The following is an extract from a letter written by distressed parents whose son became suicidal and had to be sectioned to a psychiatric hospital after playing this 'game' at his boarding school:

This time last year our fifteen-year-old son was doing very well in a high academic stream at boarding school. At this time he became involved with similarly aged boys playing the ouija board. We were unaware of this and were completely taken by surprise when in the middle of the summer term his housemaster rang and said the lad was in a state of great distress.

A week later the school recommended his transference to a psychiatric hospital for treatment because he had made several attempts on his life and was suffering from deep depression.

He spent most of the summer holidays in hospital and returned home three weeks before the beginning of the autumn term. He returned to school for one week but became unstable and distressed, and once again the school recommended that he should go back to the hospital.

The time spent in hospital was of no great assistance. Psychoanalysis did help, in that the problems caused by the ouija board could be discussed, but no rational answers could be given to explain away what our son had experienced.

Drug treatment had not the slightest effect on the depression and he made several other attempts on his life while at the hospital during sudden depressive moods. After the last attempt, for which he was sectioned, we removed him and brought him home to see whether we ourselves could help in any way.

We . . . are doing our best to give a very confused lad the uncritical love and reassurance that we hope will enable him to find his way back to a position of emotional stability. After five weeks there is already a great improvement.

As parents we have had to meet this situation completely unprepared. We had no knowledge of the way in which the occult can affect the personality and the nature of the depression it causes, but the results are devastating.

This illness has brought about his removal from boarding school and an interruption to a promising academic career.

'Depression seems to be the most common result of people having played with ouija boards,' says Canon Dominic Walker. 'Depression and fear, because they feel they've got in touch with something that is hostile. They feel they're living in a hostile world anyway, and then when they play with the ouija board, that is simply confirmed to them.'

Suicide link

Ouija has been implicated in numerous teen suicides, including the following of a girl from Sheffield.

'The girl had been jilted,' recalls Dominic Walker. 'She played with a ouija board with some friends and she asked the spirit of the board "Will I ever find love?" She got the answer back, "No man will ever love you." She killed herself. She was only nineteen.'

The verdict at the inquest was suicide. 'It came out that she had broken up with her boyfriend and was cut up about it. After the inquest her mother told me she had been playing with the ouija board the night before she killed herself and this is what had happened.'

More often than not, schoolchildren will dabble with the board to get the same kind of illicit kick they would from pulling on a cigarette behind the bike shed. It's disapproved of and that makes it *fun*. It means that any method of discouragement needs to be carefully thought out. But there are times when the school itself might not be alert to the dangers and could have unwittingly encouraged the activity.

In a small town near Plymouth, England, a teacher at a comprehensive school had to seek help after three children experimented with the ouija board to dramatic effect, as counsellor Gordon Wright recalls:

> One girl in particular had gone berserk and had been finally
> sectioned by a doctor and a psychiatrist. She jumped out of an
> upstairs window: the first of a series of attempts at suicide. She
> also hallucinated a tremendous amount. It was wondered
> whether she had been on hallucinogenic drugs, but she had not.
>   There was also a tremendous expression of fear; characteristi-
> cally involving nightmares. Perhaps the most frightening thing, as
> far as her parents were concerned, was a strange sense of
> detachment from them and from anyone at all. No-one felt as
> though they were making contact with her. She was like a zombie.
> She ended up in the local mental hospital and went through a
> long period of therapy.

The therapy seemed to have little effect. In this case, the girl began to make progress only after specific Christian prayers were said for her. 'We began to see a change from that day on,' says Gordon Wright. 'She became open to counselling and was able to pray herself.'

The girl had shown no sign of any disturbance before using the ouija board, and her apparent mental illness transpired immediately after her experiment with ouija. The change was so marked and so immediate that it was like throwing a switch: 'This was a direct reaction to her actually being involved in an occult practice,' says Gordon Wright. 'It left me in no doubt whatsoever that it was caused by playing with a ouija board. There is nothing to suggest that there was any other factor to precipitate it.'

The two other girls using the board at the time were also troubled by their experience: 'All three girls were terrified. They all started to have nightmares. They all lost their peace – their personal composure.'

Gordon Wright describes the events that led up to the disturbance:

> They started asking [the board] personal questions, like, 'When
> am I going to die?'; questions people will often ask when using
> different methods of divination.
>   The thing reacted very typically. I have heard this dozens of
> times from people using tumblers, table-rapping and suchlike.
> The ouija board had spelled out words and sentences. They
> became intrigued. They had done this on a number of occasions.

It was a fairly frequent experience. But on this occasion the thing appeared to take over and flew off the table. They were very frightened.

But what had frightened her parents the most in the days that followed was the girl's bizarre smile: 'It had been an evil smile, a kind of leer, and they had never seen it on the face of their daughter before.'

As Gordon Wright and a colleague prayed for the girl she appeared to lose consciousness for a short while, 'but when she came round the smile on her face was beautiful. That was the first time we had seen her *really* smile.'

The school put a stop to further unsupervised experiments with the ouija board. But Gordon Wright fears it was the classroom discussions on the occult, given without adequate 'health warnings', that stirred the children to curiosity in the first place. These teacher-led discussions, which he fears glamourized the occult, continued much as before. 'That distressed me a great deal,' says Gordon Wright,' because I thought they would have learned.'

Another counsellor tells of a 15-year-old girl who had become obsessed with thoughts of suicide after playing with the ouija board. She was plagued for years by the recurring mental image of herself hanging. This, and other morbid images of car crashes and people she knew in distress, only started after the ouija board session.

Anglican vicar Kevin Logan says, 'We've dealt with so many youngsters who have played around with a ouija board and have become confused and terrified; in some cases to the point where their personality starts to disintegrate and they get lost.'

As a hospital chaplain, Robert Law from Truro has had to person-ally conduct the funerals of three young people who, he believes, committed suicide as a result of occult involvement: 'Talking to their friends, you ask, "Why did they do it?" And they said they didn't want to do it, it was as if they had this compulsion. They were being pulled across the other side, was the way they described it. One was about eighteen, the others were in their early twenties.'

All three had been using the ouija board on a regular basis. 'I had one boy from Helston School: he and his brother and a mate played it for 48 hours virtually non-stop one weekend. He was frightened.'

Robert Law now runs a support group to care for carers – those who carry out the counselling. Sometimes he is invited to speak in schools. In a typical class of 25 fifth-year pupils, he has found that three or four are likely to have experimented with the ouija board.

Teenage users

Our own survey in England and Wales came up with a higher figure: 21% of 14- to 15-year-olds said they had used the ouija board occasionally. More than twice that figure had an inner conviction that this was wrong, but the majority had no qualms about it or thought it could be OK. And from our findings, out of 1,000 14- to 15-year-olds, 20 will be actively trying to contact the spirits of the dead on a weekly or monthly basis. Audrey Harper reports:

> At one school I visited at least 25 per cent of the thirteen to eighteen year-olds admitted to playing with ouija boards. Young people are at risk of being sucked into the occult at many levels. Warnings must be sounded early that even such things as ouija boards and tarot cards can be a doorway to danger.[34]

Doug Harris of the Christian organization Reachout Trust is also asked into schools to warn about the ouija board. But he says the children have usually already worked out the dangers for themselves: 'Before long there are hands going up everywhere telling me the problems they have had since they played with the ouija board or the tarot cards. There is a very serious side to this, and they know it.'[35]

One 16-year-old girl says:

> Some friends were playing ouija with me when suddenly the glass speeded up and smashed against the wall. It frightened us to death. Whatever moved that glass was a force we had no control over. Another girlfriend . . . became so scared that she and four other pals even slept in the same room. They were too scared to go to be alone. To this day I feel nervous in the dark and would never touch the ouija again.[36]

Alex

Alex was just five years old when he and some friends went to a girl's caravan for a ouija party. He was as surprised as most of his mates to find that the board seemed to work. It spelled out messages from 'spirits' including one who claimed to be a dead next-door neighbour, who assured them that everyone was friends beyond the grave and happy to be there.

They went on to contact a presence which called itself 'Linda'.

Another of the players, Clare, seemed visibly shaken. They asked her who Linda was but Clare clammed up.

As they continued to use the board 'Linda' told them that Clare had been responsible for her death and that she was going to get even. The message took on a threatening tone: 'Be careful, watch out when you're sleeping.'

Whether it was spirits, the subconscious or someone's malicious manipulation which drove the board, none of the players would have been able to say – though they assumed it was spirits. The power behind it, whatever it was, was potent. One girl said she felt ill and went icy cold to the touch. It took her several days to get over the experience.

As the evening continued there were other messages from different spirits. 'A lot of people in the caravan were considerably freaked out.' Some of them wanted to burn the board, including Alex. But he admits he found it intriguing. 'Although I didn't understand it, I had an appetite for it.'

Several went on to develop a fascination for the occult. One started going to a spiritualist church; others, including Alex, began using the tarot cards or rune stones to tell the future. Rune stones are tools of divination and magic. Their symbolic markings have their origins in Gothic mythology. Each has a special significance and the user is invited to personally identify with a particular stone. The runes can be combined with rituals to try to affect the future.

Alex and few diehards started using the ouija board at school during the lunch hours in a class that the teachers seldom visited.

'I thought it was great. I was well and truly hooked on it. It kind of made up for my sense of inadequacy.' Alex's description of himself at the time was that of a misfit; a rebel at school, often suspended, sometimes coming close to expulsion.

As he progressed more deeply into the occult he was to become increasingly disturbed and eventually suicidal.

Gary

Teenager 'Gary' also found that one thing led to another. A bit of a hippy, the ouija board was part of his mind-expansion programme. He remains convinced that the board produced results that he could not explain.

To widen his repertoire he picked up a set of runes at the high street newsagents W. H. Smith. He wasn't so unmaterialistic as to be beyond using them to help him get a girl or some extra cash. 'I was never without a girlfriend, but it didn't seem to work with the cash,' he chuckles.

'I suppose subconsciously I was tapping into something over and above myself.' Experiments with the ouija board convinced him that there was supernatural power beyond his experience. 'You can be into the runes one week and tarot cards the next. It's like a drug craving. Once you've seen it you can't unsee what you've seen. Once you've tasted it you want to do it again.'

By the age of 19 he, too, became suicidal.

Roger

We came upon 'Roger' in chapter three. He'd scared the life out of a mate with a tarot card reading. His curiosity towards the occult had been fired up earlier, as his spiritualist mum had told him how she talked to spirits around the house.

But she had been dead now for several years and Roger was in effect brought up by his older brother 'Ian', a self-styled occultist whose ways were so wild that he became well known to the local constabulary. It was he who initiated Roger into the occult.

The ouija board came as a job lot along with soft drugs, doomy Gothic music and a fascination with horror movies. In Roger's words, 'ouija became a real habit, almost addictive'.

A friend, who was into paganism, was showing off the board at a party. To Roger's surprise, the group got a message which was supposedly from his mother.

'A lot of the conversation was to check out that it really was her, by asking personal questions such as where did you get married, what did you wear on your wedding day?' All his questions, he says, were answered correctly. Now, through the ouija board, her 'spirit' was introducing the players to her new friends on the 'other side'.

Roger discounts the notion that someone in the know was making the glass move: 'It moved far too fast. There were moments when your finger was losing it and you had to try to get your finger back on.' On another occasion the glass moved so quickly it went flying off across the room.

'At the time I was fully convinced it was my mum, so much so that I told my Gran and my Dad, but now I think it was some sort of demon.' What changed Roger's mind was the frightening experience of finding these 'friendly' spirits beginning to turn nasty. 'Mum', it seems, had got him into bad company.

Roger's absorption with the occult had become increasingly

morbid and interlaced with elements of witchcraft, satanism and ritual magic. The group would go to the graveyard to collect names of the dead to contact, and for good measure would steal their grave-stones to give extra power to their rituals. 'We became so obsessed with it, we opened a grave once, at the cathedral. If we were on the ouija board we would be going at it from 11 o'clock after the pub to daylight.' The thrill of fear was too compelling, too strong, for anyone to want to go to bed.

During one long session two of his friends passed into what he describes as hallucinatory states. 'They were well under, shaking violently, saying they were slipping into a murky pool.' Another started to stare and speak in a strange voice, calling out 'help me'. He seemed scared of shadows.

From the ouija board they turned to the tarot cards, sometimes combining them both. Roger says the heady brew of dope and the occult left him badly confused and suffering from feelings of para-noia. 'Half of it was my imagination going wild, with this atmos-phere. I split up with my girlfriend over it.'

However we choose to explain his account, the experiences, authentic or imagined, were genuine enough to him.

Roger found a particularly destructive method of calming his rising fears. He realized that he could silence the emotional storm by inflicting physical pain upon himself. He began slashing his body with a razor blade.

As horrifying as it might sound, self-mutilation is not an un-common sight for psychiatrists. This self-destructive tendency reflects inner turmoil and is often linked with suicide.

One thing leads to another

That one thing can lead to another was graphically illustrated in Clevedon, England, where children from a comprehensive school were thought to be responsible for the sacrifical killing of a cat. Police sergeant Rick Palmer was in charge of the inquiry: 'Several pupils became deeply involved with ouija boards [which they] used to contact spirits, and then they took it a step further.'[37]

The same could be said of David Stillwell, of Luton in Bedfordshire:

> David . . . was only eight when he started dabbling with a ouija board out of curiosity. By the time he was 17 he'd started his own coven with a friend and was recruiting members through occult

magazines. He says: 'It became tame after a while and I decided to investigate satanism. We sacrificed rabbits, pigeons and drank their blood . . . You're too easily influenced at that age. I was lucky and got out early enough.'[38]

5

Beyond the veil

Spiritualism

> Although it is very difficult to try to put a figure on the number of cases of mental illness as a result of dealings with spiritualism, it is a very real problem which stretches nationwide.
>
> Professor Andrew Sims, Dean of the Royal College of Psychiatrists[1]

Reaching out into the unknown, pinning our hopes and faith on what we might find, perhaps even seeking an answer that we hope will give value and meaning to our lives can be a risky business. Even more so when the individual is in crisis and a powerful emotional charge is wrapped up with the quest.

Bereavement could be one such crisis, adolescence might be another. In many cases, individuals have turned to mediums to ease the despair of loss, in the hope of clinging on to contact with someone they have loved, or of gaining a new perspective as life nears it conclusion. But the search for consolation may also bring dangers, as the book *Deliverance* makes clear:

> In seeking continuing contact with the dead, spiritualists may prevent those who have lost a loved one from carrying out the necessary work of bereavement, and this may have untoward psychological consequences. There is always the danger that spiritualists, seeking guidance from the dead, may assume that the dead are necessarily wiser then the living.[2]

Spiritualism began in the 19th century, but in recent years it has evolved into a new movement called 'channelling', which is now big business in the USA. Its practitioners claim to be 'channels' for messages from various kinds of disembodied spirits.

Reginald Alex, of the Chicago-based Cult Awareness Network, argues that some channellers could well be sincere although self-deluded: he says they are 'highly susceptible' people who 'may have had a previous psychopathology' (i.e. mental illness). So is channelling a hoax or a real supernatural phenomenon? Wherever the truth may lie, the danger for those on the receiving end lies in their mental condition and state of gullibility.

Professor Carl Raschke of the University of Denver describes channelling as 'a form of pseudo-religion that performs the same function as drugs'. He is worried about its effects on those who fall prey to the habit. 'In my view,' he told a Sacramento magazine, 'it is a kind of pathology, and the more fascinated a person gets with it, the more likely it is that they can become mentally imbalanced by the process itself. Autohypnosis is a powerful tool not totally understood. It can lead to manipulation.'[3]

Taking the strain

One hundred and eight nurses, chosen at random, in Leeds, West Yorkshire, were interviewed about their spiritual experiences. David C. Lewis used an established test to give an indication of their psychological well-being: 'I discovered that those who had been involved in trying to contact the dead through spiritualism ranked lower than average on this scale of psychological well-being.' They were also found to be less happy than other nurses.[4]

From reduced psychological well-being to psychological disturbance is no great step. In *What is the New Age?* David C. Lewis cites the following example:

> A 24 year old nurse was among a group of nine who went to a seance held by one of the girl's parents. A 'spirit' was called up in the darkened living room. 'Nearly all of us were disbelieving until it really went cold in the room,' said the nurse. 'All of us got the shakes. I had a really dry feelings in my throat. I felt clammy – it makes heckles rise in my throat now to talk about it.' She wanted to leave, but morbid curiosity kept her in her place.
>
> 'I felt some presence in the room. One of the girls recognized this and spoke to it. It shook me up for the rest of the evening – also now, thinking about it.' The seance lasted only 40 minutes but the aftertaste endured much longer.
>
> Throughout the night the nurse was unable to sleep. She developed a fear of the dark which was to haunt her for months: 'It was a long time before I could walk up the stairs without a light on. I needed a light to go to sleep. I got jittery walking home in the dark on my own; if I was on my own it made my mind flip back to the events of the seance. I was afraid of the dark for . . . about two months or so.' As a result of a singly spooky seance the nurse had regressed to a child-like state of anxiety.[5]

German writer Kurt Koch recalls a young woman who was invited to a seance by friends. At first, he says, she found it beneficial and continued to go. But later: 'She began to suffer from depressions which resulted in her contacting a neurologist. During the courses of treatment she was committed to a mental hospital.' There, away from the seances which were the source of her disturbance, her condition improved. The hospital chaplain helped her to a growing faith and trust in Christ and she subsequently made a complete recovery. Kurt Koch continues, 'She was released from hospital within a matter of weeks as cured, and since that time there has been no recurrence of illness.'[6]

Koch is convinced that the only actual spirits raised at a seance are malign entities whose purpose is to deceive and entrap gullible human beings. And they do this by masquerading as spirits of the departed.

Wolves in sheep's clothing?

Over one thing at least, some spiritualists and Christians will find agreement: that with the exception of deliberate fraud, there is the possibility of genuine spirit contact at a seance. Where they profoundly disagree is over the fundamental nature of those spirits.

Most mediums claim to be helped by a spirit guide. This is often supposedly the spirit of a person who achieved some spiritual prowess during their lives. Former medium Ralph Gasson claims he came under the control of his spirit guide during his first seance:

> I had a spirit guide who claimed to be an African witchdoctor stating that he had been in the spirit world for 600 years . . . A man sitting in that same circle who also understood the African dialect conversed quite naturally with the spirit who was controlling me and interpreted what was being said into English. I myself have never known a word of any African dialect. The reader must make no mistake about it, the spirit power is real and not just mere hallucination.[7]

Occult author Dennis Wheatley describes this process as a state of possession. The medium does not possess the knowledge he or she imparts; that knowledge is held by a spirit which must possess him or her in order to impart it. Psychic researcher Jess Stearn records: 'Almost without exception, the great mediums . . . felt they were instruments of a higher power which flowed through them. They did not presume to have the power themselves.'[8]

Some parapsychologists claim that what happens at a seance is nothing to do with spirits, but is a natural phenomenon which has yet to be explained. All matter is energy, so when a medium manifests what appears to be a spirit she does so by emitting energy from within her. Any apparition is actually a manifestation of her subconscious. That position is no more provable than the existence of spirits. But even if the parapsychologists have got it right, dare we trust the subconscious murmurings of a man or a woman who is personally *convinced* he or she is able to summon spirits? And if our answer, through folly or bravery, is yes, then dare we trust the spirits he or she may summon?

Not in the case of Jim Jones, who commanded more than 900 cult members, including women and children, to commit suicide in Jonestown, Guyana. Jones had earlier proclaimed that he also received guidance from a supernatural spirit.[9]

The spiritist Emmanuel Swedenborg believed, dangerously, that he had divine sanction to communicate with spirits, and the necessary protection. He claimed to do so frequently. Yet he observed:

> When spirits begin to speak with a man, he ought to beware that he believes nothing whatever from there; for they say almost anything. Things are fabricated by them, and they lie . . . they would tell so many lies, and indeed with solemn affirmation that a man would be astonished . . . If a man then listens and believes, they press on, and deceive and seduce in divers ways . . . Let men beware therefore.[10]

Swedenborg did not speak from a Christian position. Yet he described making contact with what he believed to be deceiving demonic spirits. These, he said, were accomplished in impersonating both the living and the dead. It is here that the spiritist and Christian positions come full circle.

Where they will never agree is over the person and nature of Christ. The National Spiritualist Association of Churches (USA) states that all men are divine, and that Christ 'is one of many Saviour Christs, who at different times have come into the world to lighten its darkness. [Spiritualism] recognizes him as a world Saviour but not as "the only name" given under heaven by which men can be saved.' The document states that Jesus did not pay the ultimate price for men's sins in giving his own life in our place, as Christians believe, and claims that Jesus himself was a practising spiritualist.[11]

These statements have much in common with the views of Theosophists and other occultists, but are completely contrary to orthodox Christian belief, which declares Jesus as *the* Christ (literally, 'Anointed Saviour') and not one among many. Once this is understood it is easy to see why Christians regard spiritualism as a deception.

Possession syndrome

Christian and psychiatric views converge in the following example. From *The Practitioner* of March 1974 comes an account of a female factory worker who had been diagnosed as a schizophrenic. Five months earlier she had visited a spiritualist couple for healing. Since that time she had been subject to hallucinations, imagined she could hear her dead father's voice on the telephone and became convinced the healer was in her home. She had no previous family history of mental illness.

Dr Richard Mackarness, then an assistant psychiatrist at a hospital in Hampshire, had treated her with drugs, without success. 'Having come to the end of orthodox therapeutic resources,' he wrote, 'I began to suspect that I was dealing with a case of the possession syndrome.'

Possession syndrome is the belief, or delusion, that a person's problems are the result of possession by an evil spirit. It's a recognized condition, sometimes stemming from an inability to face one's own negative experiences and shortcomings and to compensate by projecting the blame for them onto another source.[12]

A colleague, psychiatrist Dr Kenneth McAll, had recently published an article on the subject. With the patient's permission, they took the unorthodox step of performing an exorcism. 'The result was dramatic,' wrote Dr Mackerness. 'The patient said she felt better at once and thereafter made an uninterrupted recovery. Her drugs were quickly tapered off and have not been resumed.' Dr McAll later added in his book *Healing the Family Tree*:

> We prayed very simply to God for guidance and protection, in Jesus Christ's name, said the Lord's Prayer and commanded any evil to leave peacefully. No further treatment was necessary. The patient was healed from that moment and returned home two days later to her husband and teenage son.[13]

There is no way of proving that the client was possessed. What is not in question is her *conviction* that she was, and that her recognized clinical condition set in only after consultation with a medium, and improved only after her exorcism. Could it be that such a powerful conviction in the possibility of spirit possession might in itself be enough to unstitch an individual who is already straining at the seams?

If so, then there are many who may be at risk. Belief in spirit possession is more common than rational thinkers might care to acknowledge. In a widespread survey conducted among 488 different international social groupings, 74% believed in the reality of spirit possession. Among North Americans, 52% said it was possible, while spirit possession was accepted by a full 88% of people living in the Insular Pacific. Dr Erika Bourguinon, who edited the survey, concluded: 'The beliefs are thus characteristic of the great majority of our societies.'[14]

Health warning

However widespread the belief in spirits from beyond might be, there are obvious hazards associated with making an emotional investment beyond the grave. Some aspects of spiritualism are rooted in trickery and fraud. And there is the danger that individuals could fall prey to a medium who will manipulate the emotional upheaval that follows bereavement. All in all, spiritualism more than warrants this resounding health warning given by the former medium, M. Lamar Keene:

> One of the most alarming things about the mediumistic racket is how completely some people put their lives into the hands of ill-educated, emotionally unbalanced individuals who claim a hot-line to heaven.
>
> As a medium I was routinely asked about business decisions, marital problems, whether to have an abortion, how to improve sexual performance, and similar intimate and important subjects. That people who ask such questions of a medium are risking their mental, moral and monetary health, is a shocking but quite accurate description of this matter.[15]

Adolescent misadventures

Peter Anderson writes:

Brian was a bright, fairly intelligent fourteen-year-old boy, who attended a seance casually with several other boys. Very unwisely he asked the controlling spirit when he would die . . . the answer came back, 'When you are sixteen.' He sat there ashen-faced in the classroom as he told me his story.[16]

Spiritualism is often unfairly and inaccurately caricatured as the last resort of the blue-rinse brigade. But its search for hope, meaning and identity echoes earlier adolescent yearnings. Some young people may welcome a spiritual pilot to help them set course through the choppy, uncharted waters between childhood and adulthood.

In our own survey 41% of young teenagers believed it was possible to contact the spirits of the dead. A further 28% were open to the possibility. By many accounts, spiritualism, and its close cousin necromancy, have claimed their victims among the young.

Lecturer Eddie Vass addresses schools about the dangers of the occult. There have been tricky occasions when theory has given way to practice. In the video *Doorways to Danger* he relates the following incident, which took place at a school in Cambridgeshire:

> We finished the session and I was sitting in the staff room having a cup of coffee when suddenly there was a disturbance outside. People came into the staff room and said, 'Come quick.'
>
> I went out into the foyer of the school and there was a young lady clearly demented, screaming, part of her body paralyzed, and beside herself, to the confusion of children running everywhere.
>
> Recognizing what this was, I stepped in and took her very quickly out of the foyer of the school through a door and on to the adjacent field. By now she was uncontrollable, shouting, screaming.

As a practising Christian he prayed for her, instructing what was troubling her to leave:

> At that moment she shook from head to foot, and then stood calm. I said to her, 'Could you explain what has happened?'
>
> She said, 'Well, on Saturdays I have a part time job with a hairdresser, and I found this hairdresser was a medium. Progressively, without meaning to, I got involved with her and what she was doing and, somehow, without reason, in that period we had this afternoon it suddenly sparked.'[17]

Tom Poulson is General Secretary of the Deo Gloria Trust, which has been counselling cult members for more than 25 years. He recalls an incident as a young apprentice, when two other lads, 'one a pretty hard nut', were invited to take part in a seance: 'They went off one evening and tried to contact spirits.' That was the last Tom was to see of them for the next ten days.

> Of course, word went round, 'Hey, where's John, where's Fred?' When they eventually came back to work both related how they'd felt after trying to get involved with spirits.
> They'd both been violently ill. One went into a long depression and the other guy, who was the hard nut, just said he was never, ever, going to touch anything like this again.
> Both of them began the whole thing as a bit of a laugh. That was one incident as a teenager. Since then there have been many more.

Makeshift seance

It was around midnight. Counsellor Gordon Wright was manning a crisis line in Plymouth, England, when the phone rang. The caller, a father, was clearly distressed. In the background his wife could be heard crying. 'He was phoning in to say he didn't know what to do, because they had been having trouble with their 17-year-old daughter. She was currently sitting out in the middle of the road stark naked.'

An earlier attempt to bring her indoors had failed spectacularly, when the girl had somehow managed to throw off both her parents. They called for a doctor, and were still waiting for him to arrive. As a last resort they rang the helpline. Gordon Wright summoned a woman colleague and went to the scene.

> Sure enough, there she was, still stark naked out in the street. She was clasping a transistor radio and was biting deep into it. It was making the most horrific grinding noise. I feared for her teeth.
> My lady colleague threw a coat over her and whisked her inside where her her parents were waiting. Her father and mother were in a pretty bad state. This had never happened before. The girl ran upstairs and into her bedroom and locked the door. She turned her record player up full and then she started smashing things. All you could hear was this music and things being smashed.

The doctor arrived with a duty social worker. He made his apologies and left immediately to attend another call. 'The girl was highly disturbed,' says Gordon Wright. 'But she wasn't sectioned, because the doctor had gone.' The remaining three, all Christians, then prayed for the girl throughout the night, and continued to meet for prayer over the next few weeks.

The disturbance began, says Gordon Wright, after the girl attended a seance:

> It was a makeshift seance, not one with a professional medium, and it was done for a giggle in a friend's home. They did all the things that they'd seen and heard in videos and books, and invited whoever was there to make contact, not believing for a moment that anything would happen. But for whatever reason, they left that room clearly convinced that things *did* happen.
>
> There was in fact a physical manifestation. There was a change of temperature, bits of furniture moved, and other things happened that they never got to the bottom of.

The girl was thought to be in close association with an artist who was heavily involved in black magic. Another friend who'd been at the seance was also disturbed and had to receive counselling. Both responded well to the help they were given. 'But the question I ask,' says Gordon Wright, 'is how may people go unhealed, out of the frying pan into the fire, or are admitted into mental hospitals, because they are not brought to someone who understands what has happened?'

Gordon Wright ascribes the acute disturbance that followed this experiment with spiritism as the work of a malevolent spiritual influence. By reaching out to spirits at a seance, the girl opened herself to destructive forces that could only be described as evil. A spiritual problem calls for a spiritual solution, and the spiritual pollution that she had suffered was cleaned up by prayer and the presence of Christ.

Parental involvement

We've considered risks to unstable adults who become involved in seances and vulnerable teenagers whose crises of identity or sheer curiosity draw them into the occult. But warnings have also been raised of the possible dangers to children whose parents have exposed them to occult practices. Such warnings come from different sides of the theological divide.

Psychotherapist Alan Varley has no religious convictions. (His name has been changed to protect the confidentiality of the client whose account he relates.) Yet he has had to patch up the psyches of a number of people whose bizarre convictions have brought them to breaking point.

One such client was a 15-year-old girl whose mother claimed to be a clairvoyant. She believed she had healing powers and was possessed by a great female writer who actually wrote through her. Alan Varley explains:

> She became very involved with another clairvoyant who claimed to be a witch and said she could cast spells on people. The father was alcoholic and abusive, physically and verbally. The whole atmosphere within the family was extremely nutty.
>
> The young daughter is heavily into sex with a man much older than her and has taken to drinking with paracetamol and other drugs to heighten the effect in order to obliterate herself. She is very much on the edge of running away from home, becoming a prostitute and becoming a major problem, and I'm sure that it all comes from living in this quite extraordinary, nutty and damaging home environment.
>
> She has great difficulty in establishing any firm value system or any sense of reality or up from down. She is just a very, very, confused child, and at present all I can do is a holding, sustaining action and hope to get her through to sixteen and leaving school and to college before she cracks completely.

The crucial role played by the father's abusive personality must not be diminished, but in the view of this secular psychotherapist, parental involvement with the occult had to share part of the blame for the girl's condition: 'Yes, indeed, in terms of producing the blurring of realities and loss of sense of reality within her.'

Jane

As we heard in chapter three, Jane's grandmother had been a devotee of the black arts. She initiated Jane into many of her practices, and taught her how to call up spirits at a seance.

Jane was 14 years old and jealous of her schoolmate Julie. Julie was bossy and her classwork was always better than Jane's. To make matters worse Julie cribbed her homework and cheated in exams. But the teachers seemed blind to the fact and actually liked her. Jane thought it was time to take the wind out of Julie's sails.

It was Julie's idea. She suggested they had a seance. They drew her bedroom curtains and the six of them sat cross-legged on the floor. Jane remembered her grandmother's instructions. She spread out the lexicon cards across the table top, placed an upturned tumbler in the middle and called on the spirits. She could have done so without the ouija board, but the props were for the benefit of the others.

> All the windows were shut, but after a while I became aware of a stirring within the room, and I knew the presence had arrived. The glass on the table began to move. It shifted to the first letter; a J, then to a U and continued until it had completely spelled Julie's name. Then, letter for letter, it spelt out TROUBLE. Then it stopped moving, and fell over.
>
> 'That's it,' I declared, cool and clear. 'We're finished now, time to go.'

It had taken half an hour, but in the space of thirty minutes Julie's superior expression had soured into fear and puzzlement.

> Another girl, Zoe, had drawn up her knees beneath her chin, and was clutching her legs. All the colour had drained from her face, and then she was sick, right across the rug.
>
> We cleaned up the mess. Zoe was in no fit state to help. My feeling of satisfaction ran deep and good. I felt powerful. I had achieved exactly what I had set out to do. Afterwards, things were very different at school. They respected me. They were afraid of me. Some of the other girls came up to me and asked whether I could read their palms. Usually I refused, although on rare occasions I did it as a grace to those who had earned my favour.

Grandma had taught her well.

Gary

'Gary's' first contact with the occult was at the age of 12 after the death of a schoolfriend. He went with the boy's mother to a spiritualist medium to try to contact her son. At school, Gary had been preoccupied with trying to get to the truth. Some of his teachers found him argumentative to the point of vexation. At the same time he began experimenting with drugs: 'I did everything short of heroin.' Convictions for shoplifting and burglary followed.

As we heard earlier, Gary's exploration of the occult progressed from spiritualism to the ouija board, the rune stones and the tarot. It became a fixation. By the age of 19 Gary became suicidal. 'I think it was total despair with the world as a whole. Yet at the same time my experimentation with the occult and drugs – and I can see a clear link between the two – left me very dissatisfied.'

And by now Gary had seen enough to recognize that his role model – the woman who'd introduced him to spiritualism – left much to be desired:

I had read wonderful promises of enlightenment and cosmic perception, but I observed the lifestyle of this well-educated woman who within the space of five to ten minutes could go from being perfectly rational, humorous and highly articulate, to a gibbering, screaming, irrational, schizophrenic, psychologically-warped person who hated everything.

She would be in the corner screaming her head off at anything that moved because she was totally paranoid. Her career had taken a turn for the worse, her marriage had fallen to pieces – and she had a vitriolic hatred and that could go on for hours and then change again within the space of minutes.

I would just sit there and watch all this and see how it upset my girlfriend, and I thought, well, if this is the fruit of all this, then I'm not sure I want to get into it.

But Gary had a problem. He had a creepy feeling that the same process was happening to him.

There would be times back in my flat when I would start going on psychological overdrive. I would go into self-destruct mode. It was like a neurosis or paranoia. All of a sudden it was like an intense pressure in the mind, like an anger; but internalized and self-destructive.

I could feel in my head these things happening and thought 'that's not me; that's not rational; I don't believe that'; but it was like an overwhelming rage and a fury. I would try to contain it but eventually it would get so much that the only way I could alleviate it and keep a handle on my thinking was to hit something or head-butt the wall, which is what I used to do. And I would pace up and down my room for maybe two hours until the whole thing passed.

He says he often thought about suicide but 'never had the guts to do it'. He comments, 'Maybe my compulsive nature did get me into it, my quest for truth – I do have an inquiring mind. But in trying to find out who I am, I actually lost who I was.'

Amanda

'Amanda' was 18 when she met a friend whose mother was a spiritist. Together they used a ouija board and contacted a spirit guide who told Amanda that her childhood had been a training ground for a career as a medium.

Amanda was introduced to two personal spirit guides, who claimed a special knowledge of her. The first claimed to be the spirit of her dead sister, Marjorie, who was miscarried before Amanda was born. The second was Samuel, who said he had been one of her childhood invisible friends.

The spirits asked if she would let them come into her and she agreed. She breathed them in and felt hot inside. Afterwards she found she was able to speak in different voices.

In time Amanda discovered that she was able to channel other spirits, and her mediumistic abilities became much in demand. Her interest in the occult broadened to incorporate a number of New Age healing techniques, including acupuncture, homeopathy and crystals.

A series of personality changes began to occur. Amanda believed she could feel the jealousy of her unborn sister Marjorie, who had had no life of her own:

> She would tell me that if she'd survived, I would never have lived, because she was miscarried shortly before my mother conceived me. Marjorie told me I had a duty to her to allow her some life. When I walked past the mirror, I wouldn't see myself; I would see her. I would talk to her.

Marjorie, she believed, was compelling her to shoplift. 'She made me steal little trinketry things; not even things that I liked. She was obsessed with the colour purple.'

Her parents noticed a change in Amanda's language. Her speech became filthy and she found herself turning hard and bitter. And at the back of it all was a growing fear: 'I began to go into trances outside my control.' When she started to write the spirit would take her over, producing automatic writing that she was powerless to stop.

She felt the spirit Samuel telling her that she was very special, that she was a spirit child, and that she could never be happy or fulfilled until she was with them. 'Death is nothing!' Samuel would insist. 'Death is not real. Death is life. Choose life, choose death! Be with me, we can be one!'

Through five generations of her family, there had been no history of psychiatric disorder, and up until then Amanda had never thought of suicide. But that began to change. After one trance, she came round to find a knife in her hand pointing towards herself. She was certain she was being called by Samuel to be his spirit bride. Death was her true purpose in life.

Amanda was regularly getting messages from Samuel through automatic writing or channelling, when she would speak with his voice, or even via the ouija board. During those ouija sessions she says the atmosphere in the room began to change:

> Sometimes there would be a strange smell, even a sickly-sweet smell. At other times the room would become freezing cold and there would be a horrible atmosphere as though someone murderous was walking through the room. The hairs on the back of my neck would stand up, and I would become aware of a force that was really evil.

Her happy childhood invisible friend was becoming darker and more disturbing by the hour. Amanda did not want to become Samuel's spirit bride. 'I thought it meant I would be killed, and I didn't want to die.'

She was growing increasingly troubled and unstable. Now when she looked in the mirror she saw neither her sister Marjorie nor herself. 'All I could see now was the cackling face of an old woman.'

With mounting fear, she began to recite the Lord's Prayer, but could not bring herself to say the words, 'deliver us from evil'. She prayed out loud, 'God, if you're there, you have to help me, because I'm beyond help.'

Family fascination

Cleland Thom is a lecturer in media law and former editor of a group of nine local newspapers in North London. 'My parents were both spiritualists and my father was a widely known spiritualist preacher,' he says. 'We used to hold seances together as a family.'

At the age of eight he was regularly calling on the spirits with his ten-year-old brother. 'We were absolutely fascinated by it all,' he explains. 'It was like an adventure to us.'

But he claims the adventure turned sour as spiritualism began to change his personality: 'I went from being a rosy-cheeked, outgoing young boy to someone who was moody, introverted and who locked himself away in his room.'

His interest was fired by reading Dennis Wheatley books at school. Curiosity towards the occult became an obsession. Over a period of years that obsession turned to severe depression. He began hearing voices and a cloud of fear seemed to surround him. He became convinced he was going mad: 'Entering spiritualism was like signing my own death warrant,' he says, 'but having it happen by instalments. My personality, my sexuality, my mental and emotional state were being destroyed. I felt cursed.'

Cleland Thom's account appeared in the Christian publication, *Doorways to Danger*,[18] but the following was published in the secular newspaper *The Sutton Coldfield Observer*:

> A terrified former witch, who is too terrified to reveal her identity, has issued a chilling warning . . . that those dabbling in Spiritualism will subject themselves to mental breakdown and a life of mental torment. She said she had seen many suffer mental breakdowns because of their spiritualist experiences and that she herself tried to commit suicide on several occasions.[19]

In reply, the president of the local spiritualist church wrote in the paper: 'I believe that rather than being a cause of mental illness, if correctly taught, Spiritualism can be of great benefit.'

But that was not the experience of journalist Cleland Thom, nor Jane, nor Gary, nor Amanda – who were all taught by experts. Neither is it the experience of those who have been deceived by fraudsters, in the firm belief that they were being 'correctly taught'. Not is it the conviction of doctors who raise serious psychological objections to spiritualism, nor that of theologians who dispute the notion that spiritualism can provide, in the words of one medium, 'a safe way of delving into the unknown'.

Nor was it the experience of 15-year-old Ann, whose account is related by Peter Anderson: Ann was a previously healthy, well-balanced girl who had decided to conduct the ultimate experiment, using herself as the guinea pig. She was found dead in her bed after suffocating herself with a polythene bag. Her suicide note had been sealed with wax. It read: 'If it is possible for a spirit to return, I shall return. If there are no signs of ghostly disturbance within a week of

my death, then the spirit of the human body is beyond human recall.'
The Lancashire coroner told the inquest:

> It has come to my notice that there is an interest in spiritualism at
> this girl's school. I have been told that there has been involvement
> with a ouija board, and girls are trying to contact the spirits. I
> hope that Ann's death will serve as a lesson to her school friends
> not to get involved in spiritualism – it is dangerous.[20]

6

Alternative realities

The New Age movement

New Age is a patchwork philosophy that includes ideas from
Eastern faiths, Native American traditions, Christianity,
metaphysics, parapsychology, holistic medicine, faith healing,
reincarnation, vegetarianism, astrology and occultism. Each New
Ager chooses which path or paths to follow in pursuit of spiritual
growth.
Daily Herald, 17 Dec. 1981.

So here we are in the New Age, a combination of spirituality and
superstition, fad and farce, about which the only thing certain is
that it is not new.
Time, 7 Dec. 1987.

New Age?

In a single year US citizens spent more than $100 million on crystals
– quartz stones claimed to have healing and thought-transmission
powers.[1] Healing crystals are part of the paraphernalia of the
booming New Age movement, a rag-bag of religious and philosophical oddments, incorporating Hinduism, paganism and undiluted
occultism. *Time* magazine defined it as 'an esoteric blend of
computer-age jargon and ancient religious practice, which often
invested stones with powerful magic'.

Time magazine got it right. There is little about the New Age that
is truly new. This open-ended gazetteer of esoteric ideas and old-
fashioned occult practices bids the pilgrim travel a variety of well-
known paths from divination via paganism to magic. The ultimate
destination is a Utopia described by a contributor to the *New Age
Journal* as 'a heaven on earth; a society in which the problems of
today are overcome and a new existence emerges'.[2]

The New Age movement is a loose confederation of many
disparate interests and activities, from the holistic medicine of the
middle classes to the pagan shamanism of New Age travellers. Its

utopian idealism shares many of the concerns of the Green movement, making its eco-conscious neo-paganism especially attractive to questioning young people seeking radical ways to save the planet.

It also pulls in its fair share of weirdos. One of the founder members of the British Green Party, ex-footballer David Icke, went on to claim that he was a Son of God, his wife and daughter were angels, and that tidal waves would threaten to end life on Earth by 1997.

Green and Aquarian festivals add a broader environmental appeal but draw together much the same variety of esoteric and occult practitioners as can be found at psychic festivals, ranging from mediums to shamans.

Rock festivals such as Glastonbury reveal the influence of the New Age in providing the philosophical underpinnings for a growing youth movement. Those who feel the old solutions have failed them are taking part in an end-of-millennium revival of the hippie culture. New Age travellers are turning on and dropping out – all over again. Drugs and the occult are blending together in a scene where the only reality worth striving for is an altered reality.

In the psychedelic sixties many followed the hippy trail to a higher consciousness, only to find themselves on the express to Marrakesh in search of the ultimate narcotic trip. Then yesterday's hippies got older, their hair got shorter, and many who dropped-out dropped back in again. In middle-age some are finding new ways of explaining, reinterpreting and resuming their adolescent quest, and the burgeoning industry for New Age books is eagerly devoured by a new generation in search of the holy grail.

Now, as then, the journey into enlightenment and self-oblivion may take a detour via the drug pusher, who arguably rings much the same bell somewhere in the subconscious as the assorted holy men from the East.

Kevin Logan, Anglican minister and author on the occult, writes: 'There is almost a direct correlation between the occult and drugs, where you see some being caught in the soft drugs and then graduating onto the harder stuff. The same is true of the occult.'

This connection between the occult and drugs was made by 'Gary'. Teenage life was about getting a high, and in keeping with his new-found New Age paganism, Gary switched from LSD to hallucinogenic mushrooms to tune in to their more magical mystique. In so doing, he was borrowing from an age-old tradition. He explains:

Traditionally, within animistic, occult and pagan belief, drug taking is seen as a means to an end. It is mind-expanding. Dope is used in rituals. If you are a shaman you will take hallucinogenic substances – botanics they call them – because it is a way of entering into the spirit world.

Hutchinson's Encyclopaedia defines a shaman as 'a ritual figure who acts as an intermediary between society and the supernatural world . . . also known as a medicine man, seer or sorcerer, the shaman uses magic powers . . .'

According to Gary, shamanism is a popular pastime among some New Age travellers: 'Shamanism is strong, resurgent, and up and coming, and all these guys are taking sacred herbs, drugs and potions. There is a massive resurgence in animistic tribal beliefs in our western culture.' And he points out that the drug/occult connection is being pushed further by current dance bands. This music connection is the subject of another chapter.

With hindsight, Gary now sees drugs and the occult as a kind of frantic chasing of the tail: 'That's the infuriating thing about drugs and Eastern philosophy. Like karma, they go round and round in circles all your life. It doesn't actually lead anywhere. You get disillusioned with it.'

And he warns that drugs and the occult have other things in common: you can get hooked on both and one thing leads to another.

Not all drugs are physically addictive, but most drugs are psychologically addictive, so it can become obsessive. There are very few people in my experience who haven't progressed onto harder drugs once they have started. The general progression goes something like this: most people start taking cannabis, then move on to speed or ecstacy, which then gets you into the whole hallucinogenic realm: LSD, particular types of mushroom, then crack and coke and heroin. There is a very strong link between paganism and drug taking.

New Age spirituality

The New Age paganism referred to by Gary incorporates some of the oldest occult activities in the world, and attempts to bring together mutually conflicting belief systems under a single broad banner. Its slogan might as well be that throwback to the sixties: 'If it feels good, do it.' The goal of the New Age pilgrim is to plunge into the depths of his own psyche, to gaze into the void until he realizes union with the god-force in himself.

There is no cut-and-dried New Age philosophy, but amid the mish-mash the prevailing concept of the divine borrows heavily from Eastern religions. In common with Buddhism, many New Agers see God as an impersonal force, a cosmic consciousness, rather than a personality with intelligence.

But New Age pilgrims are not restricted to any single perspective. As an alternative to plumbing the inner depths, some New Agers may regard the quest for enlightenment as a reaching up and out, until unity is attained with higher spiritual beings. This comes closer to polytheistic Hinduism, with its pantheon of gods, and explains how the New Age can incorporate practices such as channelling.

For David Spangler, one of the prophets of the New Age, Lucifer – a figure identified in the Bible with Satan – plays a central role. To be initiated into the New Age, he writes, one must be initiated into Lucifer:

> Christ is the same force as Lucifer . . . Lucifer works within each of us to bring us to wholeness, as we move into a new age, which is the age of man's wholeness, each of us in some way is brought to the point which I term the Luciferic initiation, the particular doorway through which the individual must pass if he is to come fully into the presence of his light and his wholeness . . . Luciferic initiation . . . is an initiation into the New Age.[3]

Such concerns could seem irrelevant to someone without orthodox religious convictions. But we would be wise to be concerned over the open adoration of a figure who has been described for thousands of years as an archetype of all that is deceptive and evil.

And New Age beliefs are gaining ground among the young. According to our survey, 35% of teenagers questioned now believe in the New Age concept of reincarnation, and only one in four rejects it as a possibility.

From America comes a police warning that some disturbed or dissatisfied young people are drawing encouragement from their belief in reincarnation to commit suicide:

> Due to the popular teaching of reincarnation, some youth have begun to believe that if they do not like their current circumstances . . . just 'check out' and try again. Many are doing just that – suicide.[4]

In 1977, a young woman took a friend's pistol and shot herself in the head to settle an argument. He didn't believe in reincarnation and she did.[5]

Casualties

Reference has already been made to The People's Temple, whose leader Jim Jones ordered the suicide of 913 of his followers at Jonestown in Guyana in 1979. Film footage, shot to preserve the event for posterity, shows men, women and children solemnly drinking from their little cardboard cups of cyanide-laced Kool-Aid while guards armed with pistols, rifles and crossbows stand by. Those who would not drink willingly were forcibly injected with the poison.

But what has this to do with the New Age? Only five years beforehand, Jonestown was listed in the New Age handbook, the *Spiritual Community Guide*, as a centre to 'teach Christian socialism in preparation for the New Age'.[6]

Since then the Jim Jones connection has been denied by other New Agers. But his image and his works are being perpetuated by Thee Temple ov Psychic Youth (sic) in a video production showing images of the mass suicide, bearing the caption 'Thank you, Daddy'. Poems by Jones have been incorporated into records produced by a connected music group, which has distributed a limited edition album of his last speeches – one copy for each dead body, lovingly hand-numbered in gold.

TOPY has indulged in ritualistic sado-masochistic sexual practices and the use of drugs and has been actively recruiting young people in several different countries.

Of course it is unfair to tar other New Age followers and their practices with the same brush. Many would disavow TOPY as readily as they would distance themselves from Jim Jones. But the common denominator is the same self-absorption and wide-eyed eagerness to hurtle into a psychic and spiritual void, where notions of normality are rejected and all conventional points of reference are abandoned. The words of Genesis P. Orridge, spokesman for TOPY, have a familiar ring: 'Who cares as long as it works?'

Flights of fancy

Transcendental Meditation is part of today's New Age scene. It first surfaced in the psychedelic sixties when the drug culture embraced Eastern spirituality. Now a new generation of spiritual pilgrims is following the same path.

The sixties assaulted us with Vietnam then soothed us with the opportunity to make love, not war; while the musical *Hair* ushered in the Age of Aquarius – the astrological era of harmony and under-standing. Three decades on and a new generation came to maturity, but little had changed. The nineties presented barbarism in the Balkans, political corruption, economic collapse – and a rerun of *Hair*. The ultimate alternatives – paganism and the occult – were redubbed the New Age and the hippie movement started over, complete with beads and 28-inch flares.

And one survivor who's seen it all – over and over – is physics graduate, Hindu propagandist and entrepreneur extraordinaire, the Maharishi Mahesh Yogi. In 1967 the Beatles discovered a long-haired holy man who could offer 'enlightenment'. The Maharashi was plunged into the limelight thanks to the supergroup's much-publicized pilgrimage. But where the Beatles have passed into posterity, the Maharashi has adapted his appeal chameleon-like to suit the changing culture. As the swinging sixties gave way to the Thatcherite eighties and the New Age nineties the Maharishi's message was re-tailored to suit hippy and yuppie alike.

His system of transcendental meditation became a multi-national business. Many benefits are claimed for its practitioners. Meditating twice a day for 20 minutes, whilst repeating a mantra, or chant, is said to lower the metabolic rate and cause tensions to fall away. Ads encouraging you to 'Take 20 minutes out to recharge your batteries' claim that millions use TM worldwide. It's the happy, hippy path to enlightenment, tarted up with techno-babble and made over for the new generation of New Age yuppies.

And now the Maharishi's followers have moved into politics. The Natural Law Party put forward (unsuccessful) candidates in both national and European elections in the UK. Claiming to have tapped into the 'invincible, evolutionary power' of nature, the party promises an end to war, a disease-free society and a dramatic reduc-tion in crime. All this is to be achieved by setting up a 7,000 strong team practising transcendental meditation and yogic flying. And its election pledges fly higher than its yogic hoppers: 'The Natural Law Party is the only party that can eliminate stress in society [and] bring success to all areas of life.'

A matter of mantra

Like Yoga, the Maharishi's TM is an Eastern spiritual exercise programme which has been thoroughly re-packaged for an up-beat, materially sophisticated, though spiritually naive, Western market. Its religious roots appear to have been neatly severed; the mumbo-jumbo has been junked, leaving us with an apparently beneficial, well-proven, relaxation technique.

But its esoteric central core remains untouched. TM is much more than an exercise. It is a religious practice. In 1977, New Jersey Federal Court banned the teaching of TM at state schools on the grounds that it was religious in nature, and ruled: 'no other inference is permissable or reasonable'.[7]

At the heart of this religious practice is the mantra, or prayer,. But prayer to whom? The mantra is the word or phrase on which the devotee must concentrate to the exclusion of all else, even himself. It is a Hindu incantation, as the Maharishi (literally, 'his holiness') explains:

We do something here in TM according to Vedic rites [rituals drawn from the Hindu holy scriptures], particularly chanting to produce an effect in some other world and draw the attention of those higher beings or gods living there. The entire knowledge of the mantras or hymns of the Vedas is devoted to man's connection, to man's communication with the higher beings in different strata of creation.[8]

'Higher beings . . . gods . . . some other world'? All that seems far removed from the ad-man's appeal to stressed-out yuppies to 'recharge your batteries', and appears to have more in common with Theosophy and channelling.

'Many of the innumerable mantras are, in fact, the names of fourth class deities in Hinduism', writes author Kevin Logan. He goes on to quote a TM official: 'Please note: a mantra is only the equivalent of a prayer with fixed wording.' Logan observes: 'From my understanding, TM practitioners in England are in ignorance, currently invoking heathen deities twice a day, and the majority don't even know it!'[9]

'The Maharishi . . . even goes so far as to suggest that children should contact the dead,' claims author Peter Anderson, 'so we can see from the writings of its founder that TM has very clear occult roots.' He continues: 'In TM the individual seeks to attain a state of physical immobility as well as mental passivity, and it is well known that these are two of the basic requirements for mediumship in spiritism.'[10]

The TM-Sidhi programme pushes the occult connection even further, as Kevin Logan observes in *Paganism and the Occult*:

Sidhis are the powers which can be added to basic TM, such as levitation, extra-sensory perception, telepathy, telekinesis, spiritual healing and control of mind over body . . . Meditation . . . is recognized by modern occultists as one of the four main paths of magic.[11]

Levitation

Where spiritualism has its developing circles to help individuals bolster their occult abilities and connect with their 'spirit guides', TM has its Sidhi programme. Adherents are perhaps best known for their demonstrations of yogic hopping, a variation on a theme familiar to schoolchildren who attempt to practice levitation.

British yogic flying competitions are staged annually by followers of the Maharishi, though 'flying' is a bit of an overstatement. 'Flyers believe they tap "the unified field", the meeting point of all natural and cosmic energies,' wrote *Independent* journalist Phil Reeve, reporting on the fourth such competition in Skelmersdale, Lancashire.

Devotees claim that bouncing across a mat cross-legged like a Buddha, as it appears to onlookers, can eliminate disease and reduce crime. After hopping, the next stage in developing powers of levitation is said to be hovering.

Levitation is often attempted in the school playground – one of a variety of seemingly innocent childhood games which most of us will have played at some time. They range from drawing another child forward with invisible string, experiencing lightheadedness through hyperventilation, to carrying out convincing acts of mind-reading. Most have simple enough explanations, from harmless conjuring tricks through to uncontrolled and possibly hazardous experiments in self-hypnotism.

But levitation – if it works – could have no natural explanation, and for those taking part who become convinced, rightly or wrongly, that it *does* work, the result can be fearful and disturbing.

Carolyn looks back with obvious trepidation to her schooldays and a childish 'game' which turned to terror:

> We went down to the other end of the playing fields under the willow tree to see what was going on down there. They were not doing anything that I would recognize as wrong, but there was a crowd and a girl lying down, and there were about six people on either side, who were just kind of concentrating.
>
> They had their eyes closed and [they were] basically just lifting her up, which I know now was levitation . . . At the time, to me it

was just kind of magic. Magic was never evil or wrong or anything.

Out of curiosity, she and a friend joined the circle and began to take part.

> My friend Sarah bent down, and it was going to be me that was over her; and everybody would link around us. And then she went out.
>
> I already had started to concentrate on her and her face started to distort, and you could feel that she was really having problems and I just thought, 'God, what is this that I have done, what have I got involved in?' And it unnerved me, and I began to get frightened for my friend as I did not know what was happening to her. So I really prayed, 'God, I am really sorry, help Sarah.'
>
> The group that were around me at the time turned on me and were annoyed with me: 'Look what you have done to her, it's all your fault it's all gone wrong.'
>
> There was my poor mate who was really kind of drunk – couldn't stand up or focus, nothing, and that really frightened me to see that kind of reaction in her.

We may argue that what took place was not levitation, but the power of suggestion and self-delusion. Either way, this childhood game resulted in a palpable fear, and Carolyn was traumatized for some time to come. In her words:

> When I look back, it had a big effect on my life – a significant effect on me mentally, emotionally and physically – it affected me, full stop. It messed me up . . . just that small involvement that I had.[12]

But levitation is a 'game' that may sometimes shift from playground to classroom. Protests were made to a secondary school after the following incident. A teacher got the idea from a television programme featuring psychic Uri Geller. The girl who was picked for the experiment in levitation protested, but was overruled:

> The teacher dismissed the objection, suggesting that it was harmless fun involving muscle energy and that no one knew what made it work anyway. The child felt under pressure to take part . . . and actually felt a floating sensation and something trying to push her backwards. [She believed] that that something was evil. She went home very upset.

The next day the children in the girl's class were trying levitation on their own and another child brought in a book on black magic. It is interesting to note that the children themselves made the association between levitation and black magic. The class teacher didn't take any notice, thinking it all a bit of fun.[13]

Children were badly frightened at a Devon comprehensive school after levitation and pendulum swinging (a method of divination) were introduced into the classroom by a teacher as part of the lesson. 'One of the girls was being levitated in the classroom,' recalls a counsellor. 'The children were absolutely terrified. Some said they felt an evil presence in the room.'

Afterwards, they told their schoolmates what had happened and even though they had been frightened, curiosity was aroused. There was no shortage of volunteers to experience the thrill of the unknown. Before long, other children had started playing these occult 'games', perhaps encouraged by the sanction that had been given to such practices by their teacher.

After a parent complained, levitation no longer took place in the classroom, but the girls continued their alarming game out in the playground.

The following mother's account was related in *The Independent*:

Suddenly he ['Sam'] burst in. We didn't recognize him. His whole face and body had changed. He was spitting and speaking in a voice we hadn't heard before. He said he was a demon and was going to kill the family. Then he grabbed a knife from the kitchen drawer and went for my other son . . . although it's a terrible thing for a mother to say, my son was evil and the effect of that was sheer terror.[14]

The boy in question was 15 and his mother was a teacher. Counselling revealed that 'games' with levitation, tarot cards and ouija boards led to the disturbance. The boy required psychiatric and spiritual help.

In our survey of year-ten pupils almost 29% claimed to believe that they had psychic powers. Only 1 in 12 was strongly aware that trying to develop those powers could be dangerous. So in a class of 24, if our poll is accurate – and polls are always subject to distortion – seven may believe they are psychic and most of those could be open to the possibility of developing their 'gifts' – in total ignorance of the possible dangers.

A question of development

The argument runs that if someone wants to develop their so-called psychic gifts, they would be best advised to join a developing circle where they can receive the help, guidance and support of experts. But to do so is to make two dangerous assumptions: one is that the 'experts' in question are sincere and well-meaning; and two, that practising occult powers, or what passes for them, is both safe and commendable.

For 'Amanda', her encouragement into levitation and other occult practices could not have come from a more respectable source. Her first experience of levitation took place during a Girl Guide meeting. The Guide leader introduced it as a trick. It became part of Amanda's occult repertoire that was to lead to confusion, paranoia and a terror of death at the hands of the spirits who were calling her to join them 'on the other side'.

With hindsight she sees levitation as another step on a dangerous path that she was encouraged along by adults who should have known better.

'To my mind, all these things were squeaky clean,' she explains, 'because they were being introduced by people that I respected, who were leaders in the community: teachers, my headmistress, my guide leader, and unwittingly, I suppose, my parents. So my involvement in the occult was never rebellious. It came out of my curiosity about the world and the supernatural realm.' That respectability ran all the way into the Anglican Church, where she was encouraged by a youth leader to read the tarot cards.

One 16-year-old boy who was introduced to a developing circle is no longer around to tell us his story. 'The boy hanged himself as a result of his occult involvement,' explains counsellor Gordon Wright.

He had been taken along to one of these groups at which there had been a demonstration of clairvoyance and clairaudience. [Clairvoyance is the supposed ability to see events and people ahead of time; clairaudience is supposedly being able to hear sounds and voices from the spirit realm.]

He suffered from asthma and had hands laid on him by occult healers. When he opened his eyes he believed he was able to see other people's auras and tell whether they were healthy or sick by interpreting the colour of their auras. He became almost a teenage medium.

It was his brother who found his body. In the inquest it came out that he killed himself while the balance of his mind was disturbed. It also came out that he had been involved in this group.

Gordon Wright believes the adult circle into which the boy had been drawn had been practising a form of black magic. Prior to his involvement in the group, the teenager had been something of a loner, but there had been no indication of any mental disturbance. He was not the only one. Gordon Wright says:

> I have seen several examples of teenage suicides related to the occult. There have been some gross attempts at suicide, including self-mutilation.
>
> On one occasion a girl actually cut her throat in my car. She had already slashed herself and I was taking her to the Royal Naval Hospital to get her sewn up. She pulled out a knife and slashed her throat. I still have the blood stains on my carpet and clothes.

The girl, who was deeply disturbed, had been a regular visitor to the casualty department after similar attempts. 'It started when she attended an occult healing service. She became interested in it and started going along to a group who met and encouraged out-of-the-body experiences – astral projection. She became quite involved.'

Suggestibility

Astral projection, unlike levitation, is where the spirit or soul of a person is said to leave the body and be able to travel freely and invisibly. Bizarre as this may sound, some occultists claim this ability. If we're to regard them as sincere in this belief, then an alternative explanation could be some psychological form of dissociation – a mind trick. Such a thing would not be far removed from the aim of meditation, which is the loss of awareness of self in order to be able to merge with some supposed higher consciousness.

Dick Sutphen is a professional hypnotist, who trains others in his art. He describes meditation as a 'thought stopping technique', and warns:

> I've worked with meditators on an EEG machine and the results are conclusive: the more you meditate the flatter your mind becomes, until eventually – and especially if used to excess or in combination with decognition – all thought ceases. Some

spiritual groups see this as nirvana – which is bulls**t. It is simply a predictable physiological result.

And in his view meditation might make individuals more mellow, but they also become more suggestible.[15]

To our list of occult dangers, then, must be added another: that of heightened suggestibility among those who join occult developing circles which use meditation or mind-emptying techniques.

As we shall see later, some young people have opened themselves up to more than they bargained for, as a result of being drawn into a group whose members had motives which turned out to be less than spiritual.

And even if the intent is sincere, then we need to recall the warning of psychiatrists about the psychological risk of prising open the doors which seal the vault of the deep unconscious.

Some New Age and occult practitioners may argue that they do so successfully, under controlled conditions. But as we've heard, younger and less robust individuals have taken off on flights of fancy only to sideslip into insanity or suicide, never to return.

7

Teenage dabblers

As a young boy of 13, 14, I practised magic. When you're that age, there's no limit to the scope of your imagination, so everything magic we heard of we attempted, calling forth the devil and invoking demons – we tried all these things, and with some effect.

Mark Pastellopoulous, founder of the Temple of Olympus, England.[1]

Playing with fire

The phenomenon of the teenage occult dabbler first came to light in the United States. To make sense of some bizarre crimes that were emerging, US police came up with a whole new category of criminal.

The typical dabbler was described as middle or upper class; an intelligent underachiever, creative, curious and bored; likely to have a low self-image and to be a poor social mixer.

Sergeant Randy Emon of Baldwin Park Police Department describes the type:

He would simply learn some things from his friend at school; dabble a little bit with a ouija board, go down to the library or the bookstore and pick up a book and do his own thing. Not really dangerous, but he can be moved into further areas which could be criminal or dangerous in nature.[2]

In a recent academic study in the US some 10% of young students claimed to have a friend involved in satanic activities. While satanic involvement was 'relatively unusual', the study supported the view that satanism was linked with antisocial behaviour. After questioning 1,182 teenagers, researchers found 'a clear, consistent, and significant association of antisocial behaviours within the friendship patterns of those who claimed to have friends who are satanically involved'. Teen satanists were more likely to use cocaine and marijuana, to get low grades, drop out of school, get pregnant, have an abortion or get arrested.

But the study described satanism as the effect, rather than the cause of anti-social attitudes. It was 'reactive, rather than causal, a legitimation [for antisocial behaviour], rather than a motivation'. In other words, if a teenager really wants to take youthful rebellion to excess, then there's always satanism.[3]

A US newspaper report said:

> The dabblers are drawn to satanism through drinking, drug and sex parties, heavy metal music and fantasy role-playing games such as Dungeons and Dragons. San Francisco Police Officer Sandi Gallant, considered a leading law enforcement authority on satanic crime, estimates that 1 to 3 per cent of teenagers who dabble in satanism go on to become more heavily involved.[4]

But that figure is on the low side, according to counsellor Don Holland. Addressing a state convention, he estimated that some 3 million American children and teenagers were experimenting with satanism. Of those, 5% would become deeply involved.

The UK dabbler

In the British Isles there have been fewer reported instances of occult-related teenage crime. Police have pointed to cultural differences with the USA.

The UK equivalent of the US dabbler is profiled by British cult researcher Maureen Davies. The picture that emerges is more tentative, and low key: 'These are teenage kids who have bought a book in the library and have tried to do the rituals – self-initiations and rituals like that – and got a cockerel and killed it and drank its blood.'

That's pretty much what happened to the group of scared youngsters facing Audrey Harper across the floor of a rubbish-strewn flat. In their case, it was an experiment with ritual magic which went devastatingly wrong.

Audrey Harper, a refugee from black witchcraft who is now a counsellor, was called to the darkened ground floor flat where the unemployed teenagers had been doing their utmost to summon a spirit to get them out of their predicament.

All seven were slumped against the wall. 'Their eyes were open but they were not looking at me,' she recalls. 'It was as if a camera had captured a look of sheer terror on their faces.'

The floor had been ritually marked with chalk. Among the debris were half burned candles and the pages of books that had been ripped apart. Using occult manuals signed out mainly from the local public library they had spent weeks preparing spells and incantations. Midnight struck and, standing in a circle marked out for their own protection, they began to chant.

After a while the room began to get warm, then stuffy, until they found it difficult to breathe. 'We carried on chanting,' one explained to Audrey Harper; 'we felt we were making contact and we were desperate for something to happen.'

It was as though something had entered the room. 'We couldn't see it but we felt a presence. The door slammed shut and the room suddenly got very cold. Then a strange feeling went through us and all of a sudden it was like everyone went crazy. We had to destroy everything, including each other.'

The room had been wrecked and the teenagers were clearly traumatized by whatever had taken place. 'Each had experienced a private taste of hell,' recalls Audrey Harper, 'and all needed help.'

Be as sceptical as you like about what actually took place in that room, but it bears repeating that whatever happened, even if it can be explained away as the product of several scared and hyperactive imaginations, was real enough to the young adults involved to induce group hysteria and to leave each of them disturbed and badly shaken.

Unemployment had led to boredom and hopelessness. The occult offered cheap thrills and the prospect – if their incantations paid off – of a power which they hoped would work for them.

'I was angry that such dangerous books are so readily available,' says Audrey Harper, 'and sad that intelligent young minds are being destroyed because there is nothing to occupy them.'[5]

In the UK victims of occult-related disturbance are still often lumped together with the mentally ill. But in the US, special centres have become dab hands at glueing back teenager dabblers who've come unstuck as a result of the occult.

Health hazard

Wayne A. Van Kampen is the Chief Pastoral officer of Bethesda PsycHealth Institute in Colorado. Having cared for scores of occult-damaged adolescents and victims of ritual crime, he concludes:

There is absolutely nothing in satanism that is socially acceptable in terms of healthy adolescent development. The focus is on self-fulfilment, vengeance, violence and death. There is total disregard for relational, social and religious boundaries and values.

High Point counsellor Don Holland would concur. He treats disturbed teenagers at Charter Hospital in Greensboro. Over the space of 13 months, half the youngsters referred to him for therapy had been damaged by some involvement in satanism: 'Half have dabbled in devil worship and half have been more heavily involved . . . For this generation of kids, the movement towards satanism promotes death and destruction.'

Cathleen Faber, a mental health worker at Colorado State Hospital, could recall when one in 20 patients had an interest in satanism, but in recent years she says there have been times when every client has been involved to some degree.

Chicago's Hartgrove Hospital has set up a special treatment programme for teenage satanists. Nurses and psychiatrists have been specially trained to 'treat serious behavioural problems resulting from devil worship'. Teenagers are admitted as in-patients and undergo a course of treatment lasting between four to eight weeks.[6]

The Satanic Bible

America's gift to the world was the teenager. And to the world, San Franciscan Anton LaVey bequeathed his best-selling *Satanic Bible*. It's sold some three quarters of a million copies, has been translated into many languages and is still in print. Sales have outstripped the Holy Bible two to one in some parts of America and ten to one on some college campuses.[7]

Within are rituals designed to conjure up lust in the partner of your desires; to rain destruction upon your opponents, and to invoke Satan to bestow upon you his power. The books says:

> Symbolically, the victim is destroyed through the working of a hex or curse, which in turn leads to the physical, mental or emotional destruction of the 'sacrifice' . . . if your curse provokes their actual annihilation, rejoice that you have been instrumental in ridding the world of a pest![8]

LaVey was always at pains to stress that criminal activity was neither condoned nor encouraged in his new 'Church': 'Satanism *does not* advocate rape, child molesting, sexual defilement of animals, or any other form of sexual activity which entails the participation of those who are unwilling.'[9]

Michael Aquino, who established the breakaway Temple of Set, takes the same line. Of *The Satanic Bible* he says: 'What you are looking at there is a highly polemical book. It was never meant to be taken literally in all of its commandments. Members of the Church of Satan understood that.'

But US police officers are worried about what others might make of what they read. *The Pennsylvania State Police Missing Person's Bulletin* wondered: 'It is difficult to encourage indulgence and vengeance and not to expect debauchery, mayhem and other criminal acts.'[10]

That concern was developed by Shwarz and Empey in their American study, *Satanism*:

> Suddenly there was a book which justified almost any excess or indulgence someone might wish to make. No matter what might have been intended, it was possible to read justification for it in the text.
>
> Individuals who were highly disturbed frequently read *The Satanic Bible*. Murderers and rapists were, at times, found to have the book in their homes. In reality they were often fascinated by the book because they had a source for justifying their psychopathic desires and behaviour. They were not led astray by the book; their crimes would have been committed whether it existed or not. But the book seemed to help them justify their feelings.[11]

And other commentators such as Jerry Johnston say the book has encouraged thousands of youngsters to dabble with DIY satanism:

> His writings are significant. Nearly every satanically oriented teenager or adult I've read of or talked with either started . . . through LaVey's writings or read them *en route*.[12]

LaVey might well be gratified to hear that: 'There are so many kids out there who've never read anything else,' he boasts. He might be less self-satisfied to hear these words from Sean Sellers, a teenage murderer on death row who once was the proud possessor of a well-thumbed copy of Mr LaVey's best-seller: 'A lot of people are taking *The Satanic Bible* literally.'

Roger

Some British teenagers have also been taking matters too far. Remember 'Roger'? He was initiated into the occult by his older brother 'Ian', who tried to involve a group of teenagers in a coven. Blood-letting became part of their culture.

'I used to slash myself,' says Roger, 'and drip blood onto paper and shirts to be artistic.' Another teenager used to cut himself and rub blood over his face. Sometimes they would drink it.

Ian taught them how to chant to the spirits: 'You'd chant that name over and over again,' said Roger, 'until you'd get into a trance state.' Sometimes they would heighten the experience by putting blood on their faces or in their mouths.

Curiosity sucked in more of them. Ian set up a makeshift temple in a caravan, prepared a gravestone and began his incantations. It was too much for one girl, who switched into what Roger took to be some sort of trance state. It lasted 15 minutes: 'She freaked out really badly and started screaming.'

Ian summed up the situation by announcing that she had the potential to be a witch. The girl disagreed vehemently, and that was the last they saw of her at the caravan.

Simon

'Simon' was adopted by a church minister. From about the age of 13 he became fascinated with witchcraft and was convinced he was the possessor of some great power. An older friend introduced him to an organized witch's coven, but he became so frightened by what he saw that he stopped going after several visits.

His behaviour became increasingly antisocial. A counsellor described him as 'very neurotic' and said he was deeply involved in drug-taking. To feed the drug habit he turned to theft and shoplifting. He was eventually expelled from school for pulling a knife on a teacher and became a spectator in a gang-rape carried out by a group of his friends.

Michael

The insatiably curious may seek some mentor or guide to take them deeper, and the next step may be to join an adult occult circle or even a group of satanists. The *Western Daily Press* described another dabbler who had done just that: Michael, a civil servant in his early twenties from Taunton, who regularly attends Black Masses in Somerset:

> Sex is involved and occasionally rabbits or chickens are sacrificed. But I cannot see there is anything different in me worshipping Satan than anyone else worshipping God, Mohammed or money. We meet in each other's houses where our altar is usually the kitchen table. Orgies do happen – sometimes three men and seven or eight women are involved. Most of the time we are naked. It is more like group sex with people we can trust not to have diseases like Aids.[13]

In the survey for this book, 28% of 14- to 15-year-olds said they believed in magic. More than a quarter saw nothing wrong with witchcraft and 42% thought it could be helpful. One in seven agreed with Michael that satanism was just as good as any other religion – though it's difficult to imagine many stretching that point all the way to animal sacrifice.

Animal mutilations

Britain and America have seen a wave of animal mutilations, some attributed hastily and hysterically to satanism. For others, which include the skinning and draining of blood coupled with other occultic clues, there seems no more likely explanation.

Animal sacrifice is historically well-documented within satanism. And we know the practice continues today in many countries, because it is widely documented by those who have come out of satanic circles. Glenn, a former satanist in the US, says:

> I would strap the animal into the middle of the pentagram, then I would take a portion of the blood or the body and I would drink it or eat it, and I believed that by doing this, more power and more ability was being placed into my body.[14]

'S', a former high priestess in Croydon, England, recalls:

> I had my incredibly sharp knife and there was drumming going on in the background, and I thought, you know, this is going to be amazing, and then I just cut its head off – like that, suddenly, and that was it. There's something about sacrifice; if you do it

once, you want to do it all the time. Once you've actually passed the barrier of sacrificing an animal, you get a sort of blood lust where you really want to do it, and I really wanted to do it.[15]

The occultic purpose of the blood ritual is to release the energy believed to be within the animal. This provides the power to fuel the black magic ritual. Where the cult is well-organized and structured, sacrifice will take place under controlled conditions and the remains will be disposed of, usually by burning. The ritual will escape public attention.

But if *ad hoc* satanic practices were on the rise, then one would expect a reported increase in animal mutilation. In the United Kingdom that appears to be the case. Eight days into 1994, the following case reached its conclusion at Leicester Crown Court:

> A self-confessed High Priest of devil worshippers and two of his followers have been jailed after sacrificing animals and drinking their blood. Their satanic rituals involved kicking sheep and dogs to death. The men, all from Melton Mowbray, admitted various cruelty offences and stealing artefacts from churches. A judge at Leicester Crown Court jailed them for between nine and 15 months, calling their behaviour appalling.[16]

RSPCA headquarters in Horsham, England, have received a growing number of reports on animal mutilation from their own inspectors. Mike Butcher, Chief Inspector in charge of Special Operations, said: 'I am in no doubt there is some form of animal sacrifice and abuse for ritual reasons.'

In 1992, the RSPCA succeeded in prosecuting a Chichester man who had been sacrificing chickens in black magic rituals. It came out in court that the purpose of the rituals had been to draw energy from the animals – the classic motive for ritual sacrifice. The chickens were rigged up on a pulley contraption before being slaughtered. The dead bodies of other animals were also found on the premises.

The following year the RSPCA and the police were called in to investigate what appeared to be the ritual killing of a goat and several rabbits on the Isle of Wight. The animal mutilation was linked with the desecration of graveyard crosses.

Over this period reports became widespread of the sexual assault and mutilation of horses. Many of the attacks took place in the South of England on or near the full moon, prompting Hampshire Police to speculate that it could be the work of a satanic cult. There were certainly too many to blame on a single attacker. One British vet alone has treated more than 30 animals for appallingly malicious injuries.[17] Owners set up a series of Horsewatch vigils to try to prevent the attacks.

Similar assaults on horses were recorded in the UK in 1983/4 and in Sweden and Ireland. In 1992 the body of a donkey was found near Dublin. It had been hacked to death. The press reported that it had 'satanic symbols carved on its head'. The killing was linked with the Lunar Sabbath.[18]

In a previous chapter we heard about the ritual killing of a cat on Clevedon beach. Police questioned schoolchildren who had been experimenting with the ouija board. But their dabbling went far further than that:

> Detectives have questioned children over the sacrificial killing of a cat whose charred remains were found on Clevedon beach. They believe the animal may have been staked out and sacrificed over an open fire.
>
> Police intended to question eight pupils of a comprehensive school, aged between 14 and 17, who they fear may have been lured into occult and black magic rituals.
>
> A pupil at the school told police that youngsters had worn cloaks and taken part in candlelit ceremonies at Cadbury camp, an Iron Age hilltop fort in Tickenham, near Clevedon.
>
> Headmaster Eric Dolling told reporters there had been a related outbreak of violence at the school the previous week: 'I'm taking it all very seriously. I believe they have been involved in the fringes of a group of youngsters and adults who take part in satanic activities.'[19]

Targeting the children

There have been a growing number of reports in Europe and America of children who have been drawn into such circles by adults. Jack Roper, an American occult researcher, says:

> I have young people calling me regularly, telling me that they have been involved in some sort of animal mutilation sacrifice. And the reason they say they go out to these is that they are provided with vodka, drugs, cocaine or free sex. They don't particularly like it, as one girl said to me: 'I don't really like the squealing of animals in the cemeteries when they do their rituals, but they give me free vodka.'[20]

The following description came from a British mother who said her son had been recruited into a satanic/paedophile ring while he was still at primary school:

> He talks about a Black and Decker drill being inserted into a live horse's brain. He talks about making a stallion get an erection, and then cutting the penis off with an electric saw.

The incident took place on a farm. According to the mother, the mixture of bestiality, sadism and ritual sex with children was regularly videotaped, and the tapes were shipped out of the country and sold.

Andrew

'Andrew' was drawn into a self-styled satanic group in the South of England. A counsellor, who later helped to save his life, has told his story.

Andrew was adopted at an early age. Unruly and uncontrollable, he was sent to a home for children with behavioural difficulties. Strict supervision couldn't prevent the drug-taking. At the age of 14 he was tripping out with a friend, who died of an overdose. His death turned Andrew's mind.

A passing interest in the occult turned into an obsession. He became mixed up with a man in his late twenties who was deeply into magic and the occult and had attracted a following of ten or more young people.

Under his influence Andrew began to experiment in satanism and Baal worship. One of their pastimes was the desecration of graveyards. Their rituals included the blood sacrifice of mice, birds and small animals.

Andrew became more disturbed and increasingly self-destructive. He began cutting himself with razor blades. On one occasion he tried to kill himself by slashing his body and then eventually cutting his wrist down to the bone. The counsellor and a group of other friends saved his life by sitting on him to restrain him from further blood-letting.

When Andrew recovered he headed for Glastonbury, to become a New Age traveller.

The following is taken from the diary of a teenage girl in El Paso, USA. The extract makes disturbing reading:

Sharon undressed and picked up a knife that was lying beside the [hogtied] steer. Everyone stopped dancing and stood silent. Sharon handed the knife to Jay and pulled the skin on the steer's throat taught. Jay slit the steer's throat. Sharon slit the animal's stomach open. The group pulled out the intestines. Sharon cut a strip of hide off its back approximately 2ft by 3ft. They put this hide on the ground and put the animal's guts on it.

She later describes being wrapped in the hide in presence of adults who were overseeing the ceremony and the dedication of the animal's heart to Satan. Other ritual acts included the penetration of herself and other women with the animal's severed penis, which had been trimmed and stuffed with straw. Specific details were even more sickening and would serve no useful purpose to relate here.[21]

Some US police officers claim the next step from animal mutilation is ritual murder. That's certainly the way it worked out for teenage killer Peter Roland:

At first it seemed like nothing. Then the killing started. We usually killed small animals to start with. Then came the addiction to power and blood. Heavy metal music and drugs didn't help any. It ceased to be a thrill, and became necessary. After that, anything became a target for a good kill. It wound up with a human being.[22]

Teen occult crime

Having handed the world the teenager and *The Satanic Bible*, America appears to have passed on the teenage satanist. Serious occult crime by young people has been recorded across Europe, as we'll see shortly. But we need to begin where the problem began – in the USA. Texas Sheriff Joe Evans says:

We have seen over the past several years an increasing danger developing in the area of occult activities. Many major law enforcement agencies have established Occult-Related Ritualistic Crime Departments. Drug cults, the disappearance of children, and the occult have, in numerous cases, been investigatively associated.[23]

Pete Roland of Carl Junction, Missouri, is serving life for murdering his schoolmate Stephen Newberry with a baseball bat. Pete recalls:

It basically started out with the killing of animals, then there was always the heavy metal music, and the drugs don't help. It was like something else kind of took over inside of my own mind. Just the violence, the devil, lust and greed for drugs and money.[24]

Pete was one of four Missouri teenagers who thought it would be cool fashionable fun to get into satanism. One Saturday two of them watched the video sequel to the *Texas Chainsaw Massacre*. The following day all four of them took a cat, baseball bats and some rope to an isolated spot. First they mutilated the cat and then three of them rounded on the fourth, exactly as planned, and beat him to death with baseball bats, before dumping his body in a well.

Nineteen-year-old Stephen Newberry took between 50 and 70 blows before he died. Speaking from prison, Roland, now subdued, told the TV audience of the *Geraldo Rivera* show: 'Steve's eyes were real big, you know, and he just said, "Why me, why me?" and he just looked like he was really sad, and someone said, "Because it's fun, Steve", and then we just all like vultures, you know, we went in.'

The killing was the idea of teenager Jim Hardy. It was to be a sacrifice to Satan. 'Because it's fun, Steve,' were his words. Press reports quoted Hardy saying he was fascinated with death, and his only regret was that the murder wasn't 'more exciting'.

At school the following day the victim's sister overheard Hardy, Roland and Ron Clements laughing and joking about the killing.[25]

Roland was drawn into DIY satanism by the president of his senior class at school. 'I never really felt good about myself . . . low self-esteem . . . in satanism I thought I'd get power and popularity. I felt I had a place of belonging in life.'[26]

Sean Sellers

At 17 Sean Sellers became the youngest inmate of Oklahoma's Death Row. On 1st March 1985, he was sentenced to die by lethal injection. His crimes were to kill a shop assistant in cold blood and then murder his mother and stepfather in their bed. Sellers confessed, 'Murder was a sacrifice to prove allegiance to Satan. I had broken all of the ten commandments but murder, so I needed to finish my pact.'

Sellers was still at school when he began to explore drugs, the occult, Zen meditation and finally satanism. A girlfriend who regarded herself as a witch taught him to pray to the devil. He became hooked on what he describes as an erotic excitement.

With a friend, Sellers worked his way through the published

rituals of Anton LaVey, leader of the Church of Satan, summoning what they took to be demonic forces. Together they performed, untrained and unsupervised, heady rites that at one time would have been practised only by an experienced adept within an occult society.

By now Sellers had formed his own 'coven' with nine other kindred spirits. It was after a lust ritual that he decided to break the one outstanding commandment. With one thought in mind, he and an accomplice went into a convenience store and engaged the assistant in conversation. 'My friend distracted him and I raised the gun from beneath the counter, pointed it at his head, and squeezed the trigger.' It took three shots to kill him. The young men returned to the car empty-handed, in Seller's words, 'laughing'.[27]

He recalls laughing again when he took his stepfather's revolver and shot his parents, one after the other, in the head as they slept.

Only days beforehand he had written in an essay for his English teacher: 'Satanism made me a better person. I am free. I can kill without remorse.'

Sellers, like Roland, was later to come to his senses and look back with a troubled conscience on what he had done: 'We were stripped of all love, mercy and kindness, and were consumed with hate, anger and eroticism.' He told a US TV audience:

> Satanists believe that good is evil and evil is good. That's what I believed . . . I am craftier or quicker and more cunning, why shouldn't I steal? And why is killing wrong? Every time I looked at society and saw how everyone treated everyone else out there, I saw the ideals of satanism, and so I had to believe that evil was good and good was evil.[28]

Elsewhere Sellers said:

> It's like drugs. All drug abuse begins with drug use. You don't start out saying 'I'm going to be an addict.' You just say, 'I'm going to try this and see what happens.' It's the same with satanism. Kids who think, I'll just play around with this stuff (tarot cards, ouija boards, witchcraft) don't know what they're getting into . . . before you realize it you find you're in over your head.[29]

Cause or effect?

The cases of Sellers and Roland support the notion that one thing leads to another. But unravelling cause from effect may not be that simple. Which came first: the self-styled satanism or the extreme antisocial tendencies?

Sceptics have argued that Sellers played up his satanism to try to commute his sentence. Sellers disagrees: 'I got involved in satanism . . . but I am still the one responsible. It's my responsibility and mine alone.'[30]

As far as Roland is concerned, American Satan-scare debunkers Carlson and Larue say the blame for his actions cannot be laid at the door of occultism. They point to a deeply troubled home life and a history of petty crime:

> Roland began getting in trouble with the law when he was fifteen, so it is fair to say that his emotional problems began when he was fifteen or younger – his involvement with the occult didn't begin until he was seventeen. Roland's emotional problems led him into the occult, not the other way round.[31]

However things began and for whatever reason, there is no disputing that occultism was indeed a *factor*. Whether it was the blue touch paper, the spark or the explosive itself, we may never know. We can only speculate about the role that satanism played in fuelling and channelling the rebellion, anger and frustration of these young men. But what is not for speculation is that a form of satanism was present, as part of the mix, and that people lost their lives.

It is true that these were extreme cases, but they are not in isolation. The following are just some of the recorded cases that took place over a ten-year period.

Crime catalogue

Kevin Johnson reports:

> I had a seventeen-year-old boy call me, and tell me that a year prior to his call, he was considering joining a satanic group, and he said the only thing that stopped him was that he would have to violate every one of the Ten Commandments. He said he was willing to do that except they were pushing for him to kill one of his parents, and that snapped him back to reality.

The same thing happened to Sean Sellers, only he carried it through.

In Tampa, Florida, a 19-year-old killed his mother and dedicated her death to Satan. Jonathan Erik Cantero had been a practising satanist for four years. He said the 'voice of Satan' had told him to do it. 'Ever since I got into the satanic stuff, if I wanted to get into it, I had to kill my mother.'

He stabbed her 40 times in the stomach, chest and back and attempted to sever her left hand, which had ritual significance. After killing her, he prayed over her body: 'Lord Satan, thou knowest I have stricken this woman from the earth. I have slain the womb from which I was born. I have ended her reign of desecration of my mind; she is no longer of me, but only a simple serpent on a lower plane.'[32]

In Alberquerque a 15-year-old boy was being sought by police, who believed he had killed his father with a bow and arrow. Police say he had acted in revenge because his father had torn up his *Satanic Bible*. The boy had turned his bedroom into a makeshift satanic temple. He had drawn a red pentagram on the floor and inside that had daubed 666, the number of the antichrist.[33]

Twenty-one-year-old Paul E. Birmingham Jr battered a 98-year-old woman to death on her bed. Semen stains were found on her sheets. Birmingham described being in a trance-like state when the murder was committed. Three friends testified that he had been actively involved in satanism, and had passed into similar states during satanic rituals.[34]

The naked body of a 15-year-old girl was found in sludge in Witchita. Her hands had been bound and she had been stabbed in the throat and chest. Police say she had been a member of a satanic cult. She was killed shortly after midnight on Halloween.[35]

In 1988, 21-year-old Jason Rose was sentenced to death for the murder of 19-year-old Melissa Meyer. Rose and his co-defendant, 18-year-old John Jones, declared the killing to be a sacrifice to the demon Arioch, god of chaos and evil. Rose explained on a police video, 'the runes told us to do so'. (Runes are an occultic fortune-telling device.) Rose was said to be obsessed with black metal – music with overtly satanic lyrics.

Four years earlier, in Houston, Texas, five teenagers were accused of luring a 19-year-old labourer into a field, where they beat, stabbed, choked and burned him to death because they 'wanted to watch somebody die'. 'Nothing personal', one of them had said. One was later implicated in a further stabbing, another found guilty of attempted murder. John-Michael Trimmer was 17. 'We're devil-worshippers,' he explained.[36]

In Douglasville, Georgia, 16-year-old Terry Belcher testified in court to helping 16-year-old Robert McIntyre perform a 'human sacrifice'. He assisted McIntyre to murder Theresa Simmons by strangulation after conducting a makeshift ritual. He said they were 'calling upon Satan . . . to be with us, to give him the sacrifice'. Sheriff Earl Lee described the killing as a blend of 'sex, satanic devil worship and witch-craft'.[37]

In Westport, Massachusetts, a seventeen-year-old girl was inducted into a satanic cult-cum-prostitution ring. Robin Murphy was ordered by the cult leader to slit the throat of another member, a 20-year-old woman. The leader, Carl Drew, then decapitated the victim, kicked the head around and had sex with the body. Then he marked an X on Murphy's forehead with the dead woman's blood and told her she was now a member.[38]

Seventeen-year-old Gary Lauwers, of Long Island, was stabbed 40 times by 17-year-old Ricky Kasso after a row about drugs. During the assault Kasso cried out repeatedly, 'say you love Satan!' The last thing Lauwers managed to utter was that he loved his mother. The boys had been rejected for membership by a formal satanic group, the Knights of the Black Circle. At the time of the killing Kasso was awaiting trial for grave robbery. He had allegedly stolen a skull and a left-hand, symbols thought to be used in satanic death rituals. He hanged himself in his cell.

Sixteen-year-old Ronald Lampasi killed his father and wounded his mother after making a pact with Satan, which he signed in his own blood. Donald Coday also hated his father. After praying to Satan to help him, the 16-year-old shot him nine times and killed him.[39]

There are many more cases, and many more again where the perpetrators were not teenagers but adults, and where evidence was given in court that the occult or satanism had some bearing on the frame of mind of the killer. Los Angeles author Joel Norris has said that of the 300 serial killings he has studied, 30% were connected with satanism in some way.[40]

And along with murders there have been the church desecrations and ritual animal mutilations on both sides of the Atlantic.

The devil made them do it?

But how seriously should we take defendants' claims of satanism? After all, 'the devil made me do it' is the oldest excuse in the book, and a plea of insanity is the safest bet for a softer sentence. Again, we may never know. All we can say with certainty is that US law enforcement officers are regarding the issue of occult-related crime in sufficient earnest to undertake special training. And it is not only the defence that is pointing to the influence of the occult.

It was the prosecution who brought up the issue of satanism in the Scott Waterhouse case. Eighteen-year-old Waterhouse was convicted of strangling 12-year-old Gycelle Cote. Police found semen stains on her clothing and believed the killer had masturbated over her dead body. Police records maintained that Waterhouse was a devil-worshipper. Satanic writings were found in his school locker. And the court recorded:

> We conclude that the evidence of satanism and the defendant's
> belief therein is relevant for the permissible purposes of
> proving the identity of the perpetrator as well as his intent.
> In the tape-recorded conversation introduced at his trial,
> the defendant described sex and destruction rituals as part
> of the system of satanic beliefs. The defendant stated that
> satanism represents that darker side of humanity and
> urges indulgence of man's carnal needs rather than
> abstinence.

The prosecution was successful.[41]

And satanism isn't just implicated in murders. There are the suicides, too.

Suicide

Montgomery County, USA: Two girls aided one another in a death pact. One shot her friend with a pistol and then turned the gun on herself. They were aged 12 and 13.

They had told friends they wanted to die so they could 'meet Satan'. Police said the girls had been experimenting in the occult and were known to have been interested in satanism. They were said to have had emotional problems and to be drug users, though no significant traces of drugs were found in their bloodstream.

The father of one of the girls later took out a law suit against the school, claiming his daughter had told a school counsellor that she was planning to kill herself just one week before she did so. Local police said there were around ten occult-related suicides in the area each year.[42]

Arizona, USA: Three teenage suicides among Navajo indians were linked by tribal chiefs to an upsurge in interest in satanism. All three had 666, the biblical number of the antichrist, burned into their skin. Tribal police estimated that up to 150 Navajos had joined hard-core satanic cults.[43]

Scarborough, England: In 1993, Barry and Carol Pexton asphyxiated themselves in their car. The inquest heard that they had been on an occult mission to 'get to the other side'. Their two daughters had been braced for years to face the possibility that their parents would take their lives.[44]

Southend, England: Two bank clerks, aged 18 and 20, committed suicide in their car. An inquest heard that they had been involved in black magic and fantasy role-play games.[45]

In the USA, suicide has become the second most common cause of death among 15 to 19-year-olds. The rate for that age group tripled between 1950 and 1980, while for adults it remained static. In a typical year, 600,000 US teenagers will attempt to take their lives; 5,000 will succeed, at a rate of 14 per day. In the US, the availability of guns, the abuse of drugs and alcohol and family breakdown have been cited as contributory factors.[46]

In the UK, suicide has risen by 75% among young men aged between 15 and 25 within a decade. It is now said to be the second most common cause of death among men aged between 15 and 34; 80% of young suicides are male. About 200,000 attempt suicide each year, amounting to one in ten of all hospital admissions. Between 15 and 25% are readmitted to hospital after making a further attempt within a year. Of teenagers questioned by the BBC's *Everyman* programme, 26% admitted, 'I've considered taking my life.'

Although a number of suicides recorded in this book have been linked with the occult, there is no known data to show the proportion of suicide attempts nationally or internationally that have an occult connection. To speculate would be both pointless and alarmist. Statistics are included here because adolescents have a tough enough time getting through their emergence into adulthood without deepening their identity crisis by staring into the abyss of inner space.

Most of these appalling tales of horror and wasted lives took place in the USA. Can the criminal category of Occult Dabbler be written off as America's fashion fad, or is Europe, as with so many social trends, set to follow suit?

Germany

Sondershausen, January 1994: Three 17-year-old boys were sentenced to 6-8 years for strangling a 15-year-old schoolboy. According to the prosecutor, the victim had wanted to join their satanic cult. Calling themselves Satan's Children, the group had dressed in black cloaks and danced at midnight to black metal music such as *Cannibal Lust*. During rituals in the forest of Thuringia they had cut their flesh with knives and prayed to Lucifer. One of the 17-year-olds was the son of a local politician. The defendants had allegedly tortured the boy for two hours before finally throttling him.[47]

Ludinhausen, Westphalia, 1987: 15-year-old Anja offered herself as a sacrifice to a demon. After falling into a pill-induced sleep, her throat was cut, as agreed, by fellow members of the self-styled satanic cult, *Luzificaner*. The killers were a 17-year-old boy and a 16-year-old girl, who ran away in horror as their sacrificial victim bled to death. The murder was officially linked with satanic practices.[48]

The Times reported:

> Another four children committed ritual suicide in the same year. In 1988, a grammar school pupil, sixteen, from Essen was battered to death during a Black Mass in a disused factory. More recently, two young satanists killed themselves at Forchheim in Southern Germany. There is barely a town in Germany that does not have at least one Satanist group.

In Saarbrucken, *Der Spiegel* reported the activity of ten groups of young people who came together to celebrate the Black Mass, sacrifice animals and get high on drugs. The paper described one open-air Satanic mass which was performed to the strains of heavy metal music. Drugs were passed round and the leader, a 22-year-old, called out: 'Lucifer, Lord of Darkness', before slaughtering a chicken with a knife. There was ritual mockery of Christ and Mary and all fell motionless to be penetrated in their bodies and in their spirits by Lucifer. *Der Spiegel* reported the movement had begun among university students.[49]

In Munich, police were called in by a school director after a 15-year-old student was told she would die unless she presented another person as a sacrifice on a satanic altar.[50]

In 1994, Dr Helmut Zinser, a researcher in comparative religion in Berlin, told *The Times* that one in four West Berlin pupils was regularly involved in some form of occultism. Girls were two or three times more likely to take part than boys.

France

Paris, February 1990: A Harvard University researcher produced photographs and details of two occultic groups which he claimed were performing rites in the catacombs beneath the French capital. The Faction Absurde was said to be exhuming corpses from a nearby cemetery, hiding them in the catacombs, and ritually sodomizing them. It was claimed to boast more than 100 members in their teens and twenties. A second group, La Culte de la Voie Verte, was said to actually live in the catacombs and be involved in the sexual abuse and ritual murder of young girls.[51]

Hungary

Mezokovacshaza: A 17-year-old boy killed his 13-year-old sister, stabbing her, dismembering her body and placing the organs around the room. He drew an inverted cross on the bedroom wall in her blood, and alongside, the word 'Satan'. Afterwards he tried to kill himself. Police found a printed description of a ritual which they say he had carried out almost word for word. He told them he had 'followed a command from Satan' and felt no remorse. He compared the murder to an orgasm.

Police in Budapest were called in to protect a 13-year-old girl after she had received threats that she had been chosen to be sacrificed before Christmas Eve.

The suicide of two schoolboys in Nagykavacsi, near Budapest, was linked by police with satanic literature. A police official claimed it was bring sent to Hungary from what he called the 'Satan Church of San Francisco'.

Televised debates followed and the Christian Democratic People's Party called for a ban on the advertising of occult-related books, films and videos, newly available in the country.[52]

Israel

Rehovot, 1995: Police are holding a 17-year-old suspect believed to be involved in a satanic cult. Amit Molcho, 16, was stabbed more than 20 times and left in a field. Near the body was an abandoned shack whose walls were covered with satanic graffiti.[53]

One animal welfare group in Israel has become so concerned about the rise in animal sacrifice that it has been taking evidence from teenagers. They estimate there are some 50–60 satanic cults in the country. Some hold discussions on satanism via the Internet. Several cases of teenage suicide have been linked to cult membership.

Britain

Birmingham, 1992: A 21-year-old who believed he was the devil's disciple designed and made a ritual axe for the express purpose of committing a murder. He succeeded.

Robert Green, who boasted of carrying out animal sacrifices, bludgeoned 30-year-old Thomas Coleman to death with the pointed metal head of his axe. Then on his victim's forehead he daubed a satanic symbol.

Timothy Raggett, prosecuting, said Green had become obsessed with the occult. 'He thinks of himself as a devil's disciple and his room shows that. It is covered in posters and signs, showing a manifestation of his obsession, and he has tattoos on his forehead and arms.'

Green, who was described as deranged, admitted manslaughter and was committed to hospital indefinitely.[54]

Telford: 20-year-old Andrew Newell was convicted for the murder of his flatmate, Philip Booth, a charge that he denied. Booth had died from a cluster of stab wounds to the heart. The prosecution referred to it as a ritual killing.

Newell particularly asked police not to look in a record case in his bedroom. Inside, they found occult books, a cloth, a knife, candles and a manuscript. They acknowledged that they were dealing with someone with a special interest in satanism.

Newell and Booth were fans of the heavy metal band, Iron Maiden. The manuscript contained the lyrics of one of their songs, 'The Number of the Beast':

> *Torches blazed and sacred chants were praised*
> *As they start to cry, hands held to the sky.*
> *In the night, the fires burning bright,*
> *The ritual has begun.*
> *Satan's work is done.*
> *666, the number of the Beast*
> *Sacrifice is going on tonight.*

Author Tim Tate, who made a study of the crime, records the

following: 'Underneath the last line, Newell had painted an inverted cross in human blood and inscribed the words "Lucifer", "Belial", "Baphomet", and "Satan".'[55]

Newell denied taking part in any occult ceremonies and made a plea that the killing had been in self-defence. The conviction was later altered to one of manslaughter.

What took place in Harrogate is not in contention. Keith Beck, aged 20, was jailed for life for planting a bomb in a council van, sexually assaulting a 15-year-old girl and supplying magic mushroom drugs to a boy of thirteen.

Beck, who changed his name to Grigori Rasputin, after the demonic Russian monk, attacked the girl in a so-called rite of exorcism at her home. He carved crosses on her breasts with an ornamental dagger and then had sex with her. On another occasion he was reportedly interrupted by a church minister as he was about to have sex with a 13-year-old schoolgirl during a black magic ceremony in the church.

Beck was also charged with carrying out an assault in a North Yorkshire graveyard, where he performed black magic rituals. Leeds Crown Court was told that Beck regarded himself as the devil's disciple.[56]

Britain's largest cemetery, Brookwood, in Surrey, is reportedly raided up to 12 times a year for human bones, which are thought to be used in occult ceremonies. Shane Tonks, aged 20, was arrested for being in possession of a severed head.

Mark Reynolds, 23, was convicted of killing a nun inside Aberdeen Cathedral. He was brought up a Christian but is said to have turned to satanism. Reynolds reportedly wore an inverted crucifix and claimed to be the antichrist before cutting off the nun's ear, biting her and stabbing her to death.

In June 1990, 19-year-old Richard Yeates was sentenced to eight years imprisonment for raping a woman and a 16-year-old girl. The court heard that he had chanted 'Satan, Satan' during his attacks. The prosecutor said 'The girl told police he was in a haze and had been talking to Satan. He told her he felt as though he was in another world.' Yeates is said to have informed Littlehampton police, 'I was acting as a disciple for Satan.'

In 1992, 20-year-old Tracey Barrett from Berkshire was sent to Broadmoor psychiatric hospital for 'the bizarre ritual killing' of a 59-year-old occultist.[57]

'William' came from a broken home. He was abandoned by his father from childhood and as a foreigner had another reason to see himself as outcast.

According to a counsellor, William was drawn into an occultic circle by a self-styled shaman in his twenties whose sacrificial rites with chickens later resulted in prosecution.

William joined in the drug-taking and blood ritual, and for good measure ransacked and desecrated a Catholic church, wrecking the sanctuary, smashing the artwork and drawing an occult pentagram on the altar. This time it was William who was prosecuted. He was put on probation.

It would be dangerous to overreact by stating that satanism or the occult was the prime mover behind these crimes. Misunderstanding, schizophrenia, sensational reporting or a desperate attempt at mitigation might also have inflated the role played by the occult. Detailed social and psychiatric reports would have to be examined for each before such a judgement could be made.

But even making such allowances, we have to acknowledge that an occult element was there in the minds of the perpetrators, and has been used as the excuse, justification, motive, framework, or encouragement for these crimes.

Europeans can scarcely grumble about this unwanted American import, as historically it was Europe which exported satanism to the States in the first place. Yet there appears to be a significant difference in scale. European satanism is, in the main, still the highly organized, formalized, preoccupation of a minority of consenting adults. It has been thus for perhaps a thousand years.

8

The sorceror's apprentice

Witchcraft and satanism

> In Wicca we have lost our fear of the dark, we go down the tunnel
> into Wonderland.
>
> Vivienne Crowley[1]

Earlier chapters reveal the hidden undercurrents that lurk in even
the so-called shallow waters of the occult. And as we have seen,
young people paddling in those shallows can be drawn out of
their depth into witchcraft, ritual magic and satanism. To understand the attraction and the dangers and to see where this can
lead, we need to begin to plumb the depths of the deeper end of the
occult.

Forget the popular image of the witch and her broomstick, or the
sorceror with his pointed hat and wand. Forget, too, the notion that
the practice of magic died out in the dark ages and lives on only in
fairy tales. Magic is alive and well. '"Mysteries", the largest shop for
occult items in London, opened in 1982, and has seen trade double
every six months,' writes author David Burnett.[2]

Practising witch Nigel Bourne told the London *Evening Standard*:
'There's a network – I could go to any major town and there would
be someone in the craft there.'[3]

So how widespread is witchcraft? The Pagan Anti-Defamation
League believes there may be some 5,000 practising witches in the
United Kingdom. *The Independent* newspaper[4] hikes that to
100,000, while *News At Ten* takes a wild swing and doubles it up to
200,000.[5] As for North America, author on the occult Richard
Cavendish modestly guesses at between 10,000 and 20,000.[6]

Which all goes to show how difficult it is to define precisely
what makes a witch. The *Oxford Dictionary* offers: 'Woman practising sorcery', which is incorrect. A witch may be male or female.
The dictionary goes on to define a sorceror as a 'user of the magic
arts'.

Witches

Author Richard Cavendish, who has written widely about the occult, identifies three historical stereotypes of witch. At the first level he describes the local 'wise woman', who dispenses remedies and spells, interprets omens, and may use her magic to curse as well as to bless. Her powers are inherited from her mother or grandmother, along with their secret lore. The witch Selidy Bate says:

> We do cast spells. We do try very, very hard to make the spells that we do for the benefit of the community. Things like healing, things like counselling as well. I am really the equivalent of the old village wise woman before we had things like legal centres and doctors.[7]

The second type of witch is the black witch, who, says Cavendish,

> is totally unfailingly evil. This is the woman . . . who is believed to be filled with an appalling inward malevolence and spite which she projects against her victims . . . She will also use spells, incantations and repulsive concoctions.

Cavendish's third stereotype is the satanist witch who is believed to be

> closely allied with demons, through whom she works her magic. She is a worshipper of the Devil . . . and meets with others of her kind at the 'Synagogue' or 'Sabbath', where unholy rites are celebrated.

Cavendish doubts the historical existence of the satanic witch, but believes some practitioners today may be living up to that image: 'The example of the modern witchcraft movement shows how a fictitious stereotype can appeal to people who then proceed to bring it to life . . .'[8] A former witch from Pendle in Lancashire recalls:

> We used to pray to the Sun god, the Moon god, the god of the Earth. It wasn't till I got more deeply involved that I realized things did happen, that there was a power that sucked you further and further in . . . I was doing things to people, I was cursing . . . and I liked the power that I had. The curses were for hurting other people, as I had been hurt.[9]

Branches of witchcraft

In 1921 Margaret Murray, anthropologist, Egyptologist, author and declared witch, put forward her hypothesis that a Dianic cult religion had been indigenous throughout Western Europe before Christianity. Her notion, that witchcraft had arisen from the cult of goddess worship and was widespread, is no longer regarded as having any firm factual basis. But the idea has become a touchstone to modern day Wiccans who often idealize themselves as revivalists for what they see as the native folk religion of Europe.

Nevertheless, some debate remains within occult circles as to whether the word *wicca* is from the Saxon for 'craft of the wise, or wise ones,' or from the Anglo-Saxon *wice*, meaning 'wicked'.[10]

Murray's ideas influenced Gerald Brosseau Gardner, who claimed in 1954 to have discovered a witches' coven which was still practising the 'old' religion in the depths of the New Forest.

There is much dispute among the pagan community over whether Gardner's book *Witchcraft Today* was reportage or wishful thinking. It is generally accepted that several of the features of witchcraft that he describes, such as the system of degrees, could have been drawn from his masonic background.

Regardless of its historicity, Gardnerian witchcraft, as it became known, took off and found its way to America, France and Germany in the 1960s.

The third recognized branch of witchcraft is named after Alex Sanders. Sanders was said to have been initiated into a coven by his grandmother in 1933.[11] Those who follow his system of rituals are known as Alexandrians.

To this picture we should add the ethnic witchcraft more commonly practised away from European shores. This would cover practices such as Voodoo and Santeria, which are a queasy blend of animism, French occultism and Roman Catholicism.

So what do witches believe? In common with much of the occult, witchcraft has no clear, unified system of belief. But many witches accept a plurality of gods and spirits, which makes them polytheistic.

Many also lean towards animism, observing a host of nature spirits who live in the trees, water and land. Similar myths are common to many cultures, and nature deities have been placated and invoked throughout history. But chief among the deities of witchcraft is the Goddess, the source of magic power.

The Goddess

The author and witch Doreen Valiente writes:

> There is a general belief among witches in the invocation and worship of the forces of life, the male and female aspects of nature, through which all manifestation takes place. These powers are personified as the Horned God and the Moon Goddess. They have a great many names, as befits their antiquity.[12]

Different aspects of the Goddess's character are invoked by calling upon her by one of her many different titles. Hecate, for example, is seen as the patron of witchcraft, the dark side of the Goddess.[13]

Some who practise witchcraft have made a connection between the Goddess and the old enemy of the Christian Church – Lucifer. Charles Godfrey Leland writes:

> Diana [another aspect of the Goddess] was the first created before all creation; in her were all things; out of herself, the first darkness, she divided herself; into darkness and light she was divided. Lucifer, her brother and son, herself and her other half, was the light.[14]

In the Green movement we can see the beginnings of a convergence between ecological and magical understanding. The Gaia hypothesis, for example, sees the Earth as a living, self-regulating organism. And for the pagan, to pollute and damage the Earth is to defile one's own mother.

Psychologist Carl Jung regarded the Goddess as an archetypal symbol of motherhood deep within the human unconscious. The many different forms of goddess worship would therefore be a projection of that image. The Great Mother combines depths of maternal compassion and devotion with a dark and unassailable mystery:

> . . . the magic authority of the female; the wisdom and spiritual exultation that transcend reason; any helpful instinct or impulse; all that is benign, all that cherishes or sustains, that fosters growth and fertility. The place of magic, transformation and rebirth, together with the underworld and its inhabitants are presided over by the mother.

> On the negative side, the mother archetype may connote

anything secret, hidden, dark, the abyss, the world of the dead, anything that devours, seduces and poisons, that is terrifying and inescapable like fate.[15]

The other principal deity in witchcraft is the Horned God. Margaret Murray argued that the Horned God had been worshipped widely, only to become demonized by Christianity and turned into the mythical figure of the Devil. But to the witch, the Horned God was anything but evil: 'To them this so-called Devil was God, manifest and incarnate; they adored him.'[16]

Magical streams

The *Concise Oxford Dictionary* defines magic as the 'supposed art of influencing course of events by occult control of nature or of spirits, witchcraft . . . involving invocation of devils, angels . . .' Magic is a key element of today's neo-pagan revival, and like most occult practices, its origins can be traced back millennia. The noun 'magic' stems from *magi*, the Zoroastrian priests of the mystery religion of Ancient Persia.

Other roots return to the astrological and numerological lore of the Babylonians and the philosophical speculations of Pythagoras and early Greek thinkers.[17]

Prayer, magic and sacrifice were the principal means used by the Romans to try to control the *numina*, the spirit intermediaries between man and the deities. It was believed that magic could compel them to do their bidding.[18]

From Egypt came alchemy and the quest for the divine elixir which would bring immortality. Baser instincts corrupted this into the search for the formula which would turn base metal into gold. Alchemy was the fusion of chemistry and magic, which at the time gave scientific credence to superstitious practices.

Another stream to swell the magical current was Gnosticism, whose name comes from the Greek word for knowledge. Gnostics engaged in the search for the secret, absolute, knowledge that would result in salvation, and attempted to harmonize elements of classicism with the mystery cults.

One system for obtaining this hidden understanding was the Cabala (one of several spellings), a body of Jewish occult doctrine. The Cabala was revived by 19th-century occultists and was based on the idea that everyone has magical powers which can be developed. According to one authority: 'Some occultists perverted the teachings of the Hebraic Cabala and made it a collection of recipes for gaining power over demons.'

Some Gnostics believed in dualism: that God was the creator of all things spiritual, while all things material owed their existence to Satan. Taking this belief to its logical conclusion, a number of Gnostic sects attempted to influence the material world by the practice of ritual magic intended to appeal to its alleged creator, Satan. It was out of such beliefs that satanism was born.[19]

Chaos magic

A tape distributed by an occult shop warns:

> Chaos magic is dangerous, awesome, full of potential and therefore mysterious . . . it has an ultra-sinister aspect to it . . . anyone can jump in the cauldron of chaos and discover powerful magic . . . the only rules are those imposed by one's own courage . . . We prepare to sacrifice our identity and intellect in order to interface with the void. We give ourselves up unto death.[20]

Today we have designer drugs, so we have designer magic. With the proliferation of occult literature, new and more volatile blends of magical practices are being developed in the quest for an ever greater magical 'high'. Recent years have seen a growth in interest in Chaos magic, which pulls together disparate elements from tribal shamanism and various Eastern traditions.

Chaos magic is occultic anarchy. It is a solo performance devoid of any guidelines or points of reference. The magician hurls himself into the void to merge with the god of his intentions. It has a potent appeal to the young and rebellious who prefer to make their own rules. Study tapes on the subject carry a health warning:

> All the following techniques can be dangerous to those who are nervously inclined or who are chronically ill or those with high blood pressure or heart trouble . . . all experiments are undertaken at your own risk.
> *Paths of Magic*

> Those who demand too much in their magic may return a lunatic, or may end up being absorbed by it altogether.
> *The Chaosphere*

Shamanism is increasingly in evidence at rock festivals such as Glastonbury which have pagan associations. The use of drugs is a clear common denominator with the rock culture. Shan, a Shamanistic witch, says:

> In the Shamanic Craft we do use drugs. Among Shamanic witches some of us respect the ancient use of legal and safe hallucinogens which give a mild high and help one go into a trance and meet one's god or goddess or spiritual guides; but not all witches do.[21]

A question of black or white

The Satanic Bible says:

> There is no difference between 'White' and 'Black' magic, except in the smug hypocrisy, guilt-ridden righteousness, and self-deceit of the 'White' magician himself.
> In the classical religious tradition, 'White' magic is performed for altruistic, benevolent, and 'good' purposes; while 'Black' magic is used for self-aggrandizement, personal power, and 'evil' purposes. No one on earth ever pursued occult studies, metaphysics, yoga, or any other 'white light' concept without ego gratification and personal power as a goal.[22]

Let's just assume for a moment – and it's a vast assumption – that magic actually works. If so, then that belief, held by occultists, begs several crucial questions. *How* does it work? What is the *power* that makes it work, and *where* does it come from? And *how*, *why* and *by what process* does the magician activate that power to bring about his desired change?

Magic, in the sense of summoning the spirits to do one's bidding, is common to elements of both witchcraft and satanism. Like the magnifying glass which concentrates the rays of the sun, the magician applies his will by performing a ritual to summon or release some hidden power to do his bidding.

Some see magic as a means of releasing psychic energy. Others say the power comes from a different force, that of fundamental energies within the universe; while still others insist the power is imparted by the spirit beings that govern nature, or even demons. Dr Felix Unger writes:

> Magic, like divination, is the divinely forbidden art of bringing about results beyond human power by recourse to superhuman

spirit agencies . . . living intelligent spirit beings . . . Men, by
incantations and ceremonies . . . can influence and . . . control
these spirit agents. The activity of such superphysical agents of
evil produces the extra-sensory phenomena of magic, that is,
occurrences that transcend the normal operation of physical law
and perception.[23]

Some magicians take the belief in demons literally. Others regard
them as the mythical personification of the forces they are
attempting to summon and find it helpful to hold a suitable image in
their imagination.

Many argue that magic is itself neither good nor bad, black nor
white. They claim magic power is neutral and can be used for good
or for ill, depending upon the will of the magician: 'Magic is about
as moral as electricity,' writes Isaac Bonewits.[24]

But that argument can only hold good if the source of magical
power itself can be demonstrated to be neutral. If, as some claim, the
power to perform magic comes from intelligent, personal spirit
beings or demons, then magic could only be as neutral as the spirits
behind it.

And if we make another giant assumption that those spirits are
working for the good of man (why should they, and how could we
ever be sure?), then their magical powers can only be as white as the
magician who is summoning and controlling them, and the use to
which he is putting them.

Not every occultist is convinced of the neutrality of the occult
powers he is channelling. A high priestess in Manchester has said:
'There are overriding destructive elements . . . and they *are* overriding!'[25]

A whiter shade of pale?

So where does that leave the popular notion that magic is either
black or white, good or evil; used either to heal or to harm? In our
own survey, 26% of 14- to 15-year-olds believed in black magic and
19% thought that magic, whatever its shade, was harmful. Many
commentators and practitioners would see things the same way.
There's no black or white – just shades of grey. One witch has said:
'There is no distinction between black and white witchcraft; they are
simply two sides of the human psyche.' And Kathryn Paulsen writes:
'Magic can be white only to the degree that a human being can be
good, and examples of pure white magic are therefore hard to find.'[26]

So the popular distinction between 'black' and 'white' magic is, at best, dubious. And to make any separation at all depends on two statements of faith: firstly that the source of apparent magical power is benign or, at least, neutral; and secondly that the user of such power is not subject to normal human foibles and will consistently put his power to good use.

Author and witch Stewart Farrar says: 'The rule of a white witch is to do harm to none. If you do, it's black working and it will rebound on you in the end.' This is commonly thought to be the witches' guiding principle. But however sincerely some may believe that, satanists such as LaVey regard it as self-deception. In honest recognition of normal, human, mixed motives, some practising witches prefer to refer to themselves not as white, but as 'grey'. Canon Dominic Walker comments:

> I think the real danger is that if you push white magicians and ask them if they've hexed anyone, if they've actually cursed anyone, you'll often find that they have. So you find that the whites are not so white, they're actually fairly grey.

As the saying goes, 'Power tends to corrupt, and absolute power corrupts absolutely . . .'

Drawing a line

Where the distinction between white and black magic becomes unclear, the practical division between witchcraft and satanism can also get hazy. In deference to the many well-meaning neo-pagans, it is important to attempt to clarify that distinction. One witch named Nigel says:

> Satanism is basically a reversion and perversion of Christian symbolism, whereas witchcraft, or wicca, is a totally separate autonomous organisation which has its own form of worship, which is not related to Christianity.[27]

Many witches and pagans, especially those who see themselves as a force for good, quite rightly bitterly object to being lumped together with satanists. Reg Griffiths says, 'I am a witch. Witchcraft is poles apart from satanism.'[28] One Birmingham witch adds: 'Satanists . . . have nothing to do with Wicca. Our philosophy is love, truth and justice. We love Mother Earth, Father Sun and everything nature brings us.'

Nevertheless, such notions of 'love, truth and justice' didn't prevent her from publicly brandishing an effigy of an MP who was opposed to witchcraft and threatening it with a hatpin. And she admits that magic may be used to harm an individual – if it serves the witch's notion of justice:

> Wicca works on the principle of an eye for an eye, a tooth for a tooth. If you were to send me something bad or threaten to harm me, I would be allowed to wallop you psychically. In which case I *would* make the doll and use the pins. I would cause justice to happen.[29]

So we can see that magic, whatever its shade, may have an element of compulsion; the attempt to force another individual to conform to the will of the magician by the use of a magic ritual.

Compulsion is a theme which runs throughout the more sensational 'how to do it' books on witchcraft, which for the curious, the credulous and the inadequate may be their first introduction to the subject:

> With simple witchcraft spells and rituals I show how you can make any member of the opposite sex desire you *immediately* . . . compel a reluctant lover to marry you . . . a powerful ritual that *compels* an unwanted neighbour to move away . . . In my book you read about winning the admiration and respect of people. *Stop* them exploiting you.[30]

And when compulsion becomes a cornerstone of magic, in practical terms at least, there is less to choose from between wicca and satanism. Stewart Farrar says: 'There is a sick fringe using black magic, but they usually end up destroying themselves . . . Black magic is always self-destructive. It's a suicidal path.[31]

Satanism

In an article advocating graveyard desecration, Mendez Castle writes:

> Satan, your God, is among you, black and lowering, reeking of evil and the pit. You stand transfixed before him, knowing you've only just begun to taste the divine degradation that He offers for your pleasure.[32]

There can be no question that satanism exists and is practised in various forms today. Conservative estimates have placed the number of satanists in the United Kingdom in the low thousands. Others have suggested that the small pool is spreading. In terms of percentage increase, it has been described as the fastest growing religion in Britain.

Reliable statistics are unavailable, but a survey of 1,000 customers of The Sorceror's Apprentice bookshop in Leeds, described as Britain's largest occult supplier, recorded that 4% regarded themselves as practising satanists, while 20% showed some interest in the religion.

Author Russ Parker, a member of the Manchester Deliverance Diocesan Committee, believed there were many magical and satanic groups in that city alone: 'Our team was continually called out to help people distressed through involvement with groups like this. On several occasions we had to care for people who were being physically attacked for daring to leave such groups.'[33]

Satanism's existence is confirmed by the books and literature produced by satanic organizations; their open acknowledgement of active recruitment programmes and their PR people who appear in the media. All stress that their proceedings are strictly within the law. Michael Aquino of the Temple of Set says, 'Satanism, as legitimate satanists define it, is ethical, it is above ground, it is positive.'

The First Church of Satan

Satanism broke surface in the heady liberalism of the sixties. Until then, it was an underground occupation. But in San Francisco, at the height of flower-power fever in 1966, former lion tamer and circus roustabout Anton LaVey proudly presented his offspring.

LeVey introduced satanism to showbusiness. It was LaVey who Americanized the religion, dressed it up in Hollywood hype, dragged it out into the daylight and tossed it to the younger generation.

The Church of Satan was LaVey's razzle-dazzle progeny of the permissive sixties. LaVey the strip-show organ-player. LaVey, who, ironically resplendent in a devil-suit, appeared on his own 1968 recruitment poster, before the prone and naked body of a female celebrant. '*Satan wants you . . . join now*' glowered LaVey in a self-conscious spoof of the famous Uncle Sam billboard.

The First Church of Satan gave birth to a brand of flamboyant hedonism which attracted showbiz glitterati such as Sammy Davis

Junior and Jayne Mansfield. LaVey's message was tailored for his congregation and mirrored the mood of militant libertarianism of the times. 'There is a demon inside man,' said LaVey, 'and it must be exercised, not exorcised – channelled into ritualized hatred.'[34]

LaVey's writings are claimed to have had a significant influence upon a generation of teenagers. Burton H. Wolfe writes, 'Anton LaVey brought satanism out of the closet, and the Church of Satan is the fountainhead of contemporary satanism.'

The Temple of Set

In 1975 the Church of Satan split, spawning The Temple of Set, reflecting the more scholarly and intense attitude of its founder, Michael Aquino, a Lieutenant Colonel in the United States Army. Unlike LaVey, Aquino openly acknowledged a personal devil. He declared that he had been singled out and commissioned to take on the mantle of leadership by no lesser figure than the Egyptian deity, Set. He had been calling on Satan, when he revealed himself as Set, a deity described as 'The god of darkness and sworn enemy of the gods of light . . . more ancient than the Hebraic Satan . . . the patriarch and patron of fratricide.'[35]

In the time-honoured occult tradition Set dictated his own scriptures to Aquino, thus elevating him high above contradiction. As the Church of Satan went into decline, The Temple of Set was actively seeking recruits in the United Kingdom and Europe.

Like LaVey, Aquino stresses that no criminal activity takes place within his organization. After an investigation against him, the FBI and the police dropped allegations of the sexual abuse of pre-school children at the Presidio Army day care centre. An investigation was also carried out by the Army into the alleged abuse of a three-year-old girl. Again, no action was taken. Aquino consistently denied the charges: 'We do not advocate anything evil . . . we do not advocate child molestation.'[36]

The Church of Satanic Liberation

In 1986 English teacher Paul Douglas Valentine picked up *The Satanic Bible* and couldn't put it down. But rather than throw in his lot with Anton LaVey, he decided to set up an organization of his own, where he could best express his own particular interests. Pat Pulling says the organization's emphasis is 'on sex magic: rituals based on the belief that powerful forces are released during orgasm, forces that then are available to carry out the will of the celebrant.'[37]

'My goal in life,' Valentine told a TV crew, 'is to start the wheels of the eventual destruction of Christianity through education.'[38] On another occasion, he added: 'The main focus of the Church of Satanic Liberation is to start a whole new breed of satanist. You know, start them when they're young.'

The Orthodox Temple of the Prince

In Great Britain, The Orthodox Temple of the Prince was established in 1955, four years after the repeal of the Witchcraft Act, and has Temples in Newcastle, Durham, Scarborough and Cleveland. The initiation ceremony for new members culminates in an act of ritual sexual intercourse.

Former cult leader, child psychologist Dr Raymond Bogart, reportedly confirmed that children attended temple lessons, but only with parental consent: 'Yes, I do have young children attending my temple, but no sex takes place with them until after they are sixteen.'[39]

Reports claimed Dr Bogart had served a four-year sentence for unlawful sexual intercourse with a young girl. In a subsequent article in his own defence, Dr Bogart said the girl in question had been fifteen, but maintained that he had been falsely accused.

The group claims to practise some 300 occult arts, including astrology, the tarot and magic, and admits to placing curses on individuals – but only when necessary. It has trawled for new members at public lectures and through contact ads like the following, which make no mention of their sexual predelictions. This was placed in *The Ace of Rods* magazine:

> We are looking for just a few prospective members, couples and genuine females to become an integral part of our Temples . . . Progression through ability will lead to the inner circle with certified degrees.

All the above organizations are open about their activities and have accepted, and even courted, publicly. Similarly, all have insisted that what takes place is lawful, ethical and properly regulated.

In some respects, such groups represent the public relations division of satanism. But for those that operate openly, there are others which function away from the public gaze.

Sometimes their underground magazines come to light, such as *Fenrir*, which is produced by the Order of the Nine Angles, operating out of Church Stretton in Shropshire. *Fenrir* writes about 'satanic sacrifice' and makes it plain that it is speaking literally, not figuratively, and is talking about people, not animals.[40]

There are other groups whose criminal activities force them to function in secret. That much is clear from the growing number of survivor accounts now being related to therapists and the wardship and criminal cases now reaching the courts. For where there are victims, there must be perpetrators.

Various attempts have been made to classify satanic groups. They range from Orthodox, with the emphasis on formalized ritual and ceremony, through to the self-styled and often chaotic satanic cult. Some trace their lineage back through the centuries; others, like the Church of Satan and Temple of Set, are recently established.

American police, investigating the growing problem of occultic crime, have drawn up four categories of satanism:

The Dabbler
The Religious Satanist (Orthodox)
The Non-Traditional Satanist (Modern or Cultic)
The Generational Satanist

Police Sergeant Randy Emon says, 'The non-traditionalist Satanist would take certain ideologies and develop a cult, usually polarized around some central theme . . . and use that to commit crimes. The non-traditional satanist is often the most dangerous.'[41]

The figure of Satan

Like witchcraft, satanism has no unified belief system. In line with Gnostic dualism, Satan is hailed as the god of this world who is therefore to be worshipped. As lord of the material, he is the provider of material and sensual benefit to those who, like Faust, offer themselves to his service.

Satanism has been described as an inversion and perversion of Christianity. Christ is seen as a usurper, whose throne belongs to Satan. *The Book of Satan* says:

I gaze into the glassy eye of your fearsome Jehovah, and pluck him by the beard; I uplift a broad-axe and split open his worm-eaten skull.

I dip my forefinger in the watery blood of your impotent mad redeemer, and write over his thorn-torn brow: the TRUE prince of evil – the King of the slaves![42]

Blasphemy and inversion of Christian rites feature in much of satanism, where the intention is to reverse Christian ritual to bring about the opposite effect: the invocation of Satan. Bill, a former satanist in the US, says:

In satanism you have rituals that are designed, first of all, to deliberately mock God. So in our particular type of satanism, we would mock, say, the Catholic Mass. We would consecrate communion hosts and then we would stamp on them or urinate on them or other things, believing that by doing that we were somehow abusing God.[43]

Jewish and Christian scriptures depict Satan as the ultimate source of evil. He is created and thereby inferior to God the Creator. And while not divine, he is portrayed as a spirit being who is powerful and intelligent. Like man, he was given free will, but attempted to set himself over and against God. As a result, he was ejected from heaven. Even then, what he wanted was the power and the glory that was God's by right, and from the beginning he enticed humanity to follow in his path of rebellion. All this is a stark contrast to the satanist's belief. Former black witch Doreen Irvine says:

Their main teaching is that Satan had a part in creating the world with God . . . he was wrongfully thrown out of heaven when he asked for equal power along with Jehovah God, and one day he will regain his rightful place.[44]

Christianity credits Satan with authority over other, lesser, fallen spirit beings, who joined in his revolution and so shared in his downfall. These are sometimes referred to as demons. Satan is described as the Prince of Darkness and is acknowledged by the Jewish, Christian and Muslim faiths. He is represented under different names in most religions and his many titles represent different aspects of his character. His most common, Satan, means Adversary.

His is also known as Lucifer, the light-bearer. He is described as a deceiving angel of light who blinds mankind to the truth by the glare of his own deceptive false doctrines. The following description is from the book of the prophet Isaiah, in the Old Testament:

How art thou fallen from Heaven, O Lucifer, son of the
morning! How art thou cut down to the ground . . . for thou
hast said in thine heart, 'I will ascend into Heaven, I will
exalt my throne above the stars of God . . . I will be like the Most
High.'
Isaiah 14:12–14.

Satan/Lucifer is seen primarily as God's opponent, although neither
all-powerful nor all-present, like God. He wages his war against his
Creator by attacking the pinnacle of God's creation: humanity. His
strategy is to attempt to corrupt the image of God within each individual into his own corrupt likeness.

According to standard theology Satan and his fallen hosts
(demons) employ a process of seduction in order to entice humanity
into disobedience and rebellion. Satan's forces of darkness disguise
their true identity and intentions. They masquerade as benevolent
helpers, while seeking to draw mankind increasingly under their
influence and control. The process is one of gradual enslavement
through the surrendering and undermining of the will.

We have already noted the centrality of the will to the magician or
sorceror. Satan's aim is said to be to entice man to turn over his will
to him, by ever increasing increments. His ultimate goal is to obtain
man's active service and worship.

The fall of man – humanity's first plunge into disobedience – is
depicted in the Hebrew book of Genesis as being orchestrated by
Satan. It was the first stage towards achieving his objective: disobedience and separation from God. Satan, in the form of a serpent, is
said to have enticed the first woman, Eve, to perform the only act
that God had forbidden:

Now the snake was the most cunning animal that the Lord God
had made. The snake asked the woman: 'Did God really tell you
not to eat fruit from any tree in the garden?'

'We may eat the fruit of any tree in garden,' the woman
answered, 'except the tree in the middle of it. God told us not to
eat the fruit of that tree or even touch it; if we do we will die.'

The snake replied, 'That's not true! you will not die. God said
that, because he knows that when you eat it you will be like God
and know what is good and what is bad.'

The woman saw how beautiful the tree was and how good its
fruit would be to eat and she thought how wonderful it would be
to become wise. So she took some of the fruit and ate it. Then she
gave some to her husband and he also ate it . . .

That evening they heard the Lord God walking in the garden and they hid from him among the trees.

Genesis 3:1–6, 8.

In simple pictorial terms the story depicts Satan's *modus operandi*: to divide and rule. It illustrates that:

- Satan masquerades as an advisor or friend and seldom appears in his true colours.
- He subtly casts doubt on God's word before openly accusing him of lying.
- He entices humanity to do that which is forbidden. He seduces people into breaking God's laws which have been established for their protection and to preserve their life-sustaining relationship with their Creator.
- He plants the suggestion that God's motivation for restraint is his own insecurity and desire to repress his subjects.
- He makes the seductive offer that to switch one's allegiance is to open one's eyes, and to become like God.
- He effectively redefines evil as good.

Doreen Irvine comments:

To the satanist, good is evil and evil is good. The truth is a lie and a lie is the truth. Sweet is bitter and bitter is sweet. And everything is twisted around the other way.[45]

Rational satanism

But not all satanists believe in a devil or demons. Some describe themselves as atheistic or rational satanists. If they worship any deity, it is themselves. Paul Valentine has said, 'I am God, I am Lucifer; I am Jesus; I am any god that man has ever created, because man has created the gods.'[46]

Satanism is even harder to define than witchcraft. What complicates matters is that not all satanists actually believe in Satan. Some regard the figure of Satan as the personification or symbol of the dark desires and drives that lurk within each of us. In the words of Anton LaVey: 'The satanist believes in complete gratification of his ego.'[47]

What characterizes the satanist as opposed to most witches is the conscious alignment with forces that he would acknowledge as dark. LaVey could not be plainer:

The satanist brazenly invokes those who people that infernal army of long-standing outrage, the Devils themselves! . . . The satanist realizes that only by putting himself in league with these forces can he fully and unhypocritically utilize the powers of darkness to his best advantage.[48]

Instead of invoking demons to draw dark forces into himself, the rational satanist will evoke – summon up from within – the powers, the drives and the energies he desires. To release these buried aspects of self, the rational satanist may imagine demons or devils that have the specific characteristics he is intending to manifest, and use them as icons: as a means to focus the concentration and the will. What can result, in psychological terms, is a suppressing of inhibition and the deliberate releasing of the dark and terrible desires of the id, the wild child within. Concealed behind the mask of a demon, man is capable of almost anything:

. . . any action that has seemed repulsive, reprehensible and vile to the individual should be Acted-out and set free . . . release the fiend that lies dormant in you, for he is strong and ruthless and his power is far beyond human frailty. Learn to love fear; love is to learn fear.[49]

It's a migraine-inducing, head-spinning, unpalatable brew. But again, as parents and teachers, our chief concern is not whether such bizarre beliefs could be true. What *must* exercise us is the disturbing effect of such potent convictions on young and impressionable minds; the dangers of identifying with the dark philosophies of sorcery and satanism, and how that identification with evil might affect the mental well-being of some young people and prompt others, who are unstable or vulnerable, to act.

9

Pied pipers
Ritual abuse

> Many witchcraft groups are organised in an almost completely
> closed basis. Essentially they form a 'secret society'. As such they
> have more in common with the Freemasons and the Mafia than
> with presently recognised religious groups.
> *The Pipes of Pan*, pagan magazine [1]

If dabbling in the occult can prove hazardous, then DIY satanism
has produced disastrous consequences. And that same blend of
curiosity and credulity has drawn a number of young people into
adult occult circles where they have been exploited and abused.

It would be absurd to brand anything but a fringe minority of
adult occultists as abusers. But an enthusiastic teenager may not
be in the best position to judge the company she is letting herself
in for, especially when occult circles so frequently function in
secret.

Deric R. James, writing in *The Insight Occult Annual*, divides
what he calls the practitioners of the black arts into three classes:

(a) The 'Theatricals': . . . dressing up, passwords, joss sticks,
     rituals in semi-darkness . . . many hints of 'dark secrets' . . . a
     cloak for the usual clique looking for kicks.
(b) The 'vicious' type: Nearly all practices [are] illegal and
     therefore membership is closely guarded. 'Heavy' drugs,
     perversions, sadism, ritual floggings . . . This is often the
     outlet for blackmail . . . the aim of the runners is to get
     complete power over 'useful' people such as politicians,
     journalists, doctors (who supply drugs).
(c) The real Black Lodge: Behind all the others . . . By far the
     most deadly category, since thousands of people may be
     affected by their manipulations.[2]

The writer then cites what he describes as successful criminal prosecutions involving such groups in Sussex, Norfolk, Hamburg, New
Mexico and Pennsylvania.

Please note that James' comments and the observation at the start of this chapter express the concerns of the occult community, rather than the claims of anti-occult campaigners.

Audrey Harper

Some who have put witchcraft behind them now claim the covens they belonged to openly practised black magic and the worship of Satan.

Young, homeless and in need of a friend, Audrey Harper was approached by a well-dressed young woman in a pub, and invited to a party. She envied the affluent lifestyle and was told that it was hers for the taking. Another party followed, then an invitation to a meeting at Virginia Water on 31 October – Hallowe'en night.

> I was taken blindfolded to a building. I was dressed in white and they were all dressed in black. I was asked if I wanted to join the coven. I said yes. I had a cut made – I've still got the scar – and signed my name on a parchment in my own blood, saying that my Lord and master was now Satan.
>
> There was a lot of chanting and a smell of incense. The high priest asked 'Who brings the sacrifice?' and a woman, one of the group, came forward and laid a baby on the altar. He cut the baby's throat and caught the blood in a chalice. I thought I was going to faint or throw up. I just literally froze. It was like standing there watching something, but you're not really there.
>
> The blood was warm and it was brought round. They daubed it on each hand and then they drank it and it came to me, right the way round from the left. And I just couldn't; I stood there and let this liquid stuff touch my lips and gave it back.
>
> And then it was my turn. They took this same blood from the chalice and daubed it all over me and then the high priest raped me. I was told that if I ever revealed what had happened, I would die. And I believed them.

She claimed the group deliberately introduced her to heroin, got her addicted and played on her cravings to force her to remain. One of her tasks had been the recruitment of children:

> I was told specifically thirteen to eighteen-year-olds. It was easy, London was full of runaway kids. Just go down to the station, wave some money in front of them and invite them to a party.

The first time I ever did it, I honestly had no idea what to expect, any more than they did. There was food and drinks, and then someone lit some candles, and then I began to sniff, and I thought, 'something's wrong here'. These children were drugged by candles that had been injected with hallucinatory drugs, and as you lit them, they filled the room.

Within a short time these kids had stripped off and were literally just crawling all over each other. Then people with cameras moved in. And when I saw photographs taken I got out the door and just threw up.

After that I refused to attend anything. I told the kids where to go. I just gave them money and said, 'You want a bed for the night, then here, this is where you get a bed', and just cleared off. After the first party I said 'I'm not doing it any more.' But they just told me, 'You don't own your life any more' and stuck a knife to my throat.

On other occasions Audrey Harper claims to have witnessed the rape of a 13-year-old girl who had been abducted, and the ritual abuse of children who were even younger.

The inner group would be at the top and we were all stood around, and these children were being sexually abused. There was anal sex, oral sex, and they were using inverted crosses and snakes' heads tied on to sticks. I didn't know that women could be so disgusting, because the women were as bad as the men.

In the whole of that horrific thing, the one thing that stays with me now was that not one of those kids cried. They were drugged. They were given muscle relaxants and hallucinatory drugs or something to shut them up, and I just slowly slid down the wall until I just couldn't see any more, and then I knew what evil I had got involved in.

The children were between two and eight years old, and what I found out afterwards was that they were born to people in the coven.

When she became pregnant herself she seized the opportunity to get away and had herself admitted to a hospital. In so doing she became free of the group.

She claims the coven practised black witchcraft, and was allied to a satanic temple. She has informed the police of her allegations, and now helps others who want to break free of black witchcraft and satanic cults.

Satanic crossover

Another account also alleges an overlap between darker elements of witchcraft and satanism. A former witch, 'M', claims to have witnessed the ritual murder of a 13-year-old girl in a West Country churchyard and the exhumation and desecration of a human body in a London cemetery.

As a former high priestess, she claimed to have initiated her own seven-year-old boy in a ceremony involving a human skull.[3]

From America, Bill Schnoebelen claimed to have combined witchcraft with membership of a satanic cult. Samhain, also known as Hallowe'en, was their principal festival:

> We believed it was the time when our 'Horned God' entered the underworld . . . an occasion when the gates between the worlds of the dead and the living swung wide. It was a time when we could attempt to commune with our dead . . . we knew we were carrying on old traditions which began in the time of the primeval priests of Britain, the Druids.
>
> Above us, in the ranks of the Craft, we knew that children were actually ritually slain on this night. We knew that some mothers would be asked to give up their children to the gods . . . To give up one's child was an honour, as the child would be reincarnated as a Mighty One. Their lives would be offered for the good of the land and of the earth.

Schnoebelen adds:

> Keep your children away from Hallowe'en and all its trappings . . . In our six-year struggle we watched as most of our friends in the Craft began to degenerate into misery. They were sad people with broken marriages or ruined lives to show for their labour.[4]

Sue Hutchinson is a survivor of ritual abuse and has set up a network of professional carers to counsel and help others like herself. She acts as consultant to a number of British police and health authorities, and claims first-hand contact with many ritual abuse victims. She says she too has come across practising witches who have been involved in child abuse:

> There's groups of people out there that are classified as white witches. If they want to worship the earth but are non-abusive, I

don't see that we have any right to knock them. But in black witchcraft there is a certain amount of crossover. Black witches produce spells and potions, but it's used for a bad reason. Drugs are given to children which affect the muscles, so they just lie there and are abused.

The following plea is an extract of a letter which was received by a counsellor:

Can you please help? How did you overcome your fear of them and the nightmares? I want to overcome it, I want to be free but feel still in bondage. I don't want to go to them again because of what it is doing to me. I'm so scared . . . I don't know what to do. Please can you help me. I feel cursed. I feel it's driving me insane . . . I don't sleep because of the nightmares and the reliving of it. I feel it is destroying me. I don't know what to do. Pray for the little one that she will be saved. I don't care what happens to me.

First contact

A contact ad in an occult magazine:

Small group practising ritual magic with a special interest in the Goddess invites new members. Age, sex or colour unimportant. We are based S.E. London.

Like Audrey Harper, others became involved with groups that seemed innocent on the surface, only to find they had let themselves in for more than they had bargained for.

'Elspeth' is from the south of England. She became interested in witchcraft when she was a child, and got in touch with a coven through a contact ad in an occult magazine. She told her story on British television in *The Friday Report*: 'They advertised as white witches, and later on I found out they were practising the left-hand path (black magic or satanism) instead of white magic.'[5]

After she was introduced to the 'master' she decided against joining the group. But they wouldn't let her go and resorted to threats. She was understandably scared: 'I was hit on a number of occasions, because I threatened to go to the police if they wouldn't leave me alone, and they came after me.'

She says she was bundled into a car, taken to a house and locked up. Worse was to follow: 'The master forced himself upon me, and there was another woman there, and I was subjected to a sexual ordeal. I really thought they were going to kill me.'

Afraid and alone, she even contemplated suicide. 'I thought perhaps this is the way I might rid myself of them. For a long time afterwards I felt quite sick. The thought of being humiliated stuck in my mind.'

She claims members of the coven included a number of influential people:

> Members were teachers, lawyers, even Lords; people in quite high positions in life, and they were so well covered that no one would suspect. I was lucky, but there's probably hundreds of people out there who can't get away, and it's that which concerns me.

Unlike Audrey Harper, Elspeth did not convert to Christianity, so cannot be accused of having a bias against witchcraft. In fact she continued to be active as a witch.

Her warning was echoed three years later, again on British TV, by another practising witch, Kevin Carlyon. He claimed that some of the groups set up since the fifties in the name of Wicca were in fact exploring the darker side of the occult:

> Bondage, flagellation, sex: girls are abused sexually on the altar, and many are blackmailed. They are told if they join a coven there is no way they can get out, otherwise they will have mystical powers used against them, or worst of all, they will be killed off. I mean, this does go on in this country.[6]

The problem, as Elspeth found, was the difficulty in telling good from bad, especially when dealing with manipulative strangers. The contact ad had seemed innocuous enough. It was only after she had crossed the threshold that the group revealed itself in its true colours.

With the smudging of white and black magic acknowledged by many practitioners, perhaps the most critical difference between groups is the intention of their members. But that will not always be plain from an advert – especially a deceptive one – or even from initial contact with the group.

First impressions can be deliberately deceiving. Especially where groups operate both inner and outer courts: outer courts which are appealing to new recruits, and inner courts where practices are conducted that might be 'misunderstood' by outsiders.

And through the columns of widely sold magazines like

Prediction, other young people simply open themselves up to the attention of whomever might be interested or on the prowl:

> Female Scorpio, 19, seeks coven or white witch to train/instruct her.

> Virgoan male (aged 17) seeks local coven for initiation into ritual magic.

'Some are clearly emotionally disturbed or looking for sex', *Prediction*'s editor told a national newspaper, stressing that each small ad was carefully vetted. But Canon Dominic Walker says he has known others who have fallen into the same trap as Elspeth, simply through answering such an advert:

> I've known people who've got involved in magical groups through going along to meetings that have been advertised or going along to occult shops. They have an interest in the occult, so they buy magazines and reply to advertisements and find that the group, which perhaps claims to be a white magical group, is in fact something much more sinister.
>
> Or else they join a white magical group and find it is a front for something else, and they've ended up moving on to black magical groups and then into satanism.

At the worst extreme is the ritual abuse of children, who, like Elspeth, may find themselves tricked and then trapped by their abusers.

In Greece, trials involving self-proclaimed satanists and children have shocked the nation. A school teacher was jailed for recruiting primary school pupils for devil worship, and a young couple were murdered during a black magic ceremony at the Temple of Poseidon.

Then, in a separate case in 1994, two satanists confessed to luring a 15-year-old girl to a remote hillside on the promise of introducing her to a white magic circle. Instead she was beaten and strangled and her dead body was raped before being doused with petrol and set alight. Athens police believed other local teenagers had been drawn into the cult which drank the blood of its victims and indulged in animal and human sacrifice.[7]

Could ritual abuse happen in Britain? Five years earlier, *The Times* reported the following:

> Salesman Peter McKenzie tricked girls aged six and seven into

sexual intercourse, after promising to endow them with magic powers.

McKenzie told them they could become witches in his magic circle. The court heard that no fewer than 13 little girls were taught to pray nightly to the god of 'lechery and debauchery – Asmodeus'.

The girls were recruited over a period of three years. McKenzie pleaded guilty to four charges of rape, four of attempted rape, twelve of indecent assault and four offences of unlawful sexual intercourse. The case was heard at St Albans Crown Court.

The girls were warned that if they told their parents what had happened, bad luck would befall them and they might die. Anne Rafferty opened the prosecution by saying: 'The court will hear of his systematic ensnaring of small girls from six-years-old to their early teens into what the Crown says was a web of paedophilia with overtones of witchcraft. His method was to tell the child of a type of magic. If she did as she was told, she would be lucky and progress through the ranks of witchhood.'

When the time came for the Judge to address McKenzie, he told him: 'Nobody sitting in this court could be other than totally horrified and nauseated by your conduct. They are quite frightening and terrifying offences. It has done incalculable damage to the emotional development of several of the children.'

During the court proceedings several parents and relatives had to leave as the evidence unfolded. Woman Detective Constable Lesley Kent said after the court case: 'All the children are undergoing counselling and psychiatric help and will do so for a number of years.'

The aunt of one of the girls later said: 'One eleven-year-old girl believes she is going to die in a car crash when she is seventeen. He is the most evil man in Britain.'

McKenzie procured his victims by getting the first girl he corrupted, a seven-year-old, to recruit the others.

Suffer the children

A report in the *Glasgow Sunday Mail* claimed that a coven had been set up in the city to develop the psychic powers of pre-pubescent children. The children, aged between four and eleven, were allegedly being taught to be able to see the dead, move objects by the power of the mind, and to use psychic powers against people they didn't like.

The developing circle for children came to light after a mother was invited to send her two sons, aged three and six: 'He kept pressing me to send my boys to him to join what he called his "children's coven", but there was no way I would let my children have anything to do with him.'

Professor Robert Morris, head of Edinburgh University's Department of Parapsychology, warned through the newspaper: 'Parents should be especially careful about the potential long-term damage that could be caused to children.'[8]

Established witchcraft cults, as opposed to mavericks like McKenzie, are unable to speak with one voice over their involvement with children, though many insist that they wait until the children of the cult become adults before involving them in their rituals:

> A child is brought up to love nature, to respect nature, the plants the trees and everything else, and they are not taught anything of the craft until they reach 16 years of age.
> Dot Griffiths, 'Madame Morgana'[9]

> Everybody has a preconceived idea about what a witch is, and it's always bad. It's about child abuse, blackmail, sacrifices to the devil and this sort of thing. That's not the case. Children aren't even allowed into the coven in the first place.
> Nigel Clough, witch and writer on witchcraft,[10]

> We don't let anyone under 18 train.
> Shan, 'Clan mother'[11]

And Shan has little time for Christians who point the finger at problems in the pagan community: 'I have treated people who had had their lives ruined by Christianity, by the guilt and fear which it instils.'[12]

But the late Alex Sanders, founder of the Alexandrian stream of witchcraft, clearly had no qualms about the involvement of children. And according to *Channel 4 News*, Sanders admitted to practising black witchcraft. A video made by this self-styled 'King of the Witches' shows him performing a ritual with a little child. He says: 'The little girl . . . she's my witch. Are you frightened of me?' She shakes her head.

The footage shows Sanders standing naked, while the small girl is dressed in a costume bearing a crescent moon, the symbol of the Goddess. 'We could do rituals for them . . . couldn't we?' he asks. She nods her head. They perform a brief ceremony while he sits cross-legged and naked on the floor. No sexual contact takes place between the two, but parents and teachers may question the propriety of involving a very young girl in naked witchcraft rites.[13]

'Bill' used to be a member of a North American witchcraft group which described itself as Alexandrian. The following is taken from a filmed interview with him:

> When I first got into the Alexandrian wicca it looked really good, it seemed to be white and innocent, like gathering herbs and worshipping nature. But as I got to the higher degrees, I learned that the name of the horned god was Lucifer and that the sign of the second degree was an inverted pentagram, which is of course a symbol of black magic. And it began to dawn on me that there were things here which were not quite as they should be . . . Finally [I realized] that Satan was the god of witchcraft.[14]

It must be stressed that other Alexandrian witches could probably contest that viewpoint and dispute the authenticity of the group in question. And witches of all three major streams would protest that what has been described is deviant behaviour and not the norm.

'I'm going to break . . .'

What follows is from the personal *Book of Shadows*, the occultic diary of a woman in her early twenties who was a member of a witches' coven in the Midlands. The extract illustrates her mental turmoil. The book was abandoned when police raided the site of a ritual and broke up the gathering:

11.00 pm, Tuesday, January
I can't get to sleep because my mind is going too fast. I haven't been to work for the past two days (nothing unusual). I've been thinking of what I've been thinking, all the whys? I can come up with, with the usual non-answers . . . why do I want to live? Why do I want to die?

Death seems inviting because it seems so uncomplicated, but then again, how do I know that after I die, just being nothing or part of the everything; nothing is what I will achieve . . .

I feel like I'm crazy . . . I can't control the depths within me . . . I'm killing myself, I can't sleep, I forget to eat, I can't work, keep crying, and I can hear myself scream in my head. If I don't find a way to join my outer life with my inner life, then I'm going to break.

Something similar may have happened to divorcee Julie Wykes, who was initiated into witchcraft by a boyfriend. The day after begging her local vicar to save her from the devil, the 23-year-old Dorset woman attacked her three children and then took her own life. This clearly disturbed woman inflicted multiple stab wounds on her two-year-old son and her daughters, aged four and six. Then she stabbed herself through the heart with a breadknife.[15]

An unanswerable question remains: was her disturbance the result of her involvement with witchcraft, or did she become involved with witchcraft as a result of her disturbance? Many well-intentioned Wiccans could take understandable offence over the question. But from events which led up to her death, we can see that witchcraft was a factor in this family tragedy.

Author Dr Felix Unger would go further:

> Usually violence, suicide and insanity will run through a whole family line where magical arts have been cultivated and practised. Such tragic events often involve as many as four generations.[16]

Some opponents of witchcraft question the decision to repeal the 1951 Witchcraft Act, which again made lawful the practice in the UK. The late Geoffrey Dickens MP floated the idea of a change in the law, but acknowledged that personal freedom should be protected:

> Banning witchcraft altogether would be difficult . . . and it is up to adults to do as they wish. But it must be made illegal for children to take part in any sense whatsoever.[17]

An unthinkable crime

Greek public opinion was warned to brace itself for the worst as details of a ritual abuse trial began to emerge:

> Four satanists, accused of carrying out two human sacrifices in black magic rituals, had planned to kill four more women on Christmas day, according to Greek authorities.
>
> Victims were chained and tortured after rituals had taken place and two were murdered with daggers and a gun, according to an Athens police statement.
>
> Four ringleaders, including an 18-year-old woman, confessed to torturing, raping and murdering a 14-year-old girl and a 27-year-old mother. The satanic sect was discovered when one of

four women due to be sacrificed fled to the police.

The Greek Public Order Minister said: 'Public opinion must brace itself for the worst. The investigation will go very, very deep. It will cover many key sectors of public life, ranging from the military, the Church and the education system to the influence of television films on today's youth.' The two ringleaders were jailed for life.

The Daily Telegraph, 30 Dec. 1993.

Ritual abuse is the latest sinister twist to that most appalling and unthinkable of crimes, child abuse. Persistent reports from Europe, the USA, Canada, Australia, South Africa and other industrialized countries maintain that children and young people are being drawn into occult practices by networks of abusers.

It's claimed they're being enticed into such rings by their curiosity towards fantasy, magic and the occult, or the offer of shelter, affection, drugs and uninhibited sex.

With younger children abusers are using 'magic' shows to lure them in and then to terrify them into silence. Some abusers may be paedophiles, out for sexual kicks with kids. Others, astonishing as it may sound, appear to regard the sexual abuse of children as a necessary means to some religious end. The Ritual Abuse Task Force of the LA County Commission for Women reports:

> Ritual abuse is a brutal form of abuse of children, adolescents and adults, consisting of physical, sexual and psychological abuse, and involving the use of rituals. Ritual does not necessarily mean satanic. However, most survivors state that they were ritually abused as part of satanic worship for the purpose of indoctrinating them into satanic beliefs and practices. Ritual abuse rarely consists of a single episode. It usually involves repeated abuse over an extended period of time.

Survivors and carers

However loudly our offended sensibilities scream back that this can't be happening, reports of ritual abuse won't go away. I set out to investigate the evidence for the phenomenon for my book *Blasphemous Rumours*.[18] My approach was to interview doctors, psychiatrists, psychotherapists, counsellors, solicitors and other professionals from a variety of backgrounds who claimed first-hand experience with professing survivors of abuse.

When research time ran out, I had spoken to professional carers and others who between them claimed to be dealing personally with more than 900 victims of ritual abuse in the UK alone. Even allowing for some overlap between cases the number was higher than expected.

Few professed any prior interest in the subject. Many said their first encounter with ritual abuse came when they were confronted with the problem by their fearful and damaged clients.

All produced similar and complementary, albeit incredible, stories and all fiercely disputed the prevailing wisdom that they had been brainwashed into belief by zealots and crusaders.

Furthermore, the accounts they related were consistent. Unrelated adult survivors were disclosing substantially the same things as the children who were saying the same things as one another. And accounts from the UK were substantially the same as accounts from child and adult survivors in other countries.

Backing them up was medical evidence of physical and psychological damage of a nature and intensity that would be hard to ascribe to anything other than the events they related. Such disclosures were often made at high personal cost over a long period of time under the care of skilled therapists.

That sexual abuse had taken place could usually be proven by examination. But the ritual context for that abuse depended on recollection rather than forensic evidence. Memories are not always reliable, and on both sides of the Atlantic organizations have sprung up dedicated to exposing what has become known as false memory syndrome. In a milestone case in the USA in 1994, a father won damages against a therapist after claiming that false recollections of abuse had been planted in his daughter's mind. The British False Memory Society alleges that nearly every memory of abuse recovered under therapy is false. But in 1995, the British Psychological Society came to the opposite conclusion. It reported that recovered memories of childhood trauma *were* largely reliable.[19] This has become a major area of controversy and is likely to result in a run of court cases.

It may be worth pointing out that one of the leading figures of the false memory movement in America has been exposed as an advocate of paedophilia. Writing in a Dutch magazine, he said: 'Paedophiles need to make the claim that paedophilia is an acceptable expression of God's will for love and unity among human beings.[20]

At times child victims have described things few children – or adults – are ever likely to know. Judith Dawson, a child abuse consultant in Nottinghamshire, says:

The more we listened, the more we saw the terror, the trances and heard about the rituals they described, it became clear that these kids had been born into a world where good had to be destroyed and innocence perverted. The only explanation for all they told us was satanic ritual abuse.

After all, you tell me how else can a four-year-old boy who could barely speak when he came into care, suddenly recite – word perfect – the opening words of an historic satanic chant. In Latin?[21]

Threats

An NSPCC report says:

Ritualistic abuse is real. It is secretive, powerful and dangerous. It is dangerous to the participants in such networks and to professionals trying to protect the victims of the abuse in the networks.[22]

A British survey by psychologist Sheila Youngson found 68% of professional carers had been threatened in some way. In the US, one had body parts sent to her through the post. A lawyer was abducted, threatened with a gun, shown a picture of a skinned baby and played a tape of children crying and adults chanting – all to try to persuade her to back off the case. The threat failed.

One British psychiatrist was warned over the phone to stop treating one client, and threatened with reprisals if he disobeyed. The client's account of ritual abuse, which had begun in childhood and continued into adulthood, had been consistent in every detail over 18 months. Medical evidence supported her story. The physical marks of abuse were plain to see. And to convincingly fake the psychological symptoms, she would have had to possess an expert's knowledge of post-traumatic stress disorder – and be a consummate actress. Yet she was just an ordinary housewife. The threatening phone call, made by a man who had clearly been observing the psychiatrist's movements, was the final stamp of authenticity on her story.

Scotland Yard

In 1992 a TV documentary was produced to coincide with the book *Blasphemous Rumours*. It screened clips of an underground video which showed young adults in a drugged state being ritually cut and smeared with blood beneath the watching portrait of occultist Aleister Crowley dressed in full ritual regalia. Some participants later described these sick scenes as 'performance art'. Yet the underground tape went on to show scenes that could never be aired on TV. They showed pre-pubescent boys being sexually abused and forced to commit sexual acts with men, and were captioned 'initiation rites'.

Scotland Yard confirmed the video's content: 'It contains scenes of offences of grevious bodily harm which are performed in a ritualistic fashion, in a ritualistic context,' said a spokeman for the Obscene Publications Squad.

A telephone Helpline was set up following the programme. Within the first hour there were 4,500 attempted calls. The Helpline was utterly overwhelmed by past and present survivors of ritual and sexual abuse seeking help.

> Despite their terror, many callers managed to speak of the things they had seen and done and suffered. Rape, torture, mutilation, sleep deprivation, hypnosis, ritual murder, abortion and cannibalism, all featured in calls. One little girl just cried, 'The devil's got me' over and over.[23]

For ritual abuse to be happening at all in our society today, one would expect to find historical precedents. Such precedents exist and are clear.

Historical evidence

The historical roots of ritual abuse date back centuries. It became the depraved pastime of the 15th-century French aristocracy, as author on the occult Arthur Lyons observes:

> During one eight year period, enough records were maintained so that it is certain that at least eight hundred children were ritualistically put to death, their bodies either burned or buried. Girls were often bound to the altars for torture and rape. Sodomy was practiced on small boys, the orgasm followed by strangulation.

The satanic black mass, involving the ritual murder of children and the sacrifice of aborted foetuses, was celebrated by Catherine de Medici, queen consort of King Henry II of France, and the Marquise de Montespan, mistress of King Louis XIV. There are further reports of the black mass being carried out in the 17th and 19th centuries. That decriminalized versions are practised today is openly acknowledged by contemporary satanic organizations such as the UK-based Temple of Olympus and the US-based Church of Satan.

Sex rituals

A number of contemporary occult societies practise ritual magic. For some, this may involve the ritual use of sexual intercourse and blood-letting. According to survivor accounts, criminal versions of such rituals are practised by underground cults. What makes them criminal is the same factor that makes the difference between so-called white and black magic: compulsion. These rites feature the sexual abuse of under-age children and unwilling adults.

Sexual rituals continue to be practised by a British cult, which has branches in several countries and makes reference in its literature to a world satanic network. As I write, leading members are under police investigation. The occultist Aleister Crowley is an acknowledged influence.

'A male child . . .'

Crowley's magic took him down the darkest of paths. In his *magnum opus* of 1929, *Magick in Theory and Practice*, he makes reference to the need for human sacrifice to perform his magical workings:

> It was the theory of the ancient magicians, that any living being is a storehouse of energy varying in quantity according to the size and health of the animal, and in quality, according to its mental and moral character. At the death of this animal this energy is liberated suddenly.

He continues:

> For the highest spiritual working one must accordingly choose that victim which contains the greatest and purest force. A male child of perfect innocence and high intelligence is the most satisfactory and suitable victim.[24]

Crowley's occult manual was meant to be more than some esoteric whimsy. It is presented to his readers as a course of training. But Crowley offers a get-out clause for the squeamish:

> Those magicians who object to the use of blood have endeavoured to replace it with incense . . . But the bloody sacrifice, though more dangerous, is more efficacious; and for nearly all purposes human sacrifice is best.[25]

Crowley set up an 'Abbey' at Cefalù in Sicily, to perform his rituals. These included a Gnostic version of the mass. Author Tim Tate observes:

> All the rituals at Cefalù were sexually oriented and were directed at the worship of evil for evil's sake . . . The rituals . . . lasted until 1923, when a baby disappeared from a neighbouring village. Crowley was accused of abducting it and killing it during a ritual. On 23 April, Crowley was summoned to the police station . . . to be told that Mussolini had ordered his expulsion. On 1 May, closely guarded by local police, the 'Great Beast' was summarily ejected. No charges were ever brought over the missing infant.[26]

How literally Crowley took himself is open to question, but his influence is widely and extensively acknowledged by modern-day satanic and occultic groups. And there is no knowing how literally *they* may take *him*.

A case in question concerns a drawing made by Crowley, who was something of an artist. His sketch depicted a demon, which he named Chronzon, preparing to devour a child. Apologists for Crowley would argue that the picture was nothing more than a cartoon. But one ritual abuse survivor claims the group she was in performed rituals to invoke that particular demon. Her appalling physical injuries have been verified by a police surgeon. And she claims the satanic group that abused her also performed the ritual sacrifice of children and adults.

In recent correspondence with the author of this book a senior member of a satanic organization in Britain openly acknowledged that the ritual abuse of children does take place – albeit not by members of his own network. He writes:

> The Prison Officer was expelled from the Temple last year and has since formed his own group [name supplied], of which he

styles himself Priest of Darkness III. The [group] uses pederasty as part of its pursuit of magic!

Crowley's influence over witchcraft

Though many neo-pagans may find the following uncomfortable, it seems modern witchcraft also owes a debt to the man who styled himself 'the Beast'. Richard Cavendish wrote:

> Crowley directly influenced the modern witchcraft movement . . . The chief publicist and organiser of modern witchcraft, Gerald Gardner . . . was an initiate of Crowley's . . . and hired the Beast to write witchcraft rituals for him.
>   Crowley welcomed what he saw as a popularized form of his own creed. As far back as 1915 he had written to Charles Stansfield Jones, urging him to start such a cult. 'The time is just ripe for a natural religion. People like rites and ceremonies and they are tired of hypothetical gods. Insist on the real benefits of the Sun, the Mother-force, the Father-force and so on . . . In short, be the founder of a new and greater Pagan cult.'[27]

Cavendish argues that Gardner waited until the Witchcraft Act was repealed before acting publically on Crowley's advice. His 1954 work drew upon Crowleyan magic, including flagellatory and sexual rituals; masonic symbolism and the writings of American folklorist C. G. Leland.

His book stirred up considerable interest, and, says Cavendish, many new groups were formed as a result: 'Though he was an almost forgotten man at his death, interest in Crowley has revived and he has more followers now than in his lifetime.'[28]

But if such philosophies have paved the way for ritual abuse, then where is the courtroom evidence that such a thing is taking place today?

Prosecutions

Detective Superintendent David Cole led successful police actions in two British ritual abuse cases. He recalls one:

> Smith was convicted in 1982 and sent to prison for 14 years for the defilement of a number of female children. He believed

himself to be either the reincarnation of Lucifer or the devil's representative, and he used this belief to influence children and get them to submit to sexual practices.

He fully admitted that he was very interested in satanism and believed in what he was doing. The proof of the pudding was when ritualistic material was discovered in the houses of the accused.

That was satanic abuse, because quite clearly rituals were involved to induce fear into the children. He certainly believed that he had the power of Lucifer.[29]

Accounts by survivors and their carers in the medical professions suggest that ritual abuse is occurring within four distinct contexts:

1. Criminal occult societies.
2. Paedophile rings which use the occult to frighten and control children.
3. Groups run by occult dabblers and mavericks.
4. Families where an abusive form of satanism has been the received religion for generations.

Underground criminal occult societies enforce strict codes of secrecy. Members might be blackmailed or forced to become abusers in order to implicate them and safeguard their vow of silence. So it is abuse within the remaining three categories which is more likely to come to the attention of the police and social services.

Despite repeated claims to the contrary in sections of the press, there have been successful prosecutions in cases where ritual abuse has been alleged. Criminal courts in the UK and abroad have accepted evidence that sexual and physical assault has taken place within an occultic context. Ritual abusers have been sent to jail.

In June 1993, seven life sentences were handed out to a sex offender in what was described by the police as probably the worst case of child sexual abuse yet uncovered in Britain.

The Old Bailey was given horrific details of child abuse within an extended family in West London during what were said to be satanic rituals. Four girls and three boys were repeatedly assaulted. One was held by his ankles from an open window until he agreed to sex. An eleven and a 13-year-old were driven to attempted suicide. 'These kids were bred for abuse,' said Detective Inspector Carol Bristow, who led the inquiry.

The court heard that the children were sexually abused for four successive years over Hallowe'en at what they called a 'devil' church in Northolt. They were said to have been assaulted at knifepoint by adults in black hoods and cloaks. The rector gave evidence of 'unpleasant witchcraft practices' in the church.

Charges relating to the building were dropped when inconsistencies emerged in the children's evidence, but police remain convinced that the church was a venue for abuse.

Judge Brian Capstick QC described what took place as 'about as dreadful a case as I have encountered'.[30]

In a disclosure interview, one of the children, a seven-year-old girl, said: 'My Dad took me to Hallowe'en and they tied me and touched me . . . there was a star hanging up and it had a devil on it.'[31]

Four adult members, including a mother, were charged, successfully prosecuted and jailed for incestuous rape, assault, indecency and cruelty. Police claim other adults were involved but the evidence was so appalling that it was considered likely to jeopardize the case. The others were allowed to go free.

It's a pattern that's been repeated during several British trials, where bizarre details of rituals have been dropped to avoid hindering an otherwise certain prosecution.

The non-crime

There are two simple reasons why the defendants in such cases are not charged with ritual abuse – no such crime exists in the UK statute books and few juries would believe their ears. Damning evidence can be produced of the sexual assault, but not of its context. And it is all too easy for abusers to discredit potential witnesses – especially children.

Survivor accounts describe how child victims are sometimes drugged and made to watch horror videos before being abused. Their own abuse may also be videoed and they are then forced to watch the recordings. Under cross-examination what happened in reality and what was observed on video become muddled and the child's evidence is promptly dismissed.

Several charges were thrown out in the Northolt case, above, after it was revealed the children had been made to watch movies featuring horror and hard-core pornography. Small wonder the police often settle for the safer option of sticking to forensically provable sexual offences.

But some legislators in the United States need no further convincing. They have confronted the dilemma that where there is no crime of ritual abuse, no-one can be accused of committing it; and if no-one commits it, then the crime does not officially exist. To prosecute an offender for ritual abuse, you first have to define it and make it an offence, which is what they have done. On 3 April 1990 a Bill was passed unanimously through the Idaho Centennial Legislature's House and Senate:

18-1560A RITUALIZED ABUSE OF A CHILD
A person is guilty of a felony when he commits any of the following acts with, upon, or in the presence of a child as part of a ceremony, rite or any similar observance:
(a) Actually or in simulation, tortures, mutilates or sacrifices any warm-blooded animal or human being;
(b) Forces ingestion, injection or other application of any narcotic, drug, hallucinogen or anaesthetic for the purposes of dulling sensitivity, cognition, recollection of, or resistance to any criminal activity;
(c) Forces ingestion, or external application, of human or animal urine, faeces, flesh, blood, bones, body secretions, nonprescribed drugs or chemical compounds etc.

The following is an extract from a testimony presented to the Idaho lawmakers:

I was ritually abused between the ages of three and fourteen. It began on my third birthday when my parents and grandparents relinquished their rights to me and dedicated me to Satan. From that point on the high priest of the coven my father and grandfather belonged to had control over my life. I still lived at home and went to school, yet there was a part of my life no one knew about. That part consisted of sexual abuse, bestiality, pornography, drugs and witnessing and participating in animal and human sacrifices.[32]

In 1993 a similar law was passed in Massachusetts, prohibiting 'certain ritualistic acts' including ritual mutilation, dismemberment, torture and the sacrifice of animals and humans. Moves to pass related laws were made in five other States. But in most places public opinion has yet to shift beyond wondering, with a certain cynicism, whether ritual abuse can *really* be happening, or whether the whole thing can be reassuringly dismissed as a moral panic.

In 1994, a UK Health Department inquiry found evidence of 'three substantial cases of ritual abuse'. Hot on its heels a further government study confirmed the existence of ritual abuse and declared it to be more widespread. The study, funded by the

Economic and Social Research Council and the Department of Health, identified 62 cases of ritual abuse between 1988 and 1991.

The research, conducted over two years by Manchester University, was the first national survey into the nature and extent of child sex abuse. Researchers went on to examine 20,000 child protection records from eight local authorities. They recorded: 'Extrapolating from these figures . . . there would have been 967 cases of organized abuse and 85 cases of alleged ritual abuse in England and Wales between 1988 and 1991.'

The report exposed major weaknesses in the ability of the criminal justice system to deal with child abuse, and concluded that the extent of organized abuse had been underestimated.[33]

So two official British reports confirm the existence of ritual abuse. For some the remaining stumbling-block is whether such rituals could really be the work of paid-up, card-carrying satanists who regard sexual abuse as an integral part of their belief system.

Put so starkly, the question seems absurd. Who could do – or believe – such a thing? Most liberal-minded people would rather jump through hoops than misjudge others, exhibit intolerance towards them or deny them their right to hold differing beliefs. So we tend to shy away from the question of whether ritual abuse could actually arise out of religious practice. Jean La Fontaine, who produced the first report, thinks not. And the issue did not arise in the second report.

But as far as the victims are concerned, whatever religious justification could be dreamt up for their sexual abuse and torture could only be utterly irrelevant.

Shortly before these two government reports, the first clinical book on satanist abuse was published by consultant psychotherapist Valerie Sinason. *Treating Survivors of Satanist Abuse* drew together contributions from 40 professionals in the fields of psychiatry, psychology, psychotherapy and mental health management who were dealing with the terrible reality of trying to care for ritual abuse survivors.

As Valerie Sinason, an atheist, observed at its launch: 'What the book demonstrates most vividly for me is that firstly, the torture of children and adults in peacetime democracies within the context of a religious belief can no longer be put aside as a myth.'

Other cases

And there have been successful British prosecutions for sexual abuse where the overtly satanic or occultic context has been recognized by the courts.

We noted earlier the case of Peter McKenzie. He taught girls as young as six and seven to pray to Asmodeus, the god of lechery and debauchery, while he had sexual intercourse with them during rituals. McKenzie ensnared and abused 13 girls in this way. After his prosecution families of his victims collected a 10,000 signature petition calling for tougher sentences against child abusers.

We heard how Malcolm Smith was jailed for 14 years for offences including unlawful sexual intercourse, rape and indecent assault. Smith claimed to be the devil incarnate. With his wife and sister-in-law they recruited children into a black magic ring where they were sexually abused on an altar that had been dedicated to the devil. He was successfully prosecuted in 1982 at Northampton Crown Court.

In 1992 a satanist who raped his great niece up to three times a week from the age of ten was jailed for twelve years by Liverpool Crown Court. The girl had become pregnant at the age of twelve and had been left to give birth alone to his baby. Judge Denis Clark told the defendant: 'Your fascination with the occult or devil worship played a part in impelling you towards this evil behaviour.'

In February 1989, Winchester Crown Court sentenced a sixty-year-old engineer to twelve years imprisonment on charges of incest with one of his five daughters. The man, described in court as a practising satanist, had made his own daughter pregnant five times. The jury heard that he had been 'instructed by spirits' to have sex with her. When police raided his bungalow they found a 'magic room' containing occult paraphernalia, including a pentagram on the floor, occult symbols on the walls and a black priest's robe behind the door. The court was told that police found phials of oil that had been 'used in perverted sex during black magic ceremonies.'

Other successful prosecutions in the UK and abroad where abuse took place within an occultic or satanic context are outlined in the book *Blasphemous Rumours*.[34]

The court records show it, the prosecutions prove it, and the perpetrators are behind bars for the fact – that ritual abuse exists.

Last year crimes involving Satanism recorded by the South African police occult-related crimes division included 13 missing persons, four murders, seven rapes, seven suicides, 20 attempted suicides, 26 break-ins at churches and 179 cases of desecration of graves.

The Guardian, 5th July 1995

Cult-related killers stand convicted of murder in 23 States and at least nine foreign countries. Numerous other occultists are now serving time for practising their faith through acts of arson, rape, assault, cruelty to animals and similar crimes.

Michael Newton, *Raising Hell*[35]

10

Fade to black

Rock music and the occult

> Parents used to complain about rock music because it was loud
> and the musicians had long hair. Now groups like . . . Venom . . .
> Slayer . . . King Diamond . . . 'entertain' our children with vivid
> songs of rape, sado-masochism, torture, satanic worship, sexual
> mutilation, patricide, and cannibalism.
>
> Bob and Gretchen Passantino[1]

Who can sensibly argue that what our kids fill their heads with can
have no effect on their minds, their attitudes – even their behaviour?
What finds a lodging in childhood may fester in adolescence and
erupt at the onset of adulthood.

One underground group, which produces pornography and
indulges in sado-masochism and drug abuse, has a word for the
climate of doomy introspection that it seeks to foster. It calls it *occulture*.

We have become immersed in a culture of the occult. The occult
makes money. It *sells*. From horoscopes, supernaturally-obsessed
games, cartoons, videos and TV shows to the most potent expression of adolescent striving for identity – music.

Tommy Sullivan

Fourteen-year-old Tommy Sullivan had become obsessed with
Satan. Some say it began when his Catholic school permitted a group
of students to produce a study on satanism. It was the kids' idea, and
it may have seemed a good way of letting them find out for themselves a few home truths. It seemed to have worked. Tommy Sullivan
told his classmates that satanism was the opposite to Catholicism
and was 'too scary and weird' for him.

Sister Philomena must have been relieved. There had been an
attempted burglary at a nearby Catholic church. Then the police had
stumbled upon 20 teenagers conducting occult rituals. There had
been reports of chickens being sacrificed, and recently a teenager

who was into witchcraft had committed suicide.

But then Tommy was found handing round notes which disturbed his schoolmates. In words that read backwards, he had written: 'Evil of all mankind dwells within my soul.' On another occasion he wrote:

> Satan came to me last night in a dream. He had my face. He was carrying a knife and he told me to 'preach satanism to other kids then kill everyone in your family.'[2]

Sister Philomena called in Tommy's mother, Bettyanne. Tommy's response was encouraging. He reassured his mum and dad that the obsession would stop. He promised the whole thing was in the past.

Tommy went with them to Mass, dutifully joined in, then settled down that evening to watch *Friday the Thirteenth* on video. It was ten o'clock and his parents had gone to bed. Half an hour later, Tom Sullivan, the boy's father, was snatched out of his sleep by a piercing noise. The sofa was blazing and fumes rising from the living room had triggered the smoke alarm.

His son and his wife were nowhere to be found. Tom quickly summoned his neighbours and called the police. Detective Paul Hart was a veteran of Vietnam, but described what he discovered in the Sullivan basement as 'the most brutal thing I have ever seen'.

Bettyanne Sullivan's blood was over everything. Her hands had been partially severed and her throat cut almost to the point of decapitation. Her killer had attempted to remove her eyes and the skin around them.

It was Sunday morning before a neighbour found Tommy Sullivan, buried in deep snow in nearby woods. He had cut his wrists and managed to sever his own throat all the way back to the spinal column. In the snow beside him, still open, lay the boy scout knife that he had used on his mother and then on himself.

In the smoke-damaged house, police found Tommy's books on the occult spread out in a circle in the living room. The County Prosecutor said they formed a pattern common to occult rituals where the purpose was to focus spiritual energy.

Among Tommy's possessions they found a spiral-bound notebook filled with drawings of demons and devils. A robed figure beckoned: 'Come to Satan.' Nearby were half-burned books he had borrowed from the library – on satanism. In his own room, among the heavy metal posters that covered the walls, was a small, solitary crucifix.

In the snow, close to the car that Tommy had struggled to drive, among clothes and articles he had dropped in his haste, was a chain bearing the inverted cross of satanism, and the following, made in his own writing:

> To the Greatest Demons of Hell, I Tommy Sullivan, would like to make a solemn exchange with you. If you give me the most extreme of all magical powers . . . I will kill many Christian followers who are serious in their beliefs . . . Exactly 20 years from this day I promise to commit suicide. I will tempt all teenagers on earth to have sex, have incest, do drugs, and to worship you. I believe that evil will once again rise and conquer the love of God.

Tommy Sullivan had no criminal record. No history of violence. He was bright, his schoolwork was good, and he was said to be popular. His twin passions seemed to be heavy metal music – he saved $1,000 to buy his own stereo – and the fantasy role-play game, Dungeons and Dragons. Between them they consumed his spare time.

Three weeks before the killing, his father had noted that Tommy had been repeatedly singing a song 'about blood and killing your mother'.[3]

Tommy's mother, Bettyanne, was described as a 'devout Catholic' and a 'strict disciplinarian'. Tom Sullivan told police she had nagged the boy and there had been arguments. Tommy had retreated into himself to the point where he could no longer talk to her about his feelings.[4] They had found themselves losing him as he grew increasingly distant. He resented being sent to a Catholic school, which singled him out from other children in his neighbourhood.[5] He had started drinking and had taken to walking around for hours on his own.

Stunned and appalled townsfolk assembled *en masse* and pinned the blame squarely on the devil. But Detective Paul Hart had a question: 'What kind of home life does a kid have if he turns to something like satanism? Tommy could have been sacrificing elephants in his room and his parents wouldn't have known about it.'

In cases like Tommy Sullivan's everyone is looking for a scapegoat. Ersatz satanism, heavy metal music and fantasy games versus a troubled home life, relationship breakdown and a repressed personality. Cause or effect? As ever, all we can say for certain is that these things and more were contributory factors and the obsession with evil could only have made matters worse.

Music-occult links

Links have been documented between heavy metal music and occult-related violence. The *Daily Mail* reported on a series of incidents in Lethbridge, Canada:

> A spate of suicides [has been] linked to a satanic heavy metal music cult . . . three teenagers have died and another dozen are believed to have promised to kill themselves . . . A school principal . . . passed a report to the police alleging that some Lethbridge students are involved in a satanic group controlled by adults in other cities. [One boy] left a note asking that the heavy metal song Fade to Black be played at his funeral.[6]

And from the files of the US National Criminal Justice Task Force on Occult Related Ritualistic Crimes comes the following account of death rock being used by adults as an enticement to lure adolescents into active satanism:

> There was a teen club in a large metroplex area that was run by two adults heavily involved in 'death rock'. These would identify individuals twelve to fourteen years of age who seemed to be more susceptible, and would invite them to a private part of the club. An invitation was an honour. The kids would then be lured into compromising situations after being given free sex, drugs and alcohol.
>
> The next day, when these young people would come to their senses, they would meekly go back to the group and say 'no more', when they were presented with the pictures taken of them the night before. The kids would be threatened with harm to their parents, as well as the ruin of their own reputations. Because of this, they would break down even more and participate in extremely bizarre satanic rituals.[7]

In case after case, the death-centred lyrics of heavy metal music have been linked with the suicidal or murderous tendencies of teenagers. Several are reported elsewhere in this book. Space does not permit them all.

Many – but not all – of the cases to receive publicity come from America, where lenient gun laws and the ready availability of Dad's firearm have made suicide that much easier. But in two cases it has been British rock bands that have been hauled before the courts for lyrics claimed to have driven teenagers to take their own lives.

James and Ray

It was early evening, two days before Christmas. James Vance, 18, and Ray Belknap, 19, had spent the past six hours drinking beer, smoking cannabis and listening again and again to the Judas Priest album, *Stained Class*.

They took a sawn-off shotgun and walked through a churchyard to a children's playground. Perching themselves on the roundabout, they took it in turns to place the barrel beneath their chins and shoot themselves. Ray died immediately but James survived, with appalling facial injuries. His lawyer said he looked like the Elephant Man.

He lived on in pain for three years, before dying of an overdose of drugs. He said the music had mesmerized and brainwashed him; that he had been acting under a compulsion.

The families sued the British rock band and their record company, CBS, for $6.2 million. They alleged that subliminal lyrics on the album had urged him to *Do it, do it*. Tim Post, Vance's attorney, said:

> [James] had second thoughts that he had things to live for, but he felt compelled to pull the trigger, and he began chanting, 'Do it, do it, do it,' and he did it, he pulled the trigger.[8]

After only 17 days, the case collapsed. The judge said the disputed phrase 'Do it' was only a chance combination of sounds, but he sidestepped making a clear ruling over the existence or otherwise of subliminals on the album. He was clear that the families' lawyers had failed to prove that subliminals were the cause of the suicide attempts.

Lead singer Rob Halford called it 'a great day for Judas Priest and artists all over America', and blamed the children's upbringing, rather than his music, for their suicide.

Suicide solution

Like many young people, 19-year-old John McCollum was in the habit of listening to his favourite tracks over and over again. After sating himself on British rocker Ozzy Osbourne's *Diary of a Madman* he went up to his room and put on his headphones to soak in the final side of *Speak of the Devil*. And that was how detectives found him in the morning, with the record still spinning. He had got hold of a pistol and shot himself through the right temple. One of the tracks he had been playing over and over on the family hi-fi was *Suicide Solution*. Included in the lyrics:

> *The reaper's travelling at full throttle*
> *It's catching you but you don't see*
> *The reaper is you and the reaper is me*
> *Breaking laws, knocking doors*
> *But there's no one at home*
> *Made your bed, rest your head*
> *But you lie there and moan*
> *Where to hide, suicide is the only way out*
> *Don't you know what it's really about?*

McCollum's parents decided to sue for negligence, product liability and intentional misconduct. The case was thrown out on the grounds of the First Amendment to the US Constitution – the guarantee of freedom of speech. The McCollums amended their complaint to incitement to suicide and appealed.

Their attorney alleged that the Osbourne albums contained 'a progression of songs which lead down a path from chaos, confusion and insanity to suicide'. Osbourne's music emphasized 'satanic worship and emulation, the mocking of religious beliefs and death'. He argued that it was foreseeable that susceptible individuals such as John, who were emotionally unstable, could be influenced to consider suicide. And he claimed that the track *Suicide Solution* contained subliminal lyrics which encouraged the listener to shoot himself.

The Court of Appeal was unimpressed by the argument and rejected the case. Suicide was a common theme in literature and merely discussing it could not be regarded as incitement to commit it. The Court recorded that McCollum had an alcohol problem and serious emotional difficulties. He was described by Ozzy Osbourne as 'obviously deranged'.

If so, he was not alone. The McCollum's attorney told reporters that they had been contacted by at least 20 parents who said their children had killed themselves after listening to Osbourne.'

The official line from the record industry is that such kids were probably disturbed in the first place. Trish Heimer, one of their representatives, has commented:

> I do not believe that a record and a record alone can force young
> people to do some of the things that rock music and artists are
> being blamed for today. I think people are looking for scapegoats.
> If your kid is sitting in his room, listening to the same record over

and over for eight hours, I don't care what that record is, you might think about knocking on the door and saying, 'Johnny, is everything OK in there . . . ?'[10]

Ms Heimer has a point, but McCollum's psychiatrist believes she may be missing one, too:

> When a kid is at the breaking point . . . he is susceptible to other influences, like music or MTV . . . Sadomasochism, blood and violence make big bucks for the producers of rock videos, but such things can push a kid over the edge.[11]

Who needs subliminals?

Whether subliminal lyrics do add a subconscious hook, suggestion, or even command to music has yet to be determined. In the two US court cases the very existence of subliminals was disputed. But black metal band Venom are blatant about their own use of hidden messages. Venom's album *In League with Satan* is said to contain the backmasked message, 'Raise the devil, burn, burn your daughters.' 'We like to shock,' they explained on Radio 4.[12]

Lead singer Abaddon, who winsomely takes his name from the destroying angel of the Bottomless Pit, describes himself as a practising satanist and not ashamed of it. For bands like Venom, concealing a so-called satanic message to create an impact has become an irrelevancy. The lyrics are out in the open. These are the words of Venom's song *Possessed*:

> *Look at me, Satan's child*
> *Born of evil, thus defiled,*
> *Brought to life through satanic birth . . .*
> *Listen to me and I'll tell you*
> *Things that will sicken your mind . . .*
> *I drink the vomit of the priests*
> *Make love with the dying whore . . .*
> *Satan, as my master incarnate*
> *Hail! Praise to my unholy host!*

Necrophiliac by Slayer:

> *Virgin child now drained of life*
> *Your soul cannot be free*

> *Not given the chance to rot in hell*
> *Satan's cross points to hell*
> *The earth I must uncover*
> *A passion grows to feast upon*
> *The frozen blood inside her*
> *I feel the urge, the growing need*
> *To f*** the sinful corpse*
> *My task's complete*
> *The bitch's soul*
> *Lies raped in demonic lust*

Researchers Bob and Gretchen Passantino comment:

> The fact that metal music is often important to kids who . . .
> commit suicide . . . does not prove that the music is a cause of the
> suicide. More accurately, teenagers at risk of suicide often betray
> their vulnerabilities by antisocial, destructive activities, including
> listening to destructive music. The vast majority of metal fans
> don't end up killing themselves . . . but teens who do . . . often
> also listen to destructive music.[13]

Convicted satanic murderer Sean Sellers said:

> When you've got this music playing over and over again, all the
> time, and you're hearing praise to the Devil, and praise to the
> ideas of evil, you begin to really get involved in it . . . it has an
> effect on you.

Pete Rowland was listening to the black metal band Metallica when
he was on his way to murder Stephen Newberry, Rowland said:

> I would spend four or five hours a day, every day, in my car, in my
> room, just about wherever I could listen to it. Megadeth, Slayer,
> Merciful Fate, Metallica. Just listening to music all the time, it
> puts thoughts into your mind: thoughts of killing people,
> torturing people, the power thing.

In our own survey, 62% of 14- to 15-year-olds questioned listened to
heavy metal music. More than one in eight took their fix on a daily
basis. A third admitted to finding it depressing.

The overheated and death-obsessed climate of occultism is perpetuated in some bands' stage acts. WASP simulate drinking blood on
stage; the audience at Motley Crue concerts are encouraged to chant

'Natas' – Satan backwards; GWAR throw buckets of simulated blood and excrement over their audiences. Violence and sex, simulated to stimulate, have become stock in trade. Consultant child psychiatrist Dr Robert Demski comments:

> In an effort to gain ratings, music groups exploit youthful enthusiasm and energy for the sake of money and notoriety. Violence is glorified, drugs are glamorized and personal tragedy is trivialized. By repeated exposure and peer pressure, children become desensitized to brutality and degredation.

For some bands, satanism may be simply the ultimate pose: the doom-and-gloom lyrics, the conspicuous *bad attitude*, are there for effect – to sell records. But less robust fans may share neither their cynicism nor appreciate their irony. Along with the music, they may be buying an ideology. And for overtly satanic bands that may be all to the good.

Deicide

Fun is not a word one would associate with Glen Benton, lead singer of the death-metal band Deicide, whose name, incidentally, means 'God-murder'. Benton sports an inverted cross on his forehead which is freshly burned in at monthly intervals with a branding iron. Flaring his eyes until you can see their whites, he describes his concerts as 'a focal point to express my satanism'. Asked in a TV documentary to explain his purpose, he replies: 'To create the most evilest music, and to gain entrance to the seven gates of Hell.'[14]

A sample of Deicide's lyrics:

Damned to Hell
End my life
Wrath of God
Satan, sin my soul blessed with fire
Throne of Stone
Satan I must die
In my wake seventh gate
Satan, suicide end my life
I must die

Asked if he believes in demon possessions, Benton replies, 'Of course.'

'Are *you* possessed?' the reporter presses him.

'Of course. Demonic possession to me is when you come to a certain point and . . . your body is possessed and there's no turning back, and there's no way you *can* turn back.'

'A lot of things happened to me when I was younger,' Benton explained to *Sky* magazine, 'that created my hate towards God. I was introduced to satanism when I was real young and I've been into it ever since.'

Deicide bassist Eric Hoffman is every bit as cute: 'I would like to sacrifice on stage – humans,' he adds. 'It's what people wanna see. They want the real thing. Death metal *is* satanic. We relay our music all into satanism. If you're into death metal you're into death.'

We may wince at claims like these or laugh them off, but what about the kids who become immersed in such material? Will it be water off a duck's back? And how can we be sure? The evidence suggests that some may be drowning.

Sky went on to quote therapist Dorothy Wallace, who works with satan-obsessed teenagers in the sunshine state, which has raised a crop of death-metal bands:

'I've worked with girls who've had their nipples removed . . . or the vulva cut off. They were drugged at the time and permitted it . . . now they're so horrified they can barely talk about it.' She also works with a teenager who has the mark of Satan on his testicles. 'Someone carved him up in that way. Pain is the issue. If it's not painful, it's not in Satan's name.'

Also entrusted into Wallace's care was the death metal fan who was forcibly prevented from gouging out the eye of another teenager. 'They regard it as OK to mutilate people because Satan wants them to. You earn another demon stronger than the one you've already been given. That's the goal.'

Mark Pastellopoulous has performed in two leading roles: as head of the UK-based Temple of Olympus, which practised black-magic, and of the rock band, *The Devoted Men*, which performed at London nightspots. Pastellopoulos insisted that his songs were inspired by spirits: 'Very frequently there's an other-worldiness about the words themselves, it's almost as if we are not writing the words. Our hand is performing the action, but it is not our mind.'[15]

Pastellopoulous took his music as seriously as he took his religion, which he admitted involved animal sacrifice. One might reasonably expect some fans to have taken his message seriously, too.

Norway, 1994: An Oslo court sentenced Varg Vikernes, lead

singer of the black metal group Burzum, to 21 years in prison for burning down three churches, attempted arson on a fourth and the murder of Oystein Aarseth, leader of the band Mayhem. Credited with having imported black metal music to Norway, Aarseth was initially inspired by the Gateshead band Venom, whose tongue-in-cheek demonic act was never meant to be taken literally. But somewhere in translation, this raucous metal music seems to have initiated a Norwegian crime wave . . . so far Norway has seen 13 arson attacks on churches.[16]

Dinosaurs?

So today's satanic rock can't be dismissed as 'out of date and over there' (the US). Take a deep breath and join me in a quick flip through the pages of the December 1993 edition of *Terroriser*, which bills itself as 'the UK's extreme music magazine'.

Bands advertised in a single ad include: Necromantia, described as 'Ritualistic Satanic Metal'; Mystifier, into wicca and goetia (witchcraft/black magic); Rotting Christ; Impaled Nazarene, ('Satanic'). Bands and albums gracing another ad include: *Diabolical Summoning* by Sinister; *Into the Grave* by Grave; *Forever laid to rest* by Seance and *Greetings from Hell* by Mourning. Bands named after demons include Belial and Samael.

Take these snatches from reviews, the first of *Goetia* by the Brazilian band Mystifier:

> *Goetia* is the quintet's follow up to their '91 debut offering,
> *Wicca* and is pretty harrowing stuff . . . most of the tracks are a
> bit of a mouthful, take; 'The Baphometic Goat of the Knight's
> Templar in the 12th Century' for instance, and the Brazilians
> claim they are 'imperfect men searching for the perfect evil'
> through their Satanic doom-death music . . . I could imagine the
> horned fellow giving an appreciative nod in Mystifier's direction.

And a gig by GGFH (that's Global Genocide, Forget Heaven):

> It was a brilliant set . . . coupled with videotape loops of
> autopsies, suicides and murders.

Then there were the Genitorturers who do 'piercing and bondage and things as a demonstration between songs, kind of an educational thing'; and the news that Infernal Majesty's former vocalist

Vince 'created a stir in Toronto earlier this year when he was arrested for slashing a girlfriend's wrist in an attempt to drink her blood – I kid you not!!!'

Enough. Suffice to say the scene is still thriving; only today, heavy music which became tempered into heavy metal, has splintered into fragments with names like thrash, death and black.

Goth et al.

While heavy metal dinosaurs have yet to face extinction, the occultic theme is evolving into a wider musical expression. Recent musical offshoots also peddle paganism, shamanism and morbid Gothic romanticism.

At the age of 13 'Gary' was into the occult-oriented heavy metal music of Black Sabbath, AC/DC and Iron Maiden. He explains:

> There was an attraction, particularly for the heavier, more flagrantly occultic material. It fed this obsession and fantasy and helped to shape the world that I was living in. I describe it as a log on the fire, another bit of wood that was burning in this great big bonfire of my spiritual experience.
>
> Bands on the scene today would be the Levellers, All About Eve and the Shaman, who are into a mind-expanding New Age philosophy. If you are into a band then you want to get to know about the people and their lives. So you read the magazines. If you are living in a society that lacks role models then you take your cue from them.

In the late eighties the Shamen drew fire from a Tory MP who complained they had been stamping their mail with the slogan 'Jesus is a Lie' and a satanic inverted crucifix.

The Gothic fashion craze takes its cue from Byron, Shelley and Count Dracula. Followers aim to look deathly by dressing in black, making their faces pale and picking out their features with dark lipstick and eyeliner.

The trend is closely connected to the music scene. Bands attracting a large following include Fields of the Nephilim (named after the demonic figures in the Book of Genesis), The Sisters of Mercy and The Mission.

Two London teenagers who were heavily into Goth took their obsession to the limit. They had been to see the film, *Flatliners*, about a group of medical students who decide to take the ultimate trip by experimenting with death and near-death experiences. They connected a pipe to the exhaust of their car, wound up their Gothic music on the stereo and took their own lives.

We met 'Roger' earlier. As a teenager he and a group of friends became obsessed with vampirism, to the extent of cutting themselves up, drinking their own blood, and desecrating a graveyard.

This cheerful little coterie called themselves The Black Alchemist. They got high on dope, tales of the occult and doom-laden lyrics. Bands such as The Sisters of Mercy and Bauhaus provided the soundtrack to their do-it-yourself occultism, with titles such as *After Hours, Lucretia*, and *Bela Lugosi is dead*.

'*Lucretia* I listened to again and again,' Roger recalls. 'It was a buzz with a whole atmosphere. It got my imagination moving.'

And by some accounts, heavy occultism is now spilling over into the Acid house rave scene. Author Kevin Logan describes events at a Lancashire rave:

> It was run by Hell Rave Promotions . . . half way through the night a goat was ceremoniously slaughtered . . . they promised 'a hurricane of lazer and sound to end the world – 13 demented hours for you to panic and scream' and it featured satanic numbers from heavy metal favourites.[17]

Cult bands

The music scene is a magnet for youth, and a growing number of small-scale cults are supported by bands whose aim includes recruitment.

The US Gothic band Radio Werewolf is fronted by Nikolas Schreck, a German American. Their literature makes plain their intentions:

> We are a satanic Leadership school, imparting the black magical powers that shall enable our elite to rise as future leaders in every field.
>
> The 90's shall be an inversion of the 60's . . . a hard, pitiless brutal youth instilling order upon chaos, stamping the dawning century with a new aesthetic and law.
>
> The power of satanic youth unleashed is invincible – it is a dam in the evolutionary current that has been bottled up for nearly 2,000 years.[18]

Schreck's instrument of outreach is his band, which he describes as his 'Ministry of Propaganda and Public Enlightenment'. Over a three-year period he claimed to have organized 13 public youth rallies, some of which were marked with outbreaks of violence. The purpose of those rallies is spelled out in the UK underground magazine, *Both the Ones*, in an article attributed to Werewolf Order General Secretary, Betty Purdey:

> These [rallies] represented Phase One of a long term indoctrination process. Youth were targeted first by Radio Werewolf, for in youth's fascination with music lays a powerful tool for occult conditioning . . .

The Werewolf Order boasts members in Germany, Italy and the USA, and claims to be targeting London, Brussels, Vienna and other cities. Members, who are organized into Wolfpacks, are actively encouraged to collaborate with the Church of Satan, with whom Schreck has declared allegiance. He has publicly stated:

> We would like to see most of the human race killed off because it is unworthy of the gift of life. A bloodbath would be a cleansing . . . Extermination of the weak is what we would like to see.

Schreck's organization acknowledges, but distances itself from a UK-based group which, like his own, is fronted by a band. The Temple ov Psychic Youth [sic], which acknowledges the influence of Aleister Crowley, has bases in Brighton and London but boasts a world-wide network. Its leader Genesis P. Orridge claimed: 'We use music's power of suggestion for complete liberation, to help the listener throw off all taboos.'[19] TOPY's slogan is 'Love, War, Riot.'

Orridge's band Psychic TV produced the single 'Joy', which featured Anton LaVey, founder of the Church of Satan, reciting the Lord's prayer backwards. The British Sunday newspaper *The People* ran the following account of a Psychic TV concert:

> It was a sickening sight. Those kids could see sexual groping, satanist images of Christ burning on the cross and a woman with a snake crawling over her body.[20]

The new religion?

> Rock concerts are the churches of today.
> Craig Chaquito, Jefferson Starship

Although their services might be at the Marquee, it's still a Church with its own rituals. I went to see Venom perform. It was like seeing a High Priest on stage calling the faithful to worship.
Pastor Alex Maloney, Ebenezer Church[21]

What religion – any religion – purports to offer is an understanding of life's meaning and the individual's place and role within that order. It is this sense of identity that many teenagers crave, believes Darlyne Pettinicchio, consultant to California Probation Departments:

They're desperately seeking a place to belong, a place to be special. The main focus of the heavy metaller is drugs, sex and rock 'n' roll. They see their band members as saints or even gods and they idolize them.[22]

And where their heroes lead some fans may follow. Dr Paul King writes:

Some performers portray themselves as charismatic leaders preaching sermons. The young person who becomes involved with those lyrics develops a belief system based on those lyrics. Further knowledge of the personal lives of the stars leads to greater identification.[23]

But identification with what? Pat Pulling writes:

The black metal offshoot glorifies violent sex, anti-social acts against women and children, sex with the dead, suicide and murder and satanic worship. An increasingly large number of the adolescents with whom we work report having developed an interest in the occult as a direct result of this brand of heavy metal music.[24]

The predominant recurring themes in this music are listed by the US-based Parents' Music Resource Centre:

1. Abuse of drugs and alcohol
2. Suicide.
3. Graphic violence.
4. Fascination with the occult.
5. Sexuality which is graphic and explicit.[25]

According to PMRC, the average American teenager spends upwards of four hours a day plugged into pop or rock music. Between 7th and 12th grade alone, he will listen to some 11,000 hours; equivalent to the total time spent in class throughout his entire school career.[26]

Dr Paul King is Assistant Professor of Child and Adolescent Psychiatry at the University of Tennessee. He found that 83% of the young people he was treating for psychiatric disturbances had listened to heavy metal music for several hours each day.

His three-year study of 470 juvenile drug abusers drew a further connection between the music, drugs and violence: 59% listened mainly to heavy metal music; 74% were involved in violence, and almost half with theft.[27]

Dr King spells out the connection:

Heavy metal music portrays the power and glory of evil. Adolescents with emotional and/or drug problems become further involved in delinquent behaviour, violence, acts of cruelty and Satan worship. The lyrics give purpose and meaning to those who do not identify with the values they were raised with. They often use drugs or alcohol in order to feel the power more acutely an escape into the fantasies. Drug-induced altered states of consciousness combined with the message of hatred and violence of the heavy metal *is* dangerous.[28]

The theme is echoed by researcher John Cooper in his book *The Black Mask*, but he adds a word of caution:

It is fanatical to believe that every youth who . . . enjoys heavy-metal rock music is into occultism, but young people found engaged in destructive occultism usually are hyperinvolved in thrash metal, like Ozzy Osbourne, Slayer, Venom, and Poison. The lyrics, dress, symbols and lifestyles of these . . . performers make satanism attractive to many young people from a very early age. Join the sadistic lyrics and blatantly perverse sexuality of these rock bands to the intoxication of alcohol, pot or hard drugs, and you have very heavy conditioning that might well tip a teenager into antisocial behaviour.[29]

Let's underline that caveat. It would be fanatical indeed to argue that every teenager who gets his kick from gothic, heavy, black, speed or thrash metal music is going to go out and butcher his friends and his parents and then kill himself. But we would be wise to be concerned for individuals who are already distressed, disturbed, or vulnerable, and who become obsessed with material that is dark and violent and an open celebration of death. The PMRC says:

> We realize that a normal, healthy child will not commit suicide after listening to a song. However, for a child who is disturbed after the influence of drugs and alcohol, or predisposed to suicide, messages encouraging suicide can legitimize thoughts of suicide and add further to a child's condition.

Drawing a line

At the heart of every issue of freedom and censorship lies the question of where the line must be drawn in order to protect those who are weaker or more impressionable – and who should draw it. Should rock bands exercise self-restraint, or should parents restrain their children? Or both?

UK counsellor Maureen Davies is adamant that some responsibility must rest with the bands themselves:

> Where does the buck stop? When you have a lonely teenager who is already having difficulties going through adolescence playing a tape stating, 'it's an honour to die and commit suicide', you're putting a match to gelignite. Some of these groups have got to start saying, 'the buck stops with me.'

The Parents' Music Resource Centre lobbied not for censorship, but for records and tapes to be labelled in a similar manner to videos, so consumers – be they parents or children – could have an indication of the explicitness of the lyrical content of the music before they buy. In the end, the record industry bowed to pressure and took matters into its own hands, issuing its own discreet black and white warning: 'Parental Advisory: Explicit Lyrics'. Similar steps have been taken in the UK to classify violent video games.

The move, designed to head off legislation, was described by the anti-censorship lobby as a sell-out which would lead to inevitable self-censorship. The record companies complained of being scapegoated for the seemingly insurmountable problems facing today's teenagers. Others mocked the warning stickers as being the strongest possible inducement to persuade rebellious teenagers to buy the record.

Last word then to one of the teenagers caught up in the conflict:

Rock music played a pretty big role in my life, because it just totally encouraged the whole situation. It led on to the ouija board, dungeons and dragons, the prayers – everything was based around the music, like Ozzy Osbourne . . . Metallica . . . All those sorts that I used to listen to a couple of years before started coming back in my mind and started playing on my mind and you can't escape when that music and those words are in your head; you just can't escape it . . .

Cheryl, former teenage satanist[30]

11

Dangerous obsessions

Fantasy role-play games

These games are the most effective, most magnificently packaged, most profitably marketed, most thoroughly researched introduction to the occult in man's recorded history.
Dr Gary North[1]

Of Dungeons and Dragons

Dungeons and Dragons (D&D) is gaming without frontiers, combining creative elements of fantasy with the rigours of wargaming. Millions of copies of the original have been sold worldwide, versions are now available on the Internet, and the game has thrown up scores of imitators. It has been so successful that the name has become synonymous with the whole genre. (Where reference is made to D&D by others in this chapter the term may represent any one of a variety of different role-play systems.)

Each player is cast in a starring role in an imaginative adventure of epic proportions. The scene is often set in a kind of medieval Middle Earth, where heroic characters do battle with monsters and supernatural forces in their quest for treasure.

In the game version, one player acts as the 'dungeon master' (DM) drawing up a secret map of the dungeon or landscape where the action takes place. The DM is lord of his terrain, with the power of life and death over the characters within the game. He installs cunning traps and fearsome monsters around each corner which the players must overcome if they are to reach their holy grail.

Players choose their characters at the outset and select their gifts, abilities, strengths and weaknesses at the roll of the dice. The character's race, class and occupation are chosen and his alignment with good or evil, lawfulness or chaos. Finally, characters are equipped with supplies and magic spells.

Once the game is underway, each player *becomes* that character in his imagination, visualizing what his fantasy partner sees; inhabiting his senses; thinking, acting and reacting for him: sharing in the spirit of high adventure or murder and mayhem. The games are open-ended and some have been known to go on for years. The manual says:

> Shouting the Dungeons and Dragons challenge, my players rush into the fray with their magic war hammers. Before getting an answer, their fantasy selves indulge in murder, pillage, arson, rape.[2]

> This game lets all your fantasies come true . . . where monsters, dragons, good and evil . . . fierce demons; even the gods themselves, may enter your character's life.[3]

Players need their wits about them and every ounce of ability their character can muster. Their enemies may be spirits and monsters drawn from demonology and mythology. To defeat them they will have to fight fire with fire, drawing down supernatural powers and forces to strengthen and protect them.

Welcome to the occult . . .

A handbook for advanced players says:

> This perilous exercise in dwoemercraeft summons up a powerful demon . . . The spell caster must be within a circle of protection (or a thaumaturgic triangle with protection from evil) and the demon confined to a pentagram if he or she is to avoid being slain or carried off by the summoned cacodemon . . . By tribute of fresh human blood and the promise of one or more human sacrifices, the summoner can bargain with the demon for willing service.[4]

In fantasy game instructions, the authors' imaginations often draw from the dark and disturbing traditions of the black arts.

'Some fantasy books are more like handbooks of witchcraft and devil worship', writes author David Porter, in *Danger: Children at Play*. 'There is a disturbing core of reality which is derived directly from the literature of the occult and witchcraft. Many games educate their players in the workings of the occult. The child has, in effect, bought a popular encyclopaedia of the occult and supernatural.'

One American report claims:

D&D . . . teaches demonology, witchcraft, voodoo, murder, rape, blasphemy, suicide, assassination, insanity, sex perversion, homosexuality, prostitution, Satan worship, gambling . . . barbarism, cannibalism, sadism, desecration, demon summoning, necromantics, divination, and many other occultic themes in living colour.[5]

Those views have been echoed in Adelaide, Australia, by a man who describes himself as a former witch. 'Rick X' claims to have been drawn into witchcraft by his father at the age of four: 'I've been involved in the occult for years, and the packaging of these games is the greatest introduction to witchcraft and demonology I've ever seen,' he told *The Sunday Mail*. 'Any game that involves spells and characters with supernatural powers is a cultivating area for the occult.'[6]

A cluster of glossy magazines has sprung up dedicated to fuelling the fascination. Among them is *White Dwarf*, which circulates in Britain, Australian, Canada, New Zealand, the United States and Sweden. Many others fan the fire of video games mania, where violence and the occult are common themes.

'Be warned,' said *White Dwarf's* editor, Ian Livingstone, who promised a 'believable experience of magic'; 'these games are addictive and are the most serious alternative yet to reality'.[7]

The fantasy world of role-playing games is all the more potent for being played out entirely within the mind. And a moment's glance at the gothic-horror images portrayed on fantasy game boxes and manuals will reveal the nature of this compelling mind-world which, for those with compulsive personalities, might become a fixation.

Those who do become obsessed will find themselves eating, breathing and dreaming a culture that is intrinsically dark, doomladen and violent.

Counsellors' cases

Greg, who runs a youth group, recalls a young boy who spend most of his teenage years playing Dungeons and Dragons and other fantasy role-play games: 'It was an absolute obsession and fixation for him'.

To enhance the fantasy experience and get an even greater buzz the teenager used to combine playing with drug taking. Then he decided to take the theme of the game a step further and experiment with the occult. He was hooked. Drugs, the occult and fantasy games devoured his time, energy, and attention.

Greg describes the boy's personality as obsessive and fearful. He believes a child with a less compulsive disposition would probably have pulled back long ago, but addictive personalities can get hooked on role-play games where they can immerse themselves in an alternative universe and become another person, enjoying power, influence and adventure.

Eventually, says Greg, the boy came to his senses and recognised that fantasy games and the occult had taken over most of his life. He became desperate to break free of it all and was referred to a psychiatrist who put him under medication.

'Jenny' is a counsellor from the South West of England who has been called in to help several casualties of fantasy games. She is given a pseudonym to protect the identity of her clients.

'It always starts off very innocent. It's a form of escape but it becomes an addiction – I've seen this with video games as well. The players take on these characters completely and utterly and *become* these people.

'"David" is 19. He came to me originally because he was having a lot of mental disturbances and nightmares. He was seeing dragons and ghouls, weird faces and colours. They were very disturbing. His mother said he would wake up screaming at times. He'd been dabbling with the ouija board but had also been playing a fantasy role-play game for about four years.'

David was introduced to it by a schoolmate. At first he thought it was just another board game, a way of whiling away an evening. But he later admitted to Jenny that it had become a compulsion. 'He couldn't not play it,' she explains. 'What began as once a month went to once a week, and he ended up playing it four or five nights a week for up to five hours at a time.'

As the months went by, his mother noticed the change. David had been a well-balanced, happy child, who got on reasonably well at school, fitted in socially and had friends. 'His mother had never had any trouble with him. Now he had become very disruptive. She said it was like living with a stranger.'

After six months the change was marked. 'David's schoolwork began to go really badly; he couldn't concentrate. He would sit for hours in what his mother called a semi-trance state; switched off, his brain in some other place.'

David's father had been in the forces and was often away from home. As the boy grew up he saw little of his Dad, but now David became abusive towards him and increasingly violent, sometimes wrecking rooms.

'His eyes would be wide, glazed and piercing,' says Jenny. 'His voice would change to become like his character in the game – a swordsman who chopped people's heads off. He seemed to have less and less ability to keep control of himself.'

His mother, 'Sheila', brought him round for counselling after a game session. 'He was acting extremely strangely. His body was jerking spontaneously and he was very hostile. You couldn't reason with him or get through to him at all.'

After a while he began to sit down and slowly came to. 'He became very agitated and afraid because he had no idea where he was. He was completely out of his head.'

Jenny believes David has a compulsive personality. She is convinced his addiction to the game left him mentally unhinged. Her advice was to give it up immediately and take up something in its place that he could throw himself into. After eight sessions, he took her advice. The substitute became ten-pin bowling. 'It was all a need to fill this void inside, which I think had been caused by his father. He needed to find an identity because he just couldn't identify with his Dad.'

Another mother went to Jenny because she was afraid her children were being 'taken over' by the game. Their regular partners were adults who, in her words, 'were addicted to it'. Jenny says, 'Her children *became* these characters, and changed in front of her eyes. The mother was horrified.'

One 12-year-old boy got so obsessively caught up in the role-play game that he confused his mother with a fantasy opponent and attacked her with a knife. It had taken only a few months for the game to grip him, says Jenny. 'He was really into it and even started wearing the clothes of his character. He attacked his mother with a knife because he was convinced she was the other character in the game.' The boy's father stepped in just in time and wrenched the knife out of his hand. The 12-year-old is now in the care of a child psychologist.

Suicide

'Accumulated evidence now indicates that fantasy role-playing games have been significant factors in at least 125 deaths.' So writes Pat Pulling, Jewish founder of the American organization BADD, Bothered About Dungeons and Dragons. BADD was Pat's response to the suicide of her own son at the age of 16, which she believes was linked with the game. Her book, *The Devil's Web*, is an exhaustive study of what can happen to adolescents who become obsessed with fantastic material that is compelling and consumed with death, demons and violence.

It would be an easy and welcome way out to dismiss what she says as a bereaved mother's personal obsession, and to shrug it all off as only a game. A spokesman for TSR, manufacturers of the original Dungeons and Dragons, told *The State Journal*, 'All allegations are totally false. It's easy to blame other things rather than the underlying factor. There has been no evidence that the game has been the cause of anybody's death.'[8]

While there may be no proof that such games are the root *cause* of suicide, a fixation with fantasy gaming has been stated by the police, the courts, the suicide victims and, of course, their parents:

> In the spring of 1981 our son Mike committed suicide after becoming deeply involved in Dungeons and Dragons. Mike had no mental problems prior to playing the game. His whole life began to revolve around [it]. After his death I found out from his fellow D&D players that they were into astro-projection as outlined in the D&D book. They were into casting spells. Fantasy in his mind turned into reality. He was using sulphur and garlic to conjure up demons. He spend 95 per cent of his time in his room working on D&D. We did not realize at the time that by becoming involved with D&D that could lead to a sudden depression and death.
>
> Pat and Mary Dempsey[9]

Steven Loyacono was also 16 years old when he killed himself by carbon monoxide poisoning. His diary shows a growing obsession with personal evil, madness, and with satanism. On pretence of going to the cinema, Stephen would visit a nearby occult bookshop and browse until it was almost time for his parents to pick him up. His suicide note was addressed to his D&D playmate and couched in the cod-gothic terms familiar to players of fantasy role games:

> Upon reading these words you will know that I am dead. I have now started the bresome journey to the bowels of the earth. I travel down that twisted road that winds its way down to the forsaken pit. It is time to meet my lofty maker! . . . my father will spread his wings and welcome me to his, and my, real home.[10]

Dr Charles Marsden has been described as a leading researcher into teenage suicide. He believes fantasy games are most likely to increase the pressure on those who are already disturbed. Most at risk are children with little sense of self-worth who try to prove themselves in the fantasy games and get overly involved. He told *The State Journal*:

If there is an identity problem, if they feel they don't belong, the fantasy can become real, to the point where it becomes a part of them. If they are unhappy with themselves, they may have an overwhelming desire to change the situation, and suicide is a means of that.

French deserter Antony Bourgois certainly fitted that bill. He was disturbed, had an identity problem and felt he didn't belong. He was a schizophrenic who was on the run from the French Air force.

In 1992 he fled to Oxford where he was determined to act out to the bitter end his role in the game, *The Final Ordeal*. He planned to strap a knife to his chest and then crash a car at high speed so the blade would kill him. But he wanted to take someone with him. He pressed a knife to the throat of twenty-two-year-old Lizzie Lamplugh and tried to kidnap her, but she managed to escape.

When police captured Bourgois they found a noose, a military cap covered in black magic symbols and a book on the occult. Scrawled over its pages was the name Levi Eworp, an anagram of evil power, which he believed he possessed.

Bourgois had been obsessed with death, Oxford Crown Court was told, and had posters of open graves plastered over his bedroom walls. He told a psychiatrist he had visions of killing his cellmate. He was sent to a secure psychiatric unit.[11]

And there are cases where obsession with fantasy games has gone beyond suicide.

Murder

Madrid, 1994. 52-year-old cleaner Carlos Moreno is found stabbed to death. A 20-year-old fantasy gamer and his teenage friend are accused of killing him in cold blood – to satisfy the demands of their role-play game. A scorecard gave the victim points out of 20 for attributes including strength, power and charisma. 'The guy was immortal . . . it's incredible how long an idiot takes to die,' ran a diary entry. One boy allegedly tried to silence his victim by putting his fingers in his mouth, 'which I got from the film *Hellraiser* . . .' he wrote, adding: 'If they don't catch us, the next time it will be a girl.'
The Guardian, 6th Aug. 1994

Fantasy gaming has been slow to take off in Spain, but it now has a quarter of a million regular devotees, roughly the same number as the UK, where *The Observer* described it as 'the fastest-growing hobby for teenage boys'.[12]

In the US, 16-year-old David Ventiquattro was jailed for life for murdering 11-year-old Martin Howland. The authorities linked the killing to a fantasy role-play game. Ventiquattro said he killed Martin because the game required him to 'extinguish evil'.

In 1985, two boys aged 12 and 13 tried to murder their school principal. Reports said that in their imaginations their middle school had become a dungeon and their principal a dragon. 'It was all over D&D,' claimed the police investigator.[13]

Eighteen-year-old Mary Towey was bound and gagged and strangled to death by her teenage game partners. One of them, Darren Molitor, signed his FBI confession with the names of two of his fantasy characters and told the court they had been playing 'a mind game'.[14]

After sentencing, when it could have no bearing on the outcome of his trial, he wrote:

> The 'fantasy' game becomes a 'reality' game. You begin to live it for real . . . It is an addiction. And your mind is under the control of the game.
>
> Not only is the game based on the supernatural and magic, it involves . . . serious violence . . . A character must at least murder and rob in order to survive. And if it is played, let's say, 3–5 times a week, 4–8 hours each time, the conscious mind becomes accustomed to such acts of violence . . . It is more dangerous than I can fully explain.
>
> Many have committed suicide due to the game. Another good many have either caused serious harm to themselves or other individuals . . . they took the 'game' one step too far . . . so please, for your own safety . . . and the safety of others, don't play the game anymore.[15]

Child abuse

Court cases also reveal that some adult abusers have recognized and latched on to the games' potent pulling powers. Children have been sexually assaulted after being enticed into a role-play game.

A 15-year-old girl was repeatedly raped by a prison psychologist, who with his wife, had drawn her into a fantasy game. The court heard that she was required to play the role of 'someone who would lose their powers after doing something wrong'. She was encouraged into sex by the psychologist's wife who explained, 'he always wanted a virgin as a gift'.[16]

A 24-year-old vagrant was charged with forcing five girls between the ages of 9 and 15 to perform sexual acts if they wanted to remain in an extended game of Dungeons and Dragons. Among his personal belongings was a bag containing games pieces and dice for D&D, as well as satanic material and a handbook on witchcraft.[17]

Therapy?

Fantasy role-play games have their advocates. Therapists claim to have put them to good use under supervised conditions. Psychiatrists say the game attracts teenagers because it allows them to create and rule over a world of their own making, where the usual imposed limits to freedom are removed. Some see it as a healthy way for teenagers to play out their fantasies. Others are equally vehement that instead of playing them out, they are playing them *in*.

'It's not like Monopoly,' says psychologist James Bolgiano. 'The game lasts for days . . . weeks. These characters have powers and a personality of their own, and sometimes the personality of the character becomes tangled with the actual person.'[18]

Dr Arnold Goldstein is Director of the Center for Research on Aggression at the University of Syracuse. He points to more than 150 studies which have been carried out into the therapeutic effects of role-play upon patients' attitudes. He regards carefully orchestrated, supervised, role-play as a proven technique for changing behaviour for the better. But when the roles that are played are *negative*, as in fantasy games, that therapeutic effect is reversed:

> There is every reason to suspect that the role-playing of anti-social behaviour will increase the probability of its occurrence, especially when the behaviour is practiced and rewarded as in a game-playing situation. For many, such play causes subtle changes which increases both a desensitization towards violence and a tendency to commit aggressive behaviour.

His views are endorsed by psychologist Dr John Murray, who co-edited a government study on the effects of TV violence: 'A violent role-playing game would reinforce aggressive behaviour . . . Violent toys . . . increase violent fantasies and the tendencies towards violence.'[19]

Educational tool?

Fantasy games have found their way into schools as a means of developing gifted pupils and encouraging team work and co-operation. Educational discounts entice teachers to use the material. Schools in some areas have snapped them up, but others have slapped a ban on them:

> Studies I have made of the game showed the negative effects outweighed any benefits. I can confidently say I don't want it in the schools.
> Margaret Beck, Arlington, Virginia School Board

> I have thoroughly researched this game for years and I am convinced that players at the advanced levels are adversely effected emotionally, psychologically and physically. Although the game is fun and produces some positive effects, these are outweighed by the adverse effects brought on by the game.
> Robert Landa, Attorney, Los Angeles

Cultural differences

The debate about fantasy games is being played out largely in their country of origin – America – but the British and Spanish examples above indicate that other societies should think twice before dismissing such concerns as culturally irrelevent.

As long ago as 1987, the *Daily Express* predicted 'Cult fantasy games on sale in Britain could drive players to murder and suicide.'[20] A comparison of the phenomenon in the US and Britain was made in *Police Review*[21] which found disturbances less marked in the UK because of the difference between the 'emotions and reactions' of the two cultures. *Vive la difference!*

But children are children wherever they live. In our survey, 36% of British year ten pupils said they had taken part in a fantasy role-play game. Six per cent played weekly – which boils down to at least one in every classroom.

British child carers are worried. Dianne Core of Childwatch: 'For every five children who play this game in a sensible way and look at it purely as a game, there is another who progresses onwards and upwards and wants more, because as you progress your thirst for knowledge gets greater.'

As we have noted, suicide statistics for teenagers continue to rise on both sides of Atlantic. America has the more violent society, with the greater availability of drugs, and an alarming access to firearms that offers disturbed adolescents a swifter, surer and more macho, way out. But time has shown that in social as well as economic terms, when America sneezes, other nations had better wrap up warm. American social trends have a disturbing habit of emerging elsewhere, given time.

12

Images of death

The occult and violence

> It isn't for me to pass judgement on their upbringing, but I suspect violent video films may, in part, be an explanation.
>
> Justice Morland, in the murder trial of two-year-old James Bulger

Images of death pervade our popular culture. Horror and violence intertwined with sex have become the dominant themes of video films and fantasy games. We turn on and tune in to a culture of death. Video and computer games absorb the player still further into role-play. Virtual reality takes him ever deeper, blurring deliberately the borders between fantasy and reality.

Unsurprisingly, cases are emerging of disturbed young adults pushed over the edge by a morbid obsession with death. And a growing number of accounts suggest the same thing might be happening to children.

The cases that are coming to light are backed up by research which confirms what common sense told us all along; that when all is said and done, we are what we eat. *Garbage in – garbage out*.

A chief parental preoccupation is what to feed the kids. Perhaps we should be looking a little further than food.

Chucky's children?

Chucky is the malevolent star of the horror movie, *Child's Play 3*, a murderous doll with a will of its own. And Chucky has been implicated in two real-life murders that have sickened a nation and defied comprehension.

James Bulger was two years old when he was abducted, tortured and murdered by two seemingly unremarkable ten-year-old boys. The judge described it as 'an act of unparalleled evil and barbarity', and sentenced Britain's two youngest convicted murderers to be detained at Her Majesty's Pleasure – indefinitely.

The infant's body was found on a railway line at Walton, in Liverpool. It had been torn in half by a train. Mingling with the blood of his battered face were splashes of blue paint.

Speaking for the nation, the judge struggled to understand how two normal boys of average intelligence could do such a thing. And he wondered out loud whether it had anything to do with horror movies.

The father of one of the young killers had a thing about horror films. Among the last 50 that he had hired from a single shop were, according to a press report: *Whispers* (horror containing scenes of necrophilia in a mortuary); *The Disturbance* (young man dreams he has committed various bloody murders); and *Child's Play 2* (graphic details about murders), which he lent out to the seven-year-old boy who lived nearby. It was there that his own son, shortly to become a murderer, watched it.[1]

But it was the final video that the father hired that was to cause the judge – and MPs – to pose the above question.

Child's Play 3 – There comes a time to put away childhood things, but some things won't stay put.

The father (it serves no purpose to name him or his son *again*) insists his boy never saw it. Although he admitted to lending out horror movies to his seven-year-old neighbour, his own lad – who was three years his senior – had to make do with cartoons.

So what was it that tempted, provoked or inspired these junior school pupils to commit murder? The *Daily Mail* said:

> There are startling parallels between the film's plot and the fate of little James. The video depicts a doll that comes to life and whose face is splashed at one stage with blue paint . . . James was also splashed with blue paint. The video features an abduction. The abduction of James was the beginning of the horror that overtook him. The video ends with two boys killing the doll-child on a ghost train after its face has been terribly mutilated. James was also mutilated by his two killers, who left his body on a railway track to be run over by a train.[2]

Coincidence? Maybe. The police and the father thought so, but the judge disagreed. And it was certainly no coincidence that Sky TV made the last-minute decision to pull the plug on its screening of *Child's Play 3*.

When the film was eventually shown on satellite TV, after 9.30 p.m., its reported audience included 181,000 children; 40,000 of whom were aged nine and under.

Two MPs tabled a Commons motion demanding an investigation

into 'the role played by violent films in the psychological impulses that led to this murder,' adding: 'many homes in the United Kingdom are increasingly saturated by a growing culture of violence disseminated by television, video and computer.'

And as the press joined in the struggle to shed light on what had happened, *Sunday Times* columnist Glenys Roberts recalled a strange encounter with the actor Jack Nicholson. His son had been referred to a child psychologist after becoming obsessed with what most of us would take to be a harmless movie classic, *The Wizard of Oz*. 'Burn it,' was the psychologist's reaction. 'If he is watching it again and again, there is something in it that frightens him. He is going to run it until he conquers his fear and feels nothing at all.'

Like the judge in the Bulger case, Glenys Roberts did her own thinking out loud. Did the killer of James Bulger know that his father loved him? Certainly he knew that his dad loved violent videos:

> [He] imagined his tragic actions by the railway track were those of a hero, because of the video nasties which seemed to be one of his parent's sources of enjoyment . . . to gain approval he thought he had to do bad.[3]

Suzanne Capper

Barely a month after the Bulger case, the face of Chucky was again leering out at us from the tabloids. The evil doll was cited in another case of incomprehensible brutality. Four young adults were convicted of the protracted torture and eventual murder of 16-year-old Suzanne Capper. In her week-long ordeal, before her killers doused her with petrol and set her on fire, Suzanne was tormented in the name of Chucky.

'*I'm Chucky – wanna play?*' was pounded into her ears again and again through headphones as she lay tied to an upturned bedstead. The court heard that one of her tormentors, 24-year-old Bernadette McNeilly, took on the role of Chucky. After gloating over the abducted 16-year-old in her makeshift cell, she told her co-conspirators: 'Chucky's been playing.' *The Daily Mirror* spelt out the further parallels with *Child's Play*:

> In *Child's Play*, Chucky breaks a man's arm and leg – Suzanne's arm was battered. The doll is burnt in the face with a cigarette lighter – Suzanne was burned with cigarettes. The doll kills a

psychiatrist by electrocuting him with a headset – a headset was forced over Suzanne's head. Finally the doll is apparently destroyed by fire – just like Suzanne.[4]

Just a case of the tabloids making the most of it? Perhaps. The police said there was no video in the house, but there can be no doubt that the defendants were well acquainted with Chucky. Yet horror movies alone could never be to blame. No-one *made* them do it. The defendants acted out of *choice*. They made a cold-blooded decision to torture and kill.

A plentiful supply of drugs and a bizarre lifestyle cut off from everyday reality were central features of the case. God alone knows what else went into the make-up of defendants who could torture and murder a child with such apparent nonchalance. When they set fire to Suzanne and left her for dead, they went on their way laughing and singing, 'Burn, baby burn.'

Such banal brutality defies any simple explanation. But a press report went on to spell out an occult connection:

> McNeilly and Jean Powell were fascinated by the occult, practised with tarot cards and rune stones and kept a 'black library' . . . Both were fans of the devil doll Chucky in the horror video . . . both were interested in the occult.[5]

In the wake of this second case, MP David Alton called for public recognition of the dangers to young people of involvement in the occult: 'the occult is not a game nor an alternative lifestyle . . . it is . . . extremely dangerous.' He and other MPs successfully renewed their calls for tougher restrictions on horror movies. One demanded a Royal Commission to investigate causes of violence.

Days before the Commons would vote on what action to take, a report was published by a group of leading psychologists and paediatricians. Led by Professor Elizabeth Newson, head of the Child Development Research Unit at Nottingham University, it concluded that violent video material could indeed cause direct harm to children. Professor Newson said children had been 'demoralized and desensitized' as a result of watching horror videos. Some had been so disturbed after watching even a few that they had been referred to her for treatment. She added:

> I don't want to suggest that videos are the sole cause of violence, but something that's so penetrating of children's experience has to be looked at very carefully so we can find out what it's doing to

them. I think children are being abused by having these images so easily accessible.[6]

Observer writer Melanie Phillips commented:

> The link between screen violence and behaviour is generally pooh-poohed in Britain. Yet in the United States, hundreds of studies over the past 30 years point to the same conclusion; the sheer weight of evidence is impossible to ignore. The US Surgeon General has accepted that a causal link has been established, albeit of a limited kind . . . the most likely explanation is that screen violence has a particular potency for a small number of vulnerable personalities. It is one piece in the jigsaw of criminal pathology.[7]

In the face of mounting pressure the UK government acknowledged the truth of the argument, and announced tighter controls on the hire, sale and classification of videos, designed specifically to protect children.

The Bulger and Capper cases stirred up the country. And predictably, some expressed fears of a moral panic. But film critic Michael Medved and author of the influential *Hollywood Vs America* coolly observed:

> The fact that violent imagery fails to influence *everyone* does not mean that it fails to influence *anyone*. Movie mayhem doesn't have to damage all members of the motion picture audience in order to damage our overall quality of life: even if it is only a few thousand – or a few hundred – vulnerable individuals who are encouraged to commit murderous cruelty by the bloody messages of the popular culture, the impact on society can be enormous.[8]

And as if to underline the point, France was shaken only weeks after the Bulger verdict by a case of its own. Three boys between the ages of eight and ten beat to death a vagrant. One described his favourite pastime as watching violent videos.

Michael Ryan

The English town of Hungerford in Berkshire will not forget Michael Ryan, who killed 14 people with a Kalashnikov assault rifle and wounded even more.

Much of Ryan's life seemed to be taken up in fantasy. Police described Ryan as 'a man without friends who with his mother created a world of fantasy around which much of their lives revolved'.[9] He conjured up a tough military background for himself, boasted of a rich, elderly benefactor and an exotic lifestyle which seemed always to be around the corner.

An extension of that was his involvement in the role-play game, *Further into Fantasy*. One of the myriad of fantasy games that grew from the D&D craze, this was a variation that could be played by post by anyone who could afford the subscription. Ryan played the role of Phodius Tei, priest to the evil serpent-god Set (who incidentally shares the name of the deity invoked by one of the US-based satanic networks). The players are given tasks, and Ryan received this challenge six weeks before embarking on his Hungerford massacre:

> You have been one of my greatest Terran priests and as such are worthy of the power I offer. But Phodius, you have one last point to prove . . . can you kill your fellow Terrans? Will you accept, Phodius, to go back to Terra and slay them, to devour their souls in the name of Set the immortal God?

A fortnight later, Ryan received his final message:

> When at last you awake, you are standing in a forest, there is a throbbing in your head, a madness that is the exhilaration of the serpent god. You know what you must do. Know what power is to be gained from this.[10]

Ryan's first killing was in Savernake Forest. A mother was caught by 16 rounds of automatic fire in front of her two small children while they picnicked.

Two years before the Hungerford shootings, Dr Thomas Radecki, a University of Illinois psychiatrist, surveyed the fantasy game market and observed:

> There is no doubt in my mind that the game . . . is causing many young men to kill themselves and others.

But perhaps not only the game. In his book *The Man of Lawlessness*, Tom Davies points out the many parallels between Ryan's behaviour and the character of John Rambo, played by Sylvester Stallone in the *First Blood* series of films.

The link between the role-play game and Rambo may have been

made in Michael Ryan's troubled mind, which confused fantasy with reality and became obsessed with the violent imagery served up in the name of entertainment.

Robert Sartin

Exactly one year to the day before his court appearance, 23-year-old Robert Sartin had been walking as though in a trance in the Sunday morning sunshine in Monkseaton. Directed by a voice within his head he continued loading, firing and reloading his father's shotgun until 17 people lay wounded and one man had been killed.

'It was like someone said "shoot him", he explained to a policeman. 'So I shot him. He fell against the wall and started screaming.'

The jury heard how a 41-year-old man had begged for help, to be told by Sartin, 'No, it's your day to die'. Sartin was said to have been absorbed with the character of Michael Myers, the masked killer in the Hallowe'en horror movies. In the four films, Myers murders his family one by one before being killed himself, only to return to life for each sequel.

'[Sartin] described the ability to actually see Michael, and many of the drawings he had were of Michael,' the court was told. Jurors heard that Sartin had been obsessed with the occult, pain, death and cannibalism. He paid a pilgrimage to Hungerford to see where Michael Ryan had randomly gunned down people with an assault rifle. The jury was told that Sartin had become preoccupied with what might have been in Ryan's mind:

> Sartin's mental problems were first suspected by an art teacher at school who noticed that horror and the occult dominated his work. A fourth form religious instruction exam paper was 'unnecessarily full of satanism', Prosecutor David Robson QC told the court.[11]

He added, 'Sartin had acquired a reputation for having occult powers, and young boys went in fear of him.'

Sartin told an educational psychologist that he heard voices telling him to kill his parents. He was referred to a psychiatrist who said there was nothing to worry about. Years later the court was to hear that he had been diagnosed as suffering from schizophrenia from the age of 13 or 14. Within his mind, 'a very dark river had flowed unsuspected for a number of years'.

After his arrest, Sartin told the police, 'I remember hearing people scream. I wasn't really bothered if I hit them at all. I don't feel anything for them now.'

'I'm no bloody mathematician,' said a Monkseaton neighbour of the man Sartin had killed, 'but if one man in a million has his head turned by what he sees, or what he can hire in the video shop – and you'd agree that one in a million is not a lot – then you've got five or ten potential lunatics doing what happened here yesterday.'[12]

'Why us? Why now?' puzzled the *Daily Mail*:

> Is it that there are more guns to hand? Is it because there there are more sick minds? Or is it, rather, that those whose minds are already under stress become addicted to violence on screen or poisonous fancies in print which seem to be purveyed more abundantly than ever before? Our instinct tells us that, if there is an X factor . . . it has as much to do with the images that bombard already weakened brains as with the availability of guns.[13]

For Ryan it may have been Rambo. For Sartin it was Michael Myers of *Halloween* – and perhaps another: 'There was something about the way the gunman was dressed,' said Monkseaton engineer Eric Holloway, who gave chase to Sartin. '[He was] all in black with dark glasses – and the way he held the gun seemed familiar. Later I realized this was just like Sylvester Stallone appeared in the film *Cobra*.'

Mental illness might have driven Robert Sartin to murder, but his acknowledged obsession with violent movies and the occult would appear to have fuelled his delusions. And subsequent court cases reveal that some troubled youngsters are following in the footsteps of the Hungerford and Monkseaton killers.

Following in their footsteps

Ryan and Sartin were disturbed young adults with access to lethal hardware. Darren Fowler was a 16-year-old schoolboy who managed to get hold of a shotgun.

Oxford Crown Court heard that Darren Fowler planned to kill his rival for the affections of a schoolgirl. Modelling himself on Hungerford killer Michael Ryan, he went first to the administration block at Ferrers School in Northamptonshire and opened fire indiscriminantly. The deputy head, a teacher, and two 12-year-old pupils were injured.

The court heard that Darren set out on his mission hours after watching a video called *Critters*, in which a boy takes up his father's gun.[14] A regular customer at his local video hire store, his favourite films featured Sylvester Stallone and Arnold Schwarzenegger.[15]

Eight months later, on 11 September 1988, a former Territorial Army cadet, Anthony Haskett, stalked the streets of Walsall in the West Midlands clutching a shotgun and swathed with a bandolier of cartridges. After shooting three black youths he turned the gun on himself. He was 18. In his bedroom, police found a small arsenal of weapons and military paraphernalia, including a crossbow and camouflage paste *a la Rambo*. Posters of the movie littered his walls, and a senior police officer stated the obvious: 'I think he was trying to be Rambo.'[16]

In other cases, a 20-year-old was sentenced for murder after stabbing a 15-year-old boy 72 times 'while playing Rambo'. A 16-year-old murdered his mother, his father, his brother and critically injured his sister with a brace of shotguns after a row about homework. His room was covered with Rambo posters, he gave his name as Rambo, and the police commented with stunning understatement: 'He had a definite fixation about Rambo and military things.'[17]

Imitators have not confined their attentions to Rambo. In Wisconsin, America, an 11-year-old boy was found hanging by his belt in the bathroom after watching the video *Friday the 13th: Part III*. Authorities say he was trying to copy a stunt in the film, where a character hangs himself but does not die. The boy, who was described as being 'involved in fantasies', had no history of mental disturbance.

After the release of the horror movie *The Lost Boys* several American states reported the setting up of 'Lost Boys' cults. Members were said to be involved in crime, drinking blood and playing fantasy role-play games.[18]

The film *The Omen* has also inspired some copy-cat behaviour:

> Jim, a north suburban teenager who says he is a member of a satanic group . . . denied that satanism is dangerous. 'All the things people say are evil make you happy. Sins lead to emotional, physical and mental gratification.' Jim says he has been interested in satanism since seeing the movie *The Omen* seven years ago.[19]

Hooked on violence?

A consultant psychiatrist from Glasgow, Scotland, has counselled a number of young patients who have undergone personality changes after being traumatized by horror movies. Fear itself can become addictive, Dr Prem Misra told *The Examiner*. According to one article, 'Horror videos damage kids' minds'.[20] Among his clients were:

A 15-year-old boy who awoke screaming and sweating with terror each night. His dream was always the same: a pair of bloody hands were reaching inside his body to tear out his heart and lungs. The scene was straight from the video nasty *Zombie Flesh Eaters*. Nervous exhaustion cost the boy his first full-time job, and he spent his days alone, weeping in his bedroom.

A 17-year-old girl who watched up to three horror movies each afternoon at a friend's house, overloaded on explicit scenes of death and mutilation. Eventually her mind simply shut down, and she became amnesic, to the point where she could no longer remember her friend's name or even where she had watched the videos.

An 18-year-old with a background of violence attacked a young nurse, copying a scene from the video nasty *SS Experiment Camp*. He carved patterns on her body that matched those depicted in the movie, which he had been watching. He was jailed for attempted murder.

'These videos have a literally stunning effect on the minds of youngsters,' Dr Misra told Bill Ferrady of *The Examiner*. 'Most kids will watch movies like these just once or twice and then get scared off by them. But others get hooked on them and their whole personalities can be changed.'

Overkill?

British children see some 80,000 televised acts of horror before the age of 18, according to the International Coalition against Video Violence.

By a conservative estimate, American TV is said to show a scene of violence every 16 minutes and a murder every half hour. When the average US student completes his schooling, he will have spent 11,000 hours in the classroom, against 18,000 hours watching TV. That amounts to some 36,000 murders and 67,500 acts of violence.[21]

Surveys in America, Canada, Australia and Northern Europe

show that television's most avid audience is young adolescents who watch for almost four hours every day. In fact, the only activity between the ages of 2 and 15 to which more time is devoted is sleep.[22]

British families spend more time watching the box than any of their European neighbours: 98% of homes have a television set, and the average child sits transfixed by the screen for 22 hours a week, according to a Department of the Environment survey – just three hours short of the time they spend each week in the classroom. Almost a fifth of British homes have a TV set in a child's bedroom, though there are signs that video games are beginning to compete for TV viewing.[23]

A survey of British TV by the National Viewers' and Listeners' Association in 1993 claimed that almost 15% of BBC programmes contained some occult involvement. The same was true of more than 9% of programmes on ITV. Up to 30% of programmes included scenes of violence.[24]

Britain has the highest concentration of video recorders in Europe. Their popularity as electronic babysitters continues to rise unabated. Videos can be found in 90% of homes with children.

You don't need a Ph.D. in media studies to realize that sex and violence are the dominant themes of videos for rental. And many others feature a strong element of occultism.

In one small-town video store, I counted more than 100 occult movies, including *Child's Play 3*, the video some suggest sparked off the copycat murder of toddler James Bulger. It was there on the shelf with *Child's Play 2* – barely a fortnight after the jury delivered its guilty verdicts on the infant's two child murderers.

In the survey carried out for this book, a surprising 87% of 14- to 15-year-olds professed to watching what they described as video nasties, while 88% said they were keen on occult movies. One in seven claimed to watch them every day. And many went on to supplement their diet of horror movies with books about the occult. There is a growing market in horror fiction which is targeted specifically at teenagers.

According to booksellers Waterstones, horror is now read by 65% of boys and 70% of girls. And there are signs that young children are buying horror books aimed at teenagers before graduating to full-blown adult horror by the likes of Stephen King at the ages of 11 to 12.[25]

The rise and rise of horror is beginning to alarm some academics. A 1994 study by the Children's Literature Research Centre found horror stories to be the top choice of 58% of 11- to 16-year-old girls. It concluded: 'Parents and teachers are often so delighted to see young people reading . . . that they fail to look into popular books and to think about the messages being conveyed in some fiction.'[26]

A considerable weight of research since the sixties points to the same conclusion: that exposure to morbid images of horror, death, murder, mutilation and sexual assault, can have a corrosive effect on the mind. When three other toxic ingredients are stirred in: alienation, obsession and mental vulnerability, the brew becomes poisonous and highly volatile – to both those who drink it and their unwitting victims.

In their book *The Early Window*, Professor Dr Robert Liebert and Dr Joyce Sprafkin conclude:

> Experiments continue to provide evidence of a causal relationship between violence viewing and aggression . . . Although it is equally clear that TV violence always works in conjunction with other factors . . . TV violence can provide instruction in antisocial and aggressive behaviour which will sometimes lead to direct copying.[27]

Video and computer games

The morbid obsession with violence, horror and the occult doesn't end with videotape. Small-screen images of death, demons and savagery permeate children's video games. But where TV asks for nothing more than passive acquiescence, video games require players who are active participants in the mayhem as well as the fun.

And they *can* be fun. I've been a fan of certain games since *Space Invaders* first marched across the videoscreens of our pubs and arcades. But the innocent cartoon aliens with their teletext-quality graphics heralded a high-definition, high-gore invasion that marched right into our homes.

In the US, video game machines achieved an astonishing 80% penetration into the homes of 8 to 14-year-old boys by 1993.[28] In the UK, top-selling Sega and Nintendo systems dominate the market, which is now said to be worth £750 million per year and is the most competitive in the world.

Specialist stores which once stocked little more than board games are flooded with video cartridges. Themes include sport, cartoon action, adventure, and the inevitable slash 'em and smash 'em epics. According to a British survey, 85% of arcade video games feature themes of violence, murder and destruction.[29]

While most computer games are about high-energy, snappy, zappy action, occultic themes run through a sizeable minority of titles. It's a mood which goes way beyond the 'demonic trees' that threaten Mickey Mouse in *Castle of Illusion* and the outsize spooks of *Super Mario World*.

Even New Age notions secure a place in these digital worlds, from the bizarre sub-Buddhism of *Shadowrun*, where 'whenever you kill an opponent you advance towards earning a karma point',[30] to the ninja warriors of *Shinobi II*, where your quest is to find the New Age crystals that will empower and deliver your fellow ninja.

But at a deeper, darker level, some computer role-play games take their cue from the dungeons and dragons of the original. You become the character who has to fight fire with fire and develop occult arts of your own to defeat a demonic enemy.

Video role-play games have added addiction. They are designed to be played for hours. And when is a game not a game? When it becomes an obsession.

In response to growing public concern computer game manufacturers have set up a voluntary system of classification by age to give parents advanced warning of the violent nature of their products.

Their action runs parallel to the move by the UK government to tighten up on video standards, making it a crime to supply tapes to children under age. The British Board of Film Classification now has to impose tougher thresholds and take into account whether a movie could cause potential harm to viewers.

As one MP remarked, it is now up to parents to use the system effectively to control what their children are watching.[31]

What to do?

Simple. If there is a message in these past chapters about horror-laden music, morbid video violence and occultic fantasy gaming, it is not a cry for paranoia, nor for blanket censorship, but a modest call for wide-awake, engaged and sensitive parenting, which might involve the occasional, necessary, exercising of parental discretion.

13

To parents and teachers . . .

Occult warning signs

> The best thing parents can do for their children is to *talk* to them.
> You'd be amazed at how many parents are actually afraid to
> approach their children with questions or concerns because they
> think their children won't love them anymore or that they'll lose
> them. If they're not able to broach the subject, they're going to
> lose their children anyway.
> Social worker[1]

Cause or effect?

Throughout this book, it's been stressed that occult involvement is
more likely to be a *factor* than a *cause* of adolescent disturbance.

The morbid world of the occult is disturbing in its own right, but
involvement suggests there could be something unhappy within a
child's character or circumstances to draw it towards that dark and
introspective horizon in the first place. Disillusionment, and not just
disturbance, could play a part.

But with so many factors involved there can be no simple relationship between cause and effect: while a fascination for horror movies
is unlikely to tip a child into occult involvement, that, too, could be
part of the attraction.

Why is it so important to stress and re-stress this point? Because if
we fail to address it, the alternative to complacency will not be
action, but over-reaction.

This chapter contains a series of checklists to indicate the *possible*
early warning signs of an adolescent who *could be* at risk of occult
involvement; and of an occult involvement that could itself be risky.

Some parents would argue that even a shallow interest in the
occult is wading too deep. But wherever our conscience causes us to
draw the line for our children, our common sense should draw a line
for ourselves well before we approach paranoia, or moral panic is
allowed to set in.

The occult is a symptom, rather than a cause, of a sickness. A happy and secure child, who is well-loved and well-disciplined, whose natural enthusiasm for a life worth living has been encouraged to the full, and who has a variety of healthy friendships and interests, is unlikely to surrender to its sallow and dubious charms.

The trouble is, none of us lives in an ideal world.

More than one in three British marriages ends in divorce – up 622% since 1961. Almost a fifth of families have only one parent. More than 10 million Britons are struggling below the official poverty line. Upwards of half a million parents are unable to feed their children a nutritionally adequate diet. Child abuse appears to be rising. More than 10,000 children try to get through to the Childline Helpline every day. A third of 16- to 17-year-olds claiming income support have been chucked out of their homes by their parents and carers. According to the National Children's Home some 43,000 under-17s run away from home each year, and 156,000 British children have nowhere to live.

Many young people have every reason to be disillusioned and good cause to be disturbed. Yet, according to a survey by Minitel, some 81% still claim their family is the most important thing in their lives.

The experts tell us: 'There's more disturbed and violent behaviour now. There's more desperation, more brutality. Controlling these children, helping them to get some sense of society is getting more difficult.'[2] Melanie Phillips writes: 'Parents are under pressure as never before. Children's distress and disorder and violence are rising. Families increasingly cannot cope.'[3]

If a child is deep into the occult, almost invariably there will be deeper underlying issues to do with home life and health. Taking our children's temperature is an opportunity for us adults to consider whether the lifestyles we're living are conducive to sound family health.

On the brink

If a child is standing on the brink, what would it take to push him over the edge? Cult watchers have identified a variety of factors which, in combination, could open up a teenager to an unhealthy preoccupation with the occult:

1. Absence of a belief or value system to provide a framework for stability

2. Boredom
3. Alcohol and drug abuse
4. Feeling of being unloved, not needed and not belonging
5. Recent traumatic bereavement
6. Lack of family support, acceptance and affirmation
7. Awareness of the hypocrisy of authority figures who should be role models – especially parents
8. Excessive parental expectation
9. Parental domination
10. Personal insecurity, fear of failing
11. Feelings of inadequacy or loss of control
12. Abnormal level of stress, anxiety or fear
13. Habitual repression of feelings
14. Religious conflict
15. Attraction to lack of behavioural restraint and absence of moral disapproval
16. Attraction to the promise of personal power
17. Peer pressure
18. A history of severe abuse

Checklists can be dangerous things. They can amplify anxiety and provide nourishment for paranoia. So we need to be wise about how we use them and temper needless concern with common sense.

A smattering of ticks could mean little or nothing. But too many ticks on the checklist could point to alienation which might stem from problems in the family, or even despair at the state of society. As one chaos magician has commented:

> More and more people today are feeling alienated from the civilization which has lost its mystery and its meaning and seems to be bent on an ecological disaster course.[4]

Alienation

Some of the strongest risk factors for occultic involvement include feelings of extreme alienation, a morbid fascination with destructiveness, continued use of drugs or alcohol or both, difficulty in excelling within 'the system', a sense of powerlessness, a need to control people and events, an above average intelligence and creativity, and an attraction to the mysterious.
Bob and Gretchen Passantino[5]

Alienation and powerlessness are cited by counsellors and clients alike as reasons teenagers turn to occultism. The attractions of the occult include wonderment and the draw of the mysterious, a sense of feeling special or chosen. And some occult practices offer out-and-out excitement. If the kicks are illicit and offer some frisson of danger, so much the more enticing.

Satanism, at the extreme end of the occult, holds out the promise of power to the powerless. For those sucked into its vortex, identification with satanism can be a despair-driven reaction against a society that offers no recognition, no place of security, no love, and no hope.

The classic cause of alienation is rejection. A child may feel misunderstood or uncared for, even though the parents are convinced that everything in the garden is rosy. A sense of rejection by others can lead to self-rejection, which can give rise to a hostile and destructive attitude.

An early warning sign that an intelligent child has lost faith with himself and the system may be a nosedive in his performance at school. Other signs of alienation include rejection of authority and received values and the deliberate adoption of behaviour which those in authority (parents/teachers) would regard as socially unacceptable.

Again, common sense tells us that every teenager goes through something of this as a natural part of adolescence. Not every kid who makes up with black eyeliner is a budding satanist! But the alarm bells should be ringing when alienation is taken to extremes and is marked by a sustained character change and deterioration in behaviour.

Take, for example, the girl in Humberside who had been drawn into an occult society fronted by a music group. They were deliberately targeting teens and others in their early twenties. Recruits were carefully sounded out before progressing from a mildly salacious outer circle to an inner circle where drugs, sex and blood played a major part in their rituals.

A swing in behaviour was the first indication to relatives that something was amiss. The girl became withdrawn, uncommunicative and hostile. What clinched the conviction that something was badly wrong was when she took to wearing a T-shirt with holes cut out to display her breasts. An aunt confronted the girl and she eventually spilled the story of what she had got herself into.

Spiral of rejection

Lack of love and affection can be one cause for alienation. Lack of discipline can be another. 'If only they had cared enough to yell at me,' was how one teenager expressed it. Another cause could be a sense of parental hypocrisy, where the attitude that comes over is: 'Don't do as I do; do as I say.' The crunch point could come over drug use, language, or morality. That sense of hypocrisy could extend to society:

> A lot of reasons the kids get involved in satanism is because they see hypocrisy in the Christian Church. If people are not standing up for their beliefs, then there is no reason to join in on those beliefs. It is imperative that ... Christians stand up for what they believe in ... get rid of the hypocrisy in [the] churches, start meeting the needs of the people.
> Teenage self-styled satanist Sean Sellers[6]

The next twist in the spiral of rejection could be the abandoning of family values. Again, beware of over-reaction, because every adolescent needs to push at the boundaries and test acceptable limits of behaviour in order to find his own way. As ever, it comes down to a matter of degree.

With rejection of values may come a withdrawal from the family. Teenagers need space, but then withdrawal is coupled with secretiveness and an aggressive defence of the 'right to be left alone', this could be a further symptom that the young adult in your home is switching off from you and on to something else.

Occult obsession

If that something else is the occult, and the teenager is in deep, then the warning signs should be obvious. A real fixation with the occult will be all-consuming. Your teenager will become an occult consumer.

There will be the books and tapes; signs and symbols. Typical of these would be the pentagram (five-pointed star) of witchcraft; the inverted pentagram and upside down cross of satanism, or the 666 of the Beast or antichrist. But before we wade in, we have to be sure that the message our adolescent is communicating is more than just a fashion statement.

Other occult trappings could give it away. Part of the paraphernalia could be some means of making contact with the spiritual world. This might be a tool of divination, such as rune stones, tarot cards, or the ouija board. The room might even contain a makeshift altar. Among the artefacts could be candles, a chalice and a knife.

Doom-laden music could just be a fashion trend, along with heavy metal crosses, but taken to excess, and coupled with other indicators, it could be another symptom of occult obsession. Thrash-metal, death-metal, Gothic or heavy-metal music gives itself away by the artwork on the album, lyric sheets and the names of the bands. Neo-pagan or shamanistic music may be less blatant.

The US-based Parents' Music Resource Centre offers the following advice:

> Tune in, don't tune out. Discover what your child is listening to.
> Focus on the content, not the style, so as to avoid a discussion
> over taste, rather than a discussion over inappropriate themes.
> Teach your child to think critically about what he or she listens to.

A teenager who is heavily into satanism or witchcraft will probably keep a *Book of Shadows*. This is an occultic journal or diary of rituals; a sort of ship's log of progress made on the voyage so far. This is intimate and personal and is unlikely to be left lying around. It might even be kept on computer.

To discover such stuff a parent might have to ignore the 'no-entry' sticker on the bedroom door. It's a crunch point, but come what may, if there are solid grounds for concern that a teenager is at risk, his or her room must never become a no-go zone for parents. Parental duty of protection must take precedence over the right to privacy.

Getting in too deep

The following are evidence of active, unhealthy, occult involvement:

1. Obsession with the unexplained and the supernatural
2. Obsession with occult practices, evidenced by a substantial collection of movies or books
3. Obsession with occultic heavy metal music
4. Obsession with fantasy role-play games
5. Occult symbols and drawings on notebooks, occult tattoos, jewellery
6. Occult paraphernalia in room, such as candles, chalice, knives
7. Occult prayers, rituals or death contracts
8. Withdrawal from family

 9. Shift in friendships, reluctance to explain
10. Loss of interest in normal activities
11. Drastic falling off of school grades
12. High truancy rate
13. Violent rebellion
14. Sudden behavioural changes
15. Secret behaviour
16. Self-mutilation and blood-letting
17. Deep fears and night terrors
18. Unhealthy interest in suicide
19. Drug abuse[7]

Once again, it would take more than a suspicion of such things or a few sporadic ticks on a checklist to provide proof positive of a problem. Though, from item seven onwards, *any* such behaviour should be cause for concern – and action – on the part of parents or teachers.

Drugs

Another area where teen culture and occulture can overlap is in the use of drugs. Substance abuse is worrying in its own right, and obviously cannot be regarded on its own as a symptom of occult involvement.

Other indicators that your kid has cut loose could be extreme promiscuity, self-indulgence and self-absorption. By now we are well out of the early warning zone and into deep danger. Destructive behaviour comes next, and when the anarchy is sustained and vehement and laced with vengeance, you have, in anyone's books, evidence that something has gone seriously wrong.

So, what to do?

> If you are a parent with a crisis teen, don't give up . . . Often parents who don't give up mean the difference between life and death for their children. A commitment to effective intervention and long-term constructive action is the first step on the road to recovery.
> Bob and Gretchen Passantino[8]

Targets for recruitment

We have seen evidence that a minority of DIY dabblers who get out of their depth can fall prey to the sharks of the occult world – adults who use the occult as an excuse or justification for criminal behaviour or abuse.

The US-based Cult Awareness Network has listed the characteristics typical of young people most at risk of being drawn into destructive cults. These include:

1. Aged 16 to 35 – most vulnerable between 18 and 25
2. Mid to upper socio-economic family backgrounds
3. Average to above intelligence
4. Intellectually curious and identity seeking
5. Idealistic – looking for answers to philosophical questions about life
6. In a state of transition – away from home for the first time, new environment due to new school or job, etc.; stress due to splitting up with friend or family problem, etc.[9]

A report by US police officers adds the following:

1. Low esteem/image
2. Social recluse
3. Broken homes and split families
4. Latch-key kids
5. Victims of prior sexual abuse
6. Deep need for belonging[10]

Recovering from ritual abuse

'Alan Peterson' was still at primary school when a group of adults roped him into their paedophile circle, using occult practices as a means of enticing him in and terrifying him to stay. The family was devastated, but is now working to pick up the pieces. His mother, 'Eileen' says the group recruited her child and others, sexually abused them within a ritualistic framework, and made and sold pornographic videos of the abuse.

Sexual, physical and mental abuse took place 'over a long period of time'. She says the name of Satan was invoked during the ceremonies, along with those of other gods and deities of a Druidic nature.

Alan was recruited by another schoolboy, and remained in the group for several years. During that time, says Eileen: 'his basic family beliefs and the ordinary things that you bring your child up to believe in that make him a decent human being were taken away from him.'

She had considered her primary school son too young for a pep-talk on sex and drugs. 'It's one thing to teach your child to say no to strangers, but what do you say to a schoolfriend who asks you over? You don't sit down and warn five, six and seven year olds that they may be abused by their teacher, by the policeman, by the vicar. You don't do that. And they got him earlier than the warnings did.'

By and large, she and other parents have met with a brick wall when they have taken the problem to the authorities: 'I think we're in the same situation as people who were being abused by members of the family maybe 20 years ago. People did know it was going on at the back of their minds, but to openly acknowledge that something awful is happening on your own doorstep is a different thing.'

Eileen still chides herself for not noticing the change in Alan earlier, but there were family problems and she put his growing sullenness and odd behaviour down to that. But the matter only really came to light when Alan himself decided to talk about it, because he had made up his mind to break from the group.

Eileen sought help from a childcare expert who broke the news that her son had been abused. This was confirmed by a second opinion.

'I still didn't want to believe it, so I went in and I asked Alan as calmly as I could and he just sat there with no emotion on his face and admitted what had been going on. From then, I got it in little bits at a time.

'He describes even the fear that he went through as addictive,' she says. 'Children leading an ordinary life get bored very easily. Excitement gets the adrenalin pumping – it's like a high, and I think he got addicted to the fear of them.'

Alan has had to learn that affection is no longer a cynical means to a sexual end. And as a child who is still under the legal age of consent, he has had to come to terms with his premature sexuality. He has had to be taught, as best as possible, to regain his innocence:

'For a long time he pulled away when you just put your arms around him to cuddle him, because he just wasn't quite sure what to do with the feelings you were giving. He wasn't sure that he really wanted them because he felt that bad about himself. He didn't really want anyone else to feel good about him. He has had to learn how to be loved.

'Whether he'll become an abuser in the future is a fear we're having to live with at the moment, but it's an acknowledged fear. He is worried about statistics that prove that a lot of the abused children will go on to become abusers themselves.

'They robbed Alan of his childhood. As far as I'm concerned, childhood is all about innocence, and they took that away from him.'

Perhaps the danger could have been averted, or the damage minimized, if the problem had been recognized and dealt with at an earlier stage.

'When a child does disclose,' says Eileen, 'don't close your mind, listen to what the child says. I am sure there are children who are sick, but even those need to be listened to. Don't close your mind to these kids no matter how horrific the story; listen to it, because the chances are the kids are telling the truth.'

Schools

According to Eileen Peterson, Alan's problems started at school. Undesirable elements were allowed in, and children were permitted to go off with them for periods at a time. Astonishingly, the school neither noticed nor prevented what was happening.

Schools are well placed to be the first to spot a potential problem which looks serious, and the parents will need to be informed.

Thirteen-year-old Nicole confided to her school counsellor in Montgomery County, USA, that she was planning to kill herself. According to the school authorities, the counsellor did not pass on that information. A week later Nicole and Marsha, a twelve-year-old friend, were found dead in a park. They had been shot through the head with a pistol at point-blank range. Friends of the girls told the police they had been talking about killing themselves, 'so they could meet Satan'. Police said twelve-year-old Marsha shot Nicole before turning the gun on herself. The father accused the school of failing to warn him about his daughter's suicidal tendencies, and filed a law suit.
Delaware News, April 1989

Those are extreme cases. But school libraries, class projects and even reading plans can be unwitting providers of unhelpful material. One magazine available to schoolteachers listed 170 books and videos on witchcraft and the occult which were recommended for use with children.

Concerns have been raised over primary age reading schemes which highlight witches, a video promoting a BTEC GNVQ course which uses tarot cards and crystal balls, a children's calculator which predicts horoscopes and a school syllabus called 'Fears and Superstitions.'[11]

I went to the school library. I asked for books on the occult, thinking I would find one or two. There was a whole huge section on the black arts, on witchcraft, on every aspect of the occult that you should want. As I looked, I came across a prayer to Lucifer. I didn't know who Lucifer was, but it said if you pray this prayer for a month, then you will get everything you want, and more.
Glen, former satanist, USA[12]

In the US, occultic teaching programmes promoted by New Age activists have been introduced into some schools with federal funding. One programme, adopted in Southern California, teaches that every child is God: 'Each child ... can tap into a universal mind through meditation and contacting *spirit guides* ...'[13]

In the UK, a primary school was presented with a series of activity books for younger children. They contained a game based on the Chinese divination system the *I Ching*; offered visualization and meditation exercises, and taught reincarnation, as interpreted by the spirit guide White Eagle, who 'in this New Age . . . teaches the Ancient Wisdom with fresh insight for the new Aquarian Age'.

Also in the series was an introduction to the 'spiritual science of astrology,' and an exercise for small children who were invited to make a 'cut-out doll with reincarnation dresses'.

The issue of unsuitable occultic material in schools has been taken up by Liverpool MP David Alton:

Unfortunately, school projects are contributing to the problem. Children as young as twelve are set occult-related homework, with the explanation that this 'fascinating' subject will encourage them to research and 'think for themselves'. One fourteen-year-old whose interest was aroused by a school project on astrology has become a practising satanist. Young people need our help to resist it, at home and at school. Parents must challenge teaching staff whenever they have reasons for concern.

But confrontation and challenge – however necessary – are no substitute for understanding and co-operation. Parents need teachers, and teachers need parents, and it is through working together that the interests of children are best served.

Getting involved

Spotting a problem is one thing. What a parent should do about it is another. It raises difficult questions. Should a parent act as censor? If so, how deeply should parental cuts bite? How much of this material is *too* much? When does a fashion trend become a fixation? When does a fixation become a dangerous obsession? When to cut in and where?

This will be less of a conundrum if the channels of communication have been kept open between teenagers and parents and affection and trust are evident.

Pete Roland, you may recall, was given a life sentence in the USA for the occult-related murder of his classmate, Stephen Newberry. Roland's mother, Penny Baert, spoke openly about her feelings on US TV:

> I feel very guilty that I didn't pay attention. There were some things that I saw that I should have paid attention to. I saw the album covers and they're hideous. I just assumed that if they sell it, then it's got to be OK. I saw satanic symbols on his bookwork and I'd spoken to him about it, and [I assumed] it didn't mean anything; it was a passing phase. I assumed wrong. And I would advise anybody if they see anything like that to look into it, don't ignore it, it doesn't pass. It's just something I'll never get over. Ever.'

'*I just assume that if they sell it, it's got to be OK* . . .' Since her son's incarceration Mrs Baert has met many other parents, who, like her, ignored the signs, and when they eventually did call for an explanation, settled all too easily for cheap reassurance. They were fobbed off with what they wanted to hear.

She catalogued the changes she observed in her son:

> He avoided us as a family, he didn't want to be around us. [He ate meals on his own.] No more family life; his friends didn't come around anymore. He told me that he had no regard for his life, no regard for Stephen's.[14]

Later, after he had had time to reflect, Roland was interviewed in jail and asked what advice he would give to parents whose teenagers were becoming involved in the occult:

> Show them that you really care about them. Show them love; that they're needed, that they definitely belong in the family, that they're somebody. Start showing them you're behind them.[15]

'To ignore the increasing involvement of adolescents into satanism or to pretend that it's nothing serious will not make it go away,' says Wayne A. Van Kampen of Bethesda PsycHealth Institute, Colorado. What the child needs, he believes, is help in forming positive values and in making responsible decisions about his life-style. And that will require the active involvement of both parents and teachers.[16]

Concerned parents of younger children have been offered the following advice by the British Evangelical Alliance. It relates mainly to books and games, but can be stretched to apply to TV, movies and music:

1. **At least scan your child's reading material.**
   That should give you an indication as to their diet.

2. **Always consider the overall effect of the book.**
   What values does it underline? How does it leave you feeling – positive or negative, contented or fearful?

3. **Talk openly to your children about their books.**
   Be involved and interested rather than act as a censor.

4. **Understand your children's games.**
   Get alongside them as they play. Discuss them with them.

5. **Make sure you are setting consistent standards yourself.**
   Your children will take a cue from what you watch, what you read and how you *are*.[17]

There are two traps to avoid. One is under-involvement to the point of indifference; the other is over-involvement to the point of repression. The aim is care, understanding, communication and rapport, not a censorious and heavy-handed approach that could drive a disturbed child deeper into alienation.

But before any steps can be taken, the whole family will have to face the fact that they have a problem. Next you will need to agree on a course of action to deal with it. For two-parent families, this is an opportunity to pull together. More than an opportunity – it's an imperative – any cracks between you are likely to be jemmied wide open and the relationship could crumble.

Then you will need to press on through to make contact with your troubled teenager. Confronting the problem, however sympathetically, could carry the risk of upset, anger and personal rejection. If you fail to get through, get professional help. And in the happy event that you can communicate there is unlikely to be any quick fix. Both you and your child are likely to need counselling.

Expert assistance

If drugs have been involved, or there is evidence of serious disturbance or sexual abuse, medical expertise becomes essential. It will not be possible to keep the problem 'in the family'.

Once the immediate presenting problems have been dealt with you will need the long-term assistance of a counsellor. You will also need friends and relatives who are solidly behind you. The school should be informed so that teachers can be made aware of your adolescent's special needs, which may include necessary periods of absence from the classroom.

If other teenagers are involved their parents will need to be informed. It might be possible to work with them, to face the issue together. The support of your local church could also prove invaluable.

If the worst comes to the worst you might need a change of surroundings and time to sort things out. You could have a limited opportunity to put matters right. Don't rely on your instincts: seek professional advice from an experienced counsellor.

'Where there is a suspicion that occult forces are at work in a person's life', writes psychiatrist Dr Kenneth McAll, 'a prerequisite of any subsequent treatment is a thorough medical examination'.[18]

A spiritual dimension

Some parents with strong religious convictions might be inclined to believe that deep disturbance in a child, when linked with occult involvement, must have a demonic root. The sheer nastiness of what the child is going through could convince them they are dealing with something that is evil. Dr McAll has treated up to 300 clients for occult-related disorder. He urges caution, and says every care should be taken to make an accurate diagnosis:

'[The individual] may in fact be suffering from depressive psychosis, schizophrenia or the effects of other organic psychosis. A person could be acutely neurotic; hidden aspects of his personality or an upsurge image from his deep unconscious could be the cause. Although all such diagnoses should be treated as psychiatric disorders, they do not exclude demonic control.'[19]

Dr McAll says he has treated disturbance in clients who have been involved in the following: astrology, ouija, automatic writing, horoscopes, fortune telling, divination, seances, tarot cards, witchcraft and transcendental meditation. 'Psychiatry acknowledges the reality that the occult opens the door to evil,' he says.

In cases where an occult dimension has existed, but has been overlooked and left untreated, Dr McAll believes a number of patients have simply been labelled schizophrenics and left to flounder by the medical profession.

The charity CRO (Christian Response to the Occult) also looks after individuals who have been damaged by the occult. CRO identifies a series of medical and mental side-effects arising from occult involvement. These include: prolonged and deep depression; fits of temper or violence; irrational fears; nightmares and an obsessive fixation with suicide.

No one has yet been able to draw an adequate line between the spiritual and psychological aspects of an individual. So there is room for the complementary expertise of the psychiatric profession and the church. In parts of the country, doctors and church ministers have recognized that each can offer valuable insights, and have got together to offer counselling and treatment:

> I have doctors, psychiatrists and ministers who have sent people to me for the last 20 years. We have had to deal with people barking like dogs, educated kids vomiting, having reactions going into churches, screaming and crawling on the floor like snakes. I have a person now who a psychiatrist has sent to me on the basis that they are not mentally ill, they are spiritually possessed.[20]

But how can one distinguish between mental illness and occult-related disorder? And to what degree does one lead to another? It's the age old problem of the chicken or the egg. Dr McAll's advice bears repeating: where there are strong symptoms of disturbance, don't try to sort it out yourself; call in the experts and begin with a doctor.

The job of rebuilding

Having identified the problem and embarked on a course of treatment, be it psychiatric help or counselling, next comes the task of rebuilding and providing a stable base for your disturbed adolescent.

Peer pressure is a major factor in sustaining antisocial behaviour. You might have to detach your teenager from his or her role models.

That could mean saying goodbye to some friends; cutting loose from some clubs, or even shelving some albums or videos that could just add fuel to the fire.

Explain your reasons. Aim for understanding and hope for consent, but don't be amazed if you don't get them. And don't expect to be thanked for thwarting your teenager!

You will need to be firm, but at the same time to be caring and loving. Define your boundaries. Replace the old disorder with a new routine. Ensure your teenager has enough sleep, enough food and engages in enough activity. Come alongside and get involved. Lay down limits that are realistic and workable. And when you have done so, make sure they are kept to. In everything, be utterly consistent, which will require a high degree of communication and consent between other family members. And provide positive reinforcement to balance the negative restraint.

But parental intervention can't go on forever. The last thing you want is a child who can only stand up by leaning on you. You are looking for a self-reliant and self-motivated individual, with the self-confidence to make the right decisions. And that will mean gradually increasing his space and his freedom, as the damage heals and his sense of responsibility grows.

Whatever destructive material you have taken away will need to be replaced by something positive. You have created a vacuum, now you will need to fill it. Remember the fantasy game junkie who successfully switched his attention to ten-pin bowling?

Most parents are too old and too out of touch to substitute for their teenagers' friends and interests, but you will need to firmly start the ball rolling towards others who can take their place.

Your aim is to move the child from being destructive to constructive; from being negative to positive; from irresponsibility to responsibility; from despair to hope. Your child needs new role models, and chief among these must be *you*. Your own life and attitude must point the way.

How about you?

Picking up your teenager may involve a change in your own life, even if you thought nothing was wrong to begin with.

As we heard, Pat Pulling's son committed suicide after becoming obsessed with fantasy role-play games, and she documents many similar cases in her book *The Devil's Web*:

Almost without exception, the children ... came from good families with loving parents who had taught their children well.[21]

If your child has gone through a period of alienation, then some self-examination on your part could well be necessary. Could your teenager have something to tell you by turning his back on your values? Where are you going in life? What do you have to offer that is better? What kind of example are you setting? Has your own interest or involvement in the occult fuelled his fascination? Do you spend enough time with your child? Is it time well-spent? Do you really communicate? Does he *know* your love and acceptance?

Even if none of those issues applies, then the present crisis can still be turned to good. Now could be the time for a fresh beginning for the whole family. The process of adjustment is likely to be uncomfortable, but the promise of restoration has to be worth it.

14

Breaking out

Breaking free from the occult

> Mickey was fourteen and running a tarot ring at his school. 'A teacher told us to investigate fortune telling for our homework,' he explained to counsellor Audrey Harper. He bought a horoscope magazine from a local newsagent and ordered £50 of occult paraphernalia with money stolen from his parents. 'I didn't really believe it. I thought it was just fun.' But he grew convinced there were two spirits in his bedroom. One was friendly, but the other frightened him: 'It tells me to kill my parents.' He refused an offer of counselling. 'Today,' says Audrey Harper, 'he is an adult involved in fully-fledged satanic rituals.'
>
> Audrey Harper[1]

Fortunately, not everyone ends up like Mickey. Throughout this book, we have been following the troubled fortunes of Alex, Roger, Gary and Amanda. Unlike Mickey, they broke the cycle. This is how their stories turned out, and what we can learn from them:

Alex's story

Alex, you may remember, was intelligent and a loner. Add to that the fact that he was adopted and felt an outsider, and you have a natural candidate to become what US police categorize as an 'occult dabbler'. Alex's account has much to say to parents.

He was just five years old when he was invited to a ouija party. He was hooked and started using the board during school lunch hours. From there he took up the tarot cards, and by giving readings to his schoolmates he gained popularity and found he could manipulate his friends. It gave him a taste for power and he started to crave something more potent. From the tarot he went on to DIY witchcraft.

Underneath it all, his inner loneliness remained, accompanied by a growing, irrational sense of fear. The feelings scared and intrigued him. Alex's compulsion to confront his fears became an obsession.

To try to gain mastery over them, he faced them head on by immersing himself in horror movies.

Occultic and splatter videos became his regular night-time viewing. Inevitably, nightmares followed, and haunting his sleep was a recurring vision of death. Before him was a grave. On the tombstone was Alex's name and the date of his death – his 18th birthday.

Alex became increasingly withdrawn, moody and uncommunicative. What he believed to be psychic experiences took him over until he felt as though he was losing control, 'it was as though there was always something or somebody else pulling the strings'.

He admits to making life hell for his adoptive parents, who had no idea how to handle him. They guessed he was on drugs but wouldn't or couldn't confront it. His condition deteriorated, but rather than face up to it, they let things drift.

As far as Alex was concerned, their consternation and paralysis looked pretty much like indifference. 'If they had cared they would have seen what was going on. I was in such torment most of the time; the insomnia, the fear, the paranoia. I always felt threatened wherever I was.

'I often wished they had yelled at me. They used to let me do whatever I wanted. From the age of about fourteen, while other kids had to be in by eleven I could be back whenever I liked. They knew I was smoking. If they'd sat me down and said, look at your lifestyle, look at the way you've living, and had a go at me, it might have made me think that they were actually concerned. I found out later that they had been, but they hadn't got a clue how to handle it. They were really concerned but didn't know how to show it.'

Perhaps his parents felt that by keeping Alex on a slack rein they were demonstrating their love and acceptance. But what Alex wanted above all was for his adoptive parents to get involved and *show* him they cared. 'But they felt inadequate. They were expecting a typical Dr Spock childhood and they didn't know what to do.' With so much left unsaid, the gap between them could only widen.

'There was one incident when Mum, on a light level, tried to talk to me about what I was up to, but they didn't *know* me; they didn't know what was *inside* me. I was closed off from them; very distant emotionally. There was one time when Mum asked me to explain why I punched a hole in the wall and I freaked out. I ended up in a heap on the floor, sobbing and screaming.'

Instead of seeing it through, his mother backed away: 'She just left it. If she'd stuck around for five minutes longer I might have been so drained that I might have sat down and talked to her; I don't know.

But she just stood there and looked worried for a bit, before wandering off.'

Alex's internal turmoil grew to the extent that he began cutting himself with razor blades. He started carving words into his chest and arms, and then tried to commit suicide. 'I hated myself, and I used to fantasize about dying in the most hideously graphic way possible, lying in a pool of blood. I was really under this whole thing that I was going to die by my eighteenth birthday.'

He began to fulfil elements of his own fantasy by watching like a detached observer as his own blood ran. He admits to enjoying the pain. 'I used to get emotionally hyped up listening to fast punk music: no hope, no point, no future. The whole nihilism that used to come through it hyped me again, and there's times when I used to do my arm and do my chest because the pain added to the thrill.'

From time to time his bedsheets would show traces of his blood. It didn't go unnoticed by his mother: 'She used to ask, "Why are you doing it? What's going on?" I could hardly put it down to a nose-bleed! I told her I had cut myself up.'

Even so, it was Alex who first sought medical attention. He went to the family doctor over his insomnia and bad dreams. The doctor referred him to a child psychiatrist, but, in Alex's words, 'he was about as useful as a chocolate teapot'. He had been hoping that the psychiatrist could offer him a way out, 'but he never got to the root'. His best advice was to get up in the morning, look in the mirror, and say : "I like what I see."

'He was concentrating on my self-image,' says Alex, 'and yes, while my self-image was shattered, that wasn't really the problem.'

Suicide began to seem the only option. 'There were points where I just hated life and wanted to die. I didn't want to wake up. I wanted darkness to overwhelm me. I couldn't be bothered anymore. Life wasn't worth living. I was looking at my life and wondering where I was going. I wasn't heading anywhere. I was a failure. I resign, here's my notice.' He says he tried several times to take his own life and the failure compounded his sense of defeat and resignation.

At the age of 17, he was thrown out of college. 'I remember thinking, "This is it, this is all life is about. This is the end. No point." I didn't really see myself as a person. There was nothing special about me. The psychic stuff was there, but sometimes I just felt like a freak.'

Increasingly, he was hearing voices in his head. '"END" was a word I used to hear. "No more. What's the point?" used to echo around. "Finish it. Final. There's no point."' His 18th birthday was rapidly approaching and the conviction that his coming of age would be the coming of death had not diminished.

A friend of a girlfriend 'who seemed very together' suggested he started going to church. It was one of the new churches which met in halls and homes, and attracted a lot of young people.

Alex went, invariably stoned or drunk, and always sat at the back. Despite his condition, the sense of community and the hope that he felt in the atmosphere got through to him. 'I could see something there. Maybe there was something behind it. I used to feel a sense of peace there that I'd never really experienced before.'

Gradually, some of the Christian message began to penetrate his doped-up state. 'I picked up about this God who cared and who was interested. He was interested to the level that he would watch [Jesus], the most important thing he had, viciously murdered on my behalf. This was unheard of! People don't do that for me! Alex is just the scum of the earth.'

Seven months before his 18th birthday, he was in church, stone cold sober, with no cash for drink or drugs, and says it was as though his whole life was played back before him. God seemed to be saying, 'Look at your life. You want hope: it's me.' And it was at that point he prayed for God to take hold of him.

It wasn't all plain sailing. On occasions Alex lapsed back to the ouija board, the tarot cards and dope – even to cutting himself. But not for long. And for Alex the contrast is clear: 'I can sleep. I don't live on fear. I'm not afraid of the dark or of people. There's hope in it, and a sense of being special and wanted without having to do anything.'

He's still one of the lads. A blue baseball cap is crammed over a thatch of sandy hair. There are two gold rings through his ears, and another through his nose. 'Before I had to read someone's cards to get wanted,' he says. 'Now I'm accepted and loved for what I am and who I am'.

Alex's 18th birthday came and went without incident – unless you count the celebration meal at a pub with his mum and dad. 'It was like the first day of the rest of my life. That was that. No fear at all.'

Perhaps the most bizarre and disturbing part of Alex's story, and a theme which recurs throughout this material, is the obsession with blood and the progression to self-mutilation and blood-letting.

We can rationalize this as the product of a fascination with the morbid, an obsession with gore-soaked splatter movies, and the destructive self-loathing which can follow personal rejection by others.

But even if we can begin to view such things objectively, we will never be able to help the teenager who cuts himself up in this way unless we take pains to understand what is going on in his mind.

Such things are likely to be repellent to any parent; they may make us want to back away and deny what we are seeing, to dismiss it all as some unspeakable phase which we hope will quickly pass. But unless we do speak of it, and until we try to understand the feelings behind it, and open ourselves to the risk of rejection by getting alongside the individual, we will fail to be of any help.

If there is one principal thing that parents can learn from Alex's story, it's that we must talk to our children. Understand them. Know what's going on in their heads. Watch the signs. Get involved. We mustn't be afraid of driving them away. We are more likely to win them and less likely to lose them by showing that we care enough for confrontation.

Audrey Harper has counselled clients who have cut and mutilated themselves. She says some individuals are convinced they are unlovable:

> That belief cannot change overnight. If anything, they will want to destroy any love that is shown to them. They do not love themselves, they are afraid of rejection, and they prefer to feel in control of a relationship. That is why they sometimes hurt and cut themselves. If they look ugly, no-one will love them . . . The occult is drawing people, who, for one reason or another, dislike themselves or their circumstances . . . Fear of rejection makes them constantly try to hide their true selves.[2]

Running parallel to this is the fact that blood-letting can play an important part in some occult rituals, as it did in Roger's case . . .

Roger's story

'Roger', as we have already heard, was initiated into occult practices by his brother. He entered his teens with an overdose of drugs and Gothic music and described himself as being addicted to the ouija board. An over-the-top and unhealthy fascination for horror films and vampirism developed into an obsession with blood.

Roger's gang – The Black Alchemists – would cut their bodies and drink their blood as an integral part of their magic rituals. This self-mutilation cannot be divorced from their occultism.

Blood-letting arose from Roger's bizarre practices and later became a way of silencing the mounting inner confusion which those practices produced. 'I was paranoid about everything – absolutely anything.' He became afraid of his friends and of the spirits he contacted with the board. That fear reached a peak at the age of 17.

Cutting himself became a way of resolving the conflict of clashing thoughts and emotions. 'It's like you've got three emotions spinning round your head and you are completely confused, and I hate being confused. I had to have one emotion going on, not three, so I would cut myself up and go high, and after that it would stabilize and that would bring out the depression. In the depression there is a peace, a completely "I don't care", where you don't worry about anything, and that would bring peace, and then I would just be alright.'

As with Alex, it was Roger's conversion to Christianity at the age of 18 that snapped him out of the cycle. 'I felt like I had switched to the good side. I had a reason to live. A purpose. No matter what, I had a friend.' The two and a half years since then have been a period of peace and stability.

Roger's family played a central role in his introduction to the occult. It was his mother's interest in occultism that aroused his curiosity, and his brother's involvement that drew him in beyond his depth.

As other case studies in this book indicate, a sensitive child can be knocked off balance by that kind of environment, even if the rest of the family are convinced they are taking it in their stride. The north of England psychotherapist in a previous chapter, who was tasked with trying to keep together a disturbed teenager, placed the blame squarely on her 'nutty' family, which was into abuse, alcoholism and the occult: 'All I can do is hope to get her through to sixteen and to college before she cracks completely.'

The potentially damaging effect to children of bizarre family practices should not be underestimated – even if the parents are convinced everything is 'in hand'. There may be parallels in watching X-rated movies: while an adult might be able to sit through a slasher film without flinching, a sensitive child could end up traumatized – as other studies in this book suggest.

Through their own occult involvement parents can harm their children. If we look at the origins of many people's illnesses we have found it began when mother and I were playing with the ouija board, what at first seems a harmless little game. Those who go on get caught and they can't undo it themselves.
Psychiatrist Dr Kenneth McAll

Gary's story

'Gary' followed much the same path as Roger and Alex. Again, it was an adult who tipped him over the top.

To recap: at the age of 12 a schoolfriend's mother drew him into spiritualism after her son had died. Gary was a seeker after truth, whose incessant questions and arguments frustrated his teachers. Unsatisfied and searching for a higher reality, he got into drugs and fell foul of the law by stealing to pay for them.

There were the usual icons: the heavy metal heroes. The ouija board played a part, along with runes and hallucinogenic mushrooms, which Gary got into for their mystical and pagan connotations.

While he was still in his teens Gary, too, despaired of the world around him and became suicidal. 'I'd rejected materialism. I understood that there was more to life than meets the eye; than what I could taste, touch, smell and feel; yet my experimentation with the occult promised a lot but never delivered.'

Again, Gary's personal turning point came with his conversion to Christianity, which happened in stages. 'Christianity made a dramatic difference. I had been very disillusioned and discouraged; not only with the rat race, but with the spiritual questioning that I had done.

'Christianity brought me up sharp and I think it actually revealed to me who I was. All the pressure to perform was off. I am much more secure as a person. I understand who I am.'

Gary is now in his mid-20s, and deeply involved in charity work.

Amanda's story

'Amanda' was poorly served by her parents, teachers and youth leaders who encouraged her to get into the occult in the first place.

It was a school project on the supernatural that stirred up her interest. The project became an obsession which consumed her spare time. Her work was so comprehensive that she was commended in person by her headmistress who encouraged her to continue with her investigations. Her parents were so delighted that they gave her a pack of divination cards for Christmas and followed it up with a book on the subject.

She had never been more popular. Schoolfriends, teachers at her church school, and even her Anglican youth leader egged her on with the tarot, and she was introduced to levitation at the Girl Guides.

A friend's mother took her to a seance and a 'spirit guide' had a message that she should become a medium. She invited several spirits into herself and began to channel them, relaying their messages in different voices.

It was then that she became fearful and her language turned foul. Her parents noticed the personality change.

One spirit, Samuel, kept telling her she would only be happy when she could be with them. She was certain it was a prediction of death. 'I was terrified,' she said, and called on God, if he was there, to help her.

Amanda went to see a Christian friend in West Sussex. She was taken to a church meeting where the leader had felt impressed to speak about the dangers of the occult. He said people could be set free from its harmful effects by faith in Jesus Christ.

Amanda was convinced that every word was meant for her. She took his advice and prayed, asking Jesus to help her. As she did so, she felt a tangible sense of God's presence. It made a dramatic difference.

'By this point,' she recalls, 'I had screaming voices in my head.' The cacophony had been going on for about a week. 'It was like a riot. There was no rhyme nor reason to it. It was like a lot of people, shouting, groaning, taunting and mocking; like an appalling, dreadful, migraine.' But as she prayed that prayer, the voices finally stopped.

She continued to be aware of the presence of Samuel, her spirit guide. But since she had spurned him, his presence had become increasingly hostile

With her conversion to Christianity, Amanda now regarded the spirits that had attached themselves to her in a new light. Their evil intentions had been exposed, and, far from being the spirits of people who had died, she now looked on them as demonic.

She also viewed her own psychic powers from a different perspective. She no longer saw them as abilities that she possessed, but rather as abilities that possessed her. She believed them to stem from the actions of demonic spirits that had been manipulating and making use of a willing channel.

Samuel and the remaining occult manifestations were eventually removed by prayer. But there were other adjustments to be made.

Many of Amanda's friends had been involved in the occult. They treated Amanda's rejection of their beliefs as a rejection of themselves. 'All my friends deserted me. They couldn't cope. They'd taken a lot of security from the readings and predictions I had given them. Now I was saying those were wrong. Did that mean that the future they had been looking forward to and consoled themselves with was also wrong?'

Some time ago, when a friend had had an abortion, Amanda had channelled a spirit which said it was the spirit of her dead baby. 'The spirit called her "Mummy" and said her name was "Hilary". She described herself and said she forgave her mum for what she had done. She said she was perfectly happy in the spirit world. There were spirit children that she played with, and she was looked after by various members of the family.'

But Amanda now regarded all of that as a gross error and deception. The about-face was more than her friend could bear. 'She couldn't cope. Did it mean that all the things she'd held on to were wrong?' Other friends also felt betrayed by Amanda and ignored her. 'I was in a terrible state. I didn't know what to do.'

The period of adjustment was difficult, but in the six years that followed Amanda's conversion to Christianity, her life was gradually restored to normality. She has continued on an even keel and has held down regular, responsible, employment ever since.

Her father had been an active freemason but eventually abandoned masonry because of its occultic connections. Psychiatrist Dr Kenneth McAll believes parental freemasonry, with what he calls its 'occult indulgence', can open up whole families to an occultic influence.

Amanda has gone on to counsel a lot of people who have been involved in the occult and finds a common thread in many of their personalities. 'Many,' she says, 'are insecure, with a poor self-image and a poor perception of who they are and their place in society. Many are fearful. They have the idea that they have become involved with a power which is stronger than themselves and which is out of their control.'

She has seen other cases where obsessive behaviour has been a symptom, or root, of occult involvement. One person came forward for counselling because her life seemed to have been taken over by superstition. 'She believed that unless she went through a whole series of rituals dreadful things would befall her and her family.' She couldn't go out of the house until she touched all the walls. If she failed to do this, she was afraid she wouldn't be able to return. The deeper she went into the occult, the more fearful she became, and it was this fearfulness that prompted her to seek counselling.

For Amanda, the fire was kindled by a school project and stoked by a hungry excavation of the local library. For Mike Morris, Secretary for Social Affairs of the Evangelical Alliance, her story has a familiar ring:

Our attention was brought to the issue of the occult in children's literature by a parent whose child was turned from being well-balanced into a recluse. The child had tremendous nightmares and could not form relationships. All the parents could work out was that it was heavily influenced by occultic issues within the literature. This is the sort of impact it can have on children – a sense of fear; they can become violent or unsociable in their behaviour patterns; parents speak of a major change in their personality. It can have a traumatic effect on their home life, and sometimes children will need to talk the whole issue through long and hard and repeatedly.

Filling the void

Coming out of something as compelling and all-consuming as the occult can leave a vacuum in a person's life. Laying aside beliefs and practices may mean not only a change of thinking and lifestyle, but a change of friends. Individuals might need help and support through that difficult transitional period. New people and fresh interests could be required to fill the vacuum. For Amanda, Roger, Gary and Alex, coming out of the occult also meant a change of faith.

Without equivocation I can say that the same was true for me. As a teenager, steeped in occult literature, filled with confusion and thoughts of suicide, my life turned around when I encountered the person and the presence of Jesus Christ. It was an end to my nightmares and morbid obsessions, and my semi-permanent scowl was wiped clean. It was as though an oppressive gloom had lifted. I knew I was loved. And what followed was more than just an adolescent attachment, or port in a storm. It has held good for more than 20 years.

Whatever *your* beliefs, be they any or none, I hope the evidence of these pages will have shown you that whatever you perceive the occult to be: a spiritual reality or a subjective mind game, many sensitive teenagers have been damaged and disorientated after sounding its depths. Whether or not the occult has any objective reality, it has been all too real to *them*.

Kevin Logan writes:

For those who aren't Christians, I would simply say, you don't necessarily have to believe it is spiritual – believe it is simply psychological – but whatever, please be aware that the soft occult is causing tribulation and difficulties with young people.

It causes real problems within their personalities. It brings confusion, and they find great trouble in getting a firm grip on reality. They feel as though they're losing it and they're out of control.

If they're playing with ouija boards, tarot cards, fortune telling equipment; if they're spending most of their time looking at occult videos and reading occult books, then we must be aware as responsible parents that this is something that can damage our children.

Out of ignorance

Throughout this volume we have seen examples of children who have been innocently encouraged into the occult by their teachers. One can see why. The mystery and attraction of the supernatural offers an enticing way of engaging the imagination and unlocking creativity.

But increasingly parents have been exercising their right of conscientious objection. Some have been regarded as crackpots and a few possibly are, but teachers who have troubled to read this volume will now realize that among them are parents who have legitimate cause for concern.

As surrogate parents, teachers need to think twice about condoning or encouraging occultic activities which could have a detrimental effect on more impressionable pupils. And teachers can play a more active role by watching out for signs of disturbance, and acting as an early warning system to parents.

With its myriad of conflicting beliefs and its morbid fixation with death, divination and the spirits, the occult can never provide the answer to the one issue every adolescent strives to settle: the question 'Who am I?' All the occult can ever do is point them away from reality towards a plethora of bizarre practices and drive them deeper into their own introspective doubts and fears.

As a result many vulnerable adolescents who have plunged into this abyss have paid a high price because of their own, and our, ignorance.

As parents and teachers we are charged with the task of protecting our children. When it comes to the occult, there will always be questions left unanswered, but we can no longer claim to be ignorant about the risks.

Appendix I

Religion and the Supernatural Today Survey

A survey of schoolchildren's attitudes towards religion and the supernatural has been specially commissioned for this book. The survey covers 509 year-ten pupils from five state secondary schools in England and Northern Ireland.

The following questionnaire was drawn up and carried out in conjunction with Professor Dr Leslie Francis, Mansel Jones Fellow of Trinity College, Carmarthen. Dr Francis is an acknowledged expert in the field and has conducted many similar surveys.

Religion and the Supernatural Today

This survey has been designed by Andrew Boyd, an author, and by Dr Leslie Francis, a specialist in surveys about religion. We would value your help in telling us what young people today *really* think about religion and the supernatural. Please answer all the questions honestly. You do not have to put your name on any of the pages, so you can be sure that all your answers can be given in total confidence. Findings from the survey will be published in a book. Thank you for your help.

PART ONE

Please circle the number against the answer that applies to you.

Is your school a church school?	No.	1
	Yes. Roman Catholic	2
	Yes. Church of England	3
	Yes. Protestant	4

| Is your school | Paid for by the State | 1 |
| | Independent/fee paying | 2 |

Is your school in	England	1
	Northern Ireland	2
	Scotland	3
	Wales	4
	Other, please specify	5

In which county, or county borough do you live? _____

| Which sex are you? | Male | 1 |
| | Female | (2) |

How old are you? _____ years

Do you live in a	City	1
	Suburb	2
	Town	(3)
	Village	4

Have you been baptized/Christened?	Yes	(1)
	No	2
	Don't know	3

Do you belong to a religious group?

No	1	Roman Catholic	9
Baptist	(2)	Salvation Army	10
C of E/Anglican	3	Buddhist	11
Church of Ireland	4	Hindu	12
Church of Scotland	5	Jew	13
Church in Wales	6	Muslim	14
Methodist	7	Sikh	15
Presbyterian/URC	8	Other (specify below)	16

Do you go to church on a Sunday	Nearly every week	4
(or other place of worship)?	At least once a month	3
	Occasionally	(2)
	Never	1

Do you read the Bible by yourself?	Nearly every day	(5)
	At least once a week	4
	At least once a month	3
	Occasionally	2
	Never	1

Do you pray by yourself?	Nearly every day	(5)
	At least once a week	4
	At least once a month	3
	Occasionally	2
	Never	1

Please answer the following question by putting a circle around the 'YES' or the 'NO'.

Have you been to a church	Wedding/Christening	YES	(NO)
within the last year for	Baptism	YES	(NO)
any of these services?	Funeral	YES	(NO)
	Christmas/Carol Service	YES	(NO)
	Harvest Festival Service	YES	(NO)

Please tick the box in the first column for your mother and the box in the second column for your father.

		Mother	Father
Have your PARENTS been to a church within the last year for any of these services?	Wedding/Christening		
	Baptism		
	Funeral		
	Christmas/Carol Service		
	Harvest Festival Service		

		Mother	Father
How often do your parents go to church?	At least once a week		
	At least once a month		
	Occasionally		
	Never		

PART TWO

Please answer each question by putting a circle around YES or NO

Have you ever broken any rules at school?	(YES) NO
Would you like other children to be afraid of you?	YES NO
Are you rather lively?	YES NO
Would you enjoy cutting up animals in science class?	YES NO
Did you ever take anything (even a pin or a button) that belonged to someone else?	YES NO
Do you ever feel 'just miserable' for no good reason?	YES NO
Do you often feel life is very dull?	YES NO
Do you always finish your homework before you relax?	YES NO
Can you get a party going?	YES NO
Are you easily hurt when people find things wrong with you or the work you do?	YES NO
Do you always say sorry when you have been rude?	YES NO
Do you rather enjoy teasing other children?	YES NO
Are you in more trouble at school than most children?	YES NO
Are your feelings rather easily hurt?	YES NO
Do you like playing pranks on others?	YES NO
Would you rather sit and watch than dance at parties?	YES NO
Do you often feel 'fed up'?	YES NO
At prayers or assembly, do you always sing while the others are singing?	(YES) NO
Can you let yourself go and enjoy yourself a lot at a lively party?	YES NO
Do you sometimes feel life is just not worth living?	YES NO
Did you ever write or scribble in a school or library book?	YES NO
Do other people think of you as being very lively?	YES NO
Are you always very careful with other people's things?	YES NO
Would you call yourself happy-go-lucky?	YES NO

PART THREE

Please circle the number against the number that applies to you.

Do you read your horoscope?	Nearly every day	5
	At least once a week	4
	At least once a month	3
	Occasionally	2
	Never	(1)

Do you watch films about the occult (like The Exorcist; The Omen; Poltergeist, etc.?	At least once a week	4
	At least once a month	3
	Occasionally	2
	Never	(1)

Do you watch video nasties?	At least once a week	4
	At least once a month	3
	Occasionally	2
	Never	(1)

Do you use a ouija board?	At least once a week	4
	At least once a month	3
	Occasionally	2
	Never	(1)

Do you read books about the occult?	At least once a week	4
	At least once a month	3
	Occasionally	2
	Never	(1)

Do you use tarot cards?	At least once a week	4
	At least once a month	3
	Occasionally	2
	Never	(1)

Do you use other fortune-telling items?	At least once a week	4
	At least once a month	3
	Occasionally	2
	Never	(1)

Do you play Dungeons and Dragons or similar fantasy role-playing games?	At least once a week	4
	At least once a month	3
	Occasionally	2
	Never	(1)

Do you listen to Heavy Metal music?	Every day	5
	At least once a week	4
	At least once a month	3
	Occasionally	2
	Never	(1)

PART FOUR

Please read the sentence carefully and think, 'Do I agree with it?'

If you <u>Agree Strongly</u>, put a ring round ...... (AS)   A   NC   D   DS
If you <u>Agree</u>, put a ring round .... AS   (A)   NC   D   DS
If you are <u>Not Certain,</u> put a ring round ..... AS   A   (NC)   D   DS
If you <u>Disagree</u>, put a ring round................ AS   A   NC   (D)   DS
If you <u>Disagree Strongly</u>, put a ring round .. AS   A   NC   D   (DS)

I find it boring to listen to the Bible .... AS   A   NC   D   (DS)
I know that Jesus helps me .... (AS)   A   NC   D   DS
Saying my prayers helps me a lot .... (AS)   A   NC   D   DS
The Church is very important to me .... AS   (A)   NC   D   DS
I think going to church is a waste of time .... AS   A   NC   D   (DS)
I want to love Jesus .... (AS)   A   NC   D   DS
I think church services are boring .... AS   A   NC   D   (DS)
I think people who pray are stupid .... AS   A   NC   D   (DS)
God helps me to lead a better life................ (AS)   A   NC   D   DS
I like to learn about God very much .... (AS)   A   NC   D   DS
God means a lot to me .... (AS)   A   NC   D   DS
I believe that God helps people................... (AS)   A   NC   D   DS
Prayer helps me a lot .... (AS)   A   NC   D   DS
I know that Jesus is very close to me .... (AS)   A   NC   D   DS
I think praying is a good thing.................... (AS)   A   NC   D   (DS)
I think the Bible is out of date.................... AS   A   NC   D   DS
I believe that God listens to prayers .... (AS)   A   NC   D   DS
Jesus doesn't mean anything to me .... AS   A   NC   D   (DS)
God is very real to me .... (AS)   A   NC   D   DS
I think saying prayers does no good............. AS   A   NC   D   (DS)
The idea of God means much to me............. (AS)   A   NC   D   DS
I believe that Jesus still helps people .... (AS)   A   NC   D   DS
I know that God helps me .... (AS)   A   NC   D   DS
I find it hard to believe in God.................... AS   A   NC   D   (DS)
I believe in Satan.. (AS)   A   NC   D   DS
I believe in black magic .... (AS)   A   NC   D   DS
I believe it is possible to
contact spirits of the dead .... (AS)   A   NC   D   DS
I believe in ghosts....................................... AS   A   NC   D   (DS)
I believe in my horoscope .... AS   A   NC   D   (DS)
I believe fortune tellers
can tell the future .... AS   A   NC   D   DS
Any kind of witchcraft is wrong................. (AS)   A   NC   D   DS

Witchcraft can be helpful
providing it hurts no-one .... AS   A   NC   D   (DS)
Satan is God's enemy .... (AS)   A   NC   D   DS
I like Heavy Metal music............................ AS   A   NC   D   (DS)
Heavy Metal music makes me feel good ..... AS   A   NC   D   (DS)
Heavy Metal music is depressing................. (AS)   A   NC   D   DS
Dabbling in the occult is harmful .... (AS)   A   NC   D   DS
God is a real person or being...................... (AS)   A   NC   D   DS
God is a universal force.............................. AS   A   NC   D   (DS)
God is in everything .... AS   A   NC   D   (DS)
I believe in magic .... (AS)   A   NC   D   DS
All religions lead to the same God .... AS   A   NC   D   (DS)
It doesn't matter which religion you
follow, as long as you are sincere .... AS   A   NC   D   (DS)
I believe in reincarnation – when we
die we come back as another person............ AS   A   NC   D   (DS)
Sometimes I get impatient to see what
will happen in the afterlife.......................... AS   A   NC   D   (DS)
I believe it is wrong to use a ouija
board to try to contact spirits .... (AS)   A   NC   D   DS
I believe that God will judge each
of us when we die....................................... (AS)   A   NC   D   DS
I believe that Jesus was just
a good man.. AS   A   NC   D   (DS)
I believe that satanism is just as good
as any other religion.................................. AS   A   NC   D   (DS)
I believe that Jesus was another
prophet like Mohammed .... AS   A   NC   D   (DS)
Religion is only for weak people.................. AS   A   NC   D   (DS)
I believe that white magic is just as
harmful as black magic .... (AS)   A   NC   D   DS
I believe that Jesus Christ is
alive today... (AS)   A   NC   D   DS
I believe trying to tell the future
could be harmful.. (AS)   A   NC   D   DS
No-one has the right to tell me
what is morally right and wrong .... AS   A   NC   D   (DS)
I believe everyone has psychic powers
that can be developed................................. AS   A   NC   D   (DS)
I believe it can be harmful to try to
develop psychic powers.............................. (AS)   A   NC   D   DS
My parents have the right to tell me
what is morally right and wrong .... (AS)   A   NC   D   DS

The Bible can show me what is morally right and wrong	(AS) A	NC	D	DS
I am fascinated by the supernatural	AS A	NC	D	(DS)
There is nothing wrong with watching video nasties	AS A	NC	D	(DS)
I believe people must ask Jesus to come into their lives to become a real Christian	(AS) A	NC	D	DS
I believe a person is a Christian because he or she lives in a Christian country	AS A	NC	D	(DS)
I believe a person is a Christian if he or she was baptized as a baby	AS A	NC	D	(DS)

Thank you!

Appendix II
Analysis of key data

The questionnaire was filled in by pupils from non-denominational schools who typically described themselves as having no denominational affiliations. Fewer than 5% regarded themselves as adherents of a non-Christian religion. Their average age was 14 to 15.

Parts of the survey asked pupils whether they agreed, disagreed with or were undecided about certain statements, such as 'I believe in God'. Opinions were usually divided, and it is the prevailing view that has been highlighted below.

For the sake of clarity and accessibility relevant information is presented here in lay terms and percentages have been rounded up or down to the nearest percentage point.

Religious belief

God

47% found it hard to believe in God. Only 18% thought he was a real person or being. 24% were inclined to regard him as a universal force. Most were uncertain who, or what, God was, and were unsure about whether God would judge them when they died.

Only 1 in 11 children agreed strongly that God was very real to them, while the weight of opinion was split almost evenly between those who considered him to be unreal or were undecided.

Only 7% agreed strongly with the statement: 'God helps me to lead a better life.' 43% disagreed or disagreed strongly.

There was a general uncertainty about the value of prayer. 52% said they never prayed by themselves, though most conceded prayer might have some benefit. Only 37% believed that God actually listened to prayer.

69% never read the Bible, and most were undecided about whether or not the Scriptures were out of date.

Jesus

Jesus fared a little better than God. 43% said he meant something to them, while only 27% said he meant nothing. But almost a third were unsure exactly *what* Jesus did mean. 38% thought he was just a good man and 59% couldn't be certain whether he was a prophet like Mohammed. Most were undecided about whether Jesus still helps people.

45% disagreed with the statement: 'Jesus Christ is alive today'. Only 16% thought he was, while a slightly higher (and perhaps contradictory) 22% believed they had to ask Jesus into their lives to become a real Christian.

Religion

The notion that someone was a Christian simply because he or she lived in a Christian country was firmly rejected by 67% . Only one in six believed that a person was a Christian if he was baptized as a baby, although 62% had themselves undergone baptism.

60% regarded themselves as belonging to no denomination, and 66% said they never went to church – not even at Christmas. The next highest category (22%) went only occasionally. 59% thought church services were boring.

As far as their parents were concerned, 60% said their mothers never went to church and the same was true of 70% of their fathers.

43% agreed that it didn't matter which religion you followed, as long as you were sincere. 38% had yet to make up their minds on that question, while only 18% disagreed.

Yet a contradictory 25% thought all religions led to the same God, against 31% who disagreed with that notion. Most had no firm view on it.

More children believed in reincarnation than disbelieved in it (35% versus 25%), but 40% were undecided.

Personal morality

There was confusion over the issue of moral authority.

53% said no one had the right to tell them what was morally right or wrong, and 27% said that also went for their parents. While 57% thought on reflection that their parents *did* have the right to make pronouncements over personal morality. Only one in five thought the Bible could offer moral guidance.

94% admitted to having broken school rules. 77% owned up to having taken something which belonged to someone else. 14% said they would like other children to be afraid of them.

Outlook on life

45% said they sometimes felt life was not worth living. 73% sometimes felt 'just miserable' for no good reason. 72% *often* felt fed up, and 68% admitted to *often* feeling that life was very dull. 36% agreed they sometimes got impatient to see what would happen in the afterlife.

The occult

42% admitted to being fascinated by the supernatural.

Dabbling in the occult is harmful: A hefty majority weren't sure about that, and many were cautious, but about one in six seemed to think the occult could be beneficial. The breakdown was as follows:

Dabbling in the occult is harmful:
Disagree strongly	6%
Disagree	9%
Not certain	46%
Agree	17%
Agree strongly	20%

Ouija board: More than a fifth of the pupils asked said they had used the ouija board – 1 in 50 said they did so on a regular basis. But the overwhelming majority had never touched it:

Do you use the ouija board?
Never	79%
Occasionally	19%
Monthly	1%
Weekly	1%

More than a quarter could see nothing wrong in using a ouija board:

Is it wrong to use a ouija board to try to contact spirits?
Disagree strongly	11%

Disagree	17%
Not certain	27%
Agree	24%
Agree strongly	21%

Horoscopes: A majority of children said they read their horoscope daily, and a narrow majority said they actually believed in them. Only 11% said they never read their stars:

Do you read your horoscope?

Never	11%
Occasionally	28%
Monthly	4%
Weekly	25%
Daily	31%

I believe in my horoscope:

Disagree strongly	15%
Disagree	13%
Not certain	34%
Agree	23%
Agree strongly	15%

Tarot Cards: 90% said they never used them, but 8% said they used them occasionally, and a further 2% said they consulted the tarot on a weekly or daily basis.

Fortune telling: Most were sceptical about the ability of fortune tellers to look into the future, but 23% – almost one in four – believed they could. A majority of children said they never used fortune-telling items, but almost one in seven said they used them occasionally:

Do you use fortune-telling items? (Other than the tarot):

Never	81%
Occasionally	14%
Monthly	2%
Weekly	3%

36% thought trying to tell the future could be harmful. An equal proportion was undecided. The remaining 28% seemed to think fortune telling could be beneficial.

Psychic powers: 29% of young teenagers thought they and others possessed psychic powers. Only a quarter could see any possible danger in trying to develop them.

Spirit contact: Most believed it was possible to contact spirits.

I believe it is possible to contact spirits of the dead:
Disagree strongly	18%
Disagree	12%
Not certain	28%
Agree	27%
Agree strongly	14%

Ghosts: 51% believed in ghosts; 26% were uncertain, while only 22% were sceptical.

Magic: There were mixed views about magic. 28% believed in it while the rest were unsure or inclined to be sceptical. When it came to black magic, 21% were believers, 51% were not, and the rest were uncertain. 64% had no firm view about the statement: white magic is just as harmful as black.

Witchcraft: More than a quarter saw nothing wrong with witchcraft, and most thought it could be helpful, providing it didn't hurt anyone.

Any kind of witchcraft is wrong:
Disagree strongly	10%
Disagree	17%
Not certain	38%
Agree	16%
Agree strongly	19%

Witchcraft can be helpful providing it hurts no one:
Disagree strongly	14%
Disagree	12%
Not certain	31%
Agree	32%
Agree strongly	10%

Satan: Half didn't believe in Satan and 28% had yet to make up their minds. Only 8.5% strongly agreed that they did believe in Satan. Half thought he was God's enemy. 41% weren't sure. One in seven thought satanism was just as good as any other religion, though most disagreed with that.

Occult culture

Dungeons and Dragons: 36% played Dungeons and Dragons or similar.

Do you play Dungeons and Dragons or similar fantasy role-play games?

Never	63%
Occasionally	26%
Monthly	4%
Weekly	6%

Heavy Metal Music: Opinions were divided on heavy metal. Most weren't fans or said they only listened occasionally. But more than a third were into it, and one in eight said they listened on a daily basis:

Do you listen to heavy metal music?:

Never	39%
Occasionally	38%
Monthly	2%
Weekly	9%
Daily	13%

57% disagreed with the statement that heavy metal music made them feel good, and a third went so far as to call it depressing.

Occult books and movies: 44% said they read books about the occult, while twice that figure watched occult movies. Almost one in seven said they did so every day.

Video nasties: 87% claimed to have watched video nasties – one third said they did so on a regular basis. And 71% believed there was nothing wrong with watching them. Only 12% said they had never seen one. (See commentary below.)

Commentary

The survey confirms that teenagers have little time for what they would regard as moral high-handedness. Rebellious teens live up to their image, with more than a quarter denying parental authority and more than half reluctant to acknowledge that anyone has the right to adjudicate over what is right and wrong.

In a post-Christian society, traditional Christian belief seems to have been relegated to a residual role among the young. In this at least, young people appear to be taking their cue from their parents and abandoning the Church, which is regarded as boring and unimportant.

God and Christ are still notionally present, but who they are and what they might mean have become hazy. Fewer than one in four regard God as 'very real to me', and fewer than one in six agree with the central Christian doctrine of the resurrection: that Jesus Christ is alive today.

Openness towards the view that God is a universal force, rather than a personal Creator, and the inclination to believe in reincarnation could indicate a drift from traditional Christian teaching towards Eastern beliefs and New Age philosophy.

Fewer than a third held to the Judaeo/Christian doctrine that God will judge each of us when we die. 44% were undecided. This central Christian belief, expressed in Hebrews 9:27, stands in stark contradiction to the doctrine of reincarnation: 'Man is destined once to die, and after that to face judgement.'

With teenage suicide rates continuing to rise, there could be cause for concern here. A deeply depressed adolescent is likely to agree with the substantial minority in the survey who find life sometimes not worth living. If he also happens to be one of the 35% who believe in reincarnation, and one of the 36% who express occasional impatience to experience the afterlife, then the notion of cutting his losses and starting over could hold a fatal attraction. Reincarnation could be used as a justification for suicide.

When it came to dabbling in the occult, 37% of youngsters expressed reservations about its safety, but almost half were unaware of its inherent dangers. And many more seemed to be in ignorance that astrology, which is endemic among the young, is, in fact, an occult art.

While only one in five turns to the Bible for guidance, and almost a third deny any parental authority, 88% of 14- to 15-year-olds seek advice from their stars. Almost a third read their horoscopes daily and an even higher percentage say they believe what they read.

Astrology is by far the most popular means of divination among the young, though one in five uses other fortune-telling devices, and one in ten consults the tarot cards.

An alarming number showed a willingness to use the ouija board. Most thought it was possible to contact the spirits of the dead and more than a quarter saw no problem in using ouija to do so. 21% said they had actually tried it.

Young people expressed a tolerance towards the practice of witch-craft and have succumbed to the occultist's view that magic itself is morally neutral. Most young people drew no moral distinction between black and white magic and 42% were in favour of witch-craft, providing it was not used to hurt anyone, though half expressed their reservations about satanism.

This willingness by the young to accept or embrace occult prac-tices is unsurprising, given their acknowledgement of the role played in their lives by the culture of occultism.

Fantasy role-play games like *Dungeons and Dragons* have captured a wide constituency. More than one in three have played them, and 6% took part on a weekly basis.

One in eight took a daily fix of heavy metal music, although a third of young people found it depressing.

88% watched occult movies and almost half read occult books. An astonishing 87% also claimed to have watched video nasties, and most saw no problem in doing so. This could be bravado, or might be explained by the fact that the questionnaire offered no official definition for the video nasty, so respondents were guided by their own understanding. The only sound conclusion we can draw is that most young people have a macho attitude to video violence and say they've watched movies which they personally regard as being particularly horrific or unpleasant.

Conclusion

What we can safely conclude is that the issues raised in this book concern much more than a hidden minority. There is widespread acceptance of the occult and occult practices among the young.

In the business of entertainment, occultism is a major earner, and what emerges is a picture of the teen consumer as easy prey. Young people are soft targets for a burgeoning commercial occultism, which seems reckless to the potential for emotional or psychological damage among those who consume its wares.

Out of a thousand year-ten pupils 210 are likely to have used the ouija board to contact spirits of the dead, 880 will seek – and 380 will believe – the advice of their stars, while 270 will go on to consult occult tools of divination for more explicit guidance about their future.

Most sound-minded, well-balanced and secure young people will hopefully shrug the whole thing off. But some may not. And what about the others: the sensitive, the disturbed and the vulnerable?

One occultist has likened his practice to handling volatile chemicals. No one in his right mind would let untrained children loose in a laboratory. Dare we sit back and watch while this unplanned, unsupervised and altogether dangerous experiment into the occult unfolds?

Further material

Between Christ and Satan, Kurt Koch, Evangelization Publishers, 1970.
Blasphemous Rumours: Is Satanic Ritual Abuse Fact or Fantasy?, Andrew Boyd, HarperCollins, 1991.
Chasing Satan, Dianne Core, Gunter Books, 1991.
Children at Risk, David Porter, Kingsway, 1987.
Children for the Devil, Tim Tate, Methuen, 1991.
Close Encounters with the New Age, Kevin Logan, Kingsway, 1991.
Dancing with the Devil, TVF, Channel 4, 1991, reporter Steven Wells.
Dawning of the Pagan Moon, David Burnett, MARC, 1991.
Deliverance Means Love, Audrey Harper, Kingsway, 1992.
Devil Worship, The Rise of Satanism, Jeremiah Films Inc., P.O. Box 1710, Hemet, California 92343.
Doorways to Danger, video, CRO.
Gods of the New Age, Caryl Matrisciana, Marshall Pickering, 1990.
James Randi, Psychic Investigator, Boxtree, 1991.
Madame Blavatsky's Baboon, Peter Washington, Secker, 1993.
Paganism and the Occult, Kevin Logan, Kingsway, 1988.
Playing with Fire, Weldon and Bjornstad, Moody Press, 1984.
Satanism and the Occult, Kevin Logan, Kingsway, 1994.
Satan's Snare, Peter Anderson, Evangelical Press, 1988.
The Devil's Alphabet, Dr Kurt Koch, Marshall, Morgan and Scott (now Marshall Pickering).
The Devil's Web, Pat Pulling, Word, 1990.
The Early Window: Effects of Television on Children and Youth, Liebert and Sprafkin, Pergamon Press, 1988.
The Hidden Dangers of the Rainbow, Constance Cumbey, Huntingon House, 1983.
The New Age and You, Roger Ellis and Andrea Clarke, Kingsway, 1992.
The New Age Cult, Walter Martin, Bethany House, 1989.
The Occult, Russ Parker, IVP, 1989.
The Occult and Young People, Roger Ellis, Kingsway, 1989.
Understanding Alternative Medicine, Roy Livesey, Life Changing Books, 1985.
Video Violence and Children (Report of the British Parliamentary Inquiry), Barlow and Hill (Eds.), St Martin's Press, 1985.
Web of Darkness, Sean Sellers, Victory House Inc., 1990.
What is the New Age?, Michael Cole, Jim Graham, Tony Higton, David Lewis, Hodder & Stoughton, 1990.
What your Horoscope Doesn't Tell You, Charles Strohmer, Word, 1988.
When the Devil Dares Your Kids, Bob and Gretchen Passantino, Eagle, 1991.

Notes

Introduction
1. Russ Parker, *The Occult* (IVP, 1989), p. 19.
2. Canon Dominic Walker, Co-Chair of the Christian Deliverance Study Group.
3. Survey by Surrey University for *Is Anybody There?* (Channel 4, 31st Oct. 1987), quoted in Kevin Logan, *Paganism and the Occult*, Kingsway, 1988, p. 7.
4. Logan, *op. cit.*, p. 164.
5. 'Mysticism goes mainstream', *American Health* (Jan.–Feb. 1987), quoted in John Ankerberg, *The Facts on the Occult* (Harvest House, 1991), p. 8.
6. Ellis & Clarke, eds., *New Age and You*, Kingsway, 1992, p. 26.
7. Logan, *op. cit.*, p. 37. Survey in 1987.
8. CWN Series, quoted in *International Daily News Bulletin* No. 184, Feb.–Mar. 1991.
9. Bill Keahon, head of Suffolk County Major Offense Bureau, interviewed in *New York Times*, quoted in *Police*, Feb. 1987.
10. *Geraldo Rivera Specials*.
11. Rachel Storm, 'The black magic games that turn into terror', *The Independent*, 17th Oct. 1988.

Chapter 1: Through a glass darkly
1. 'Occult', *Encyclopaedia Britannica*, Micropaedia, Vol. 7, p. 469.
2. Dr Ron Enroth, quoted in Ankerberg & Weldon, *The Facts on the Occult* (Harvest House, 1991), p. 10.
3. Both quoted in 'Superpowers?', *Equinox* (Channel 4, 6th Oct. 1991).
4. Dr Kurt Koch, cited *The Devil's Alphabet* (Marshall, Morgan & Scott), p. 121.
5. Quoted in Jerry Johnson, *The Edge of Evil* (Word, 1989).
6. *The Times*, 25th May 1989, reviewing Tanya Luhrmann, *Persuasions of the Witch's Craft* (Blackwell, 1989).
7. Peter Brookesmith, ed., *The Occult Connection* (Black Cat, 1984), p. 6.
8. Dr Susan Blackmore, Bristol University, addressing the British Parapsychological Association, quoted in Kevin Logan, *Paganism and the Occult* (Kingsway, 1988), p. 163.
9. Dr Roger Moss, consultant psychiatrist, quoted in *Doorways to Danger* (Evangelical Alliance, 1987).
10. *Ibid.*
11. Mar. 1974, quoted in Kenneth McAll, *Healing the Family Tree* (Sheldon Press, 1990).
12. 10th Nov. 1989.

13. High Priestess of Dianic Witchcraft, *Kilroy* (20th May 1988).
14. David Austen, UK representative of the Temple of Set, *Newsline* (Sky TV, 15th Oct. 1990).
15. *Evening Mail*, 20th May 1988.

Chapter 2: In the stars
 1. Kurt Koch, *Between Christ and Satan* (Evangelization Publishers, Germany, 1970).
 2. *The Daily Telegraph*, 25th Jul. 1988.
 3. James Randi, *Psychic Investigator* (Boxtree, 1991), pp. 126, 141.
 4. Peter Anderson, *Satan's Snare* (Evangelical Press, 1988), p. 41.
 5. *When the Devil Dares Your Kids* (Eagle, 1991).
 6. Kurt Koch, *The Occult and Christian Counselling*, p. 95.
 7. Audrey Harper, *Deliverance Means Love* (Kingsway, 1992), pp. 46f.
 8. *Doorways to Danger* video (Evangelical Alliance).

Chapter 3: On the cards
 1. *The Independent*, 14th Jun. 1990.
 2. Brian Innes, *The Occult Connection* (Black Cat, 1984); Wade Baskin, *Satanism* (Citadel Press, 1972).
 3. *Daily Express*, 24th Jan. 1986.

Chapter 4: Spirit of the glass
 1. Ingrid Millar, Mike Ridley & Kim Bartlett, 'Ouija board spelled out terror for sad Sinead', *The Sun*, 13th Dec. 1990.
 2. Kevin Logan, *Paganism and the Occult* (Kingsway, 1988), p. 128.
 3. Edmund C. Gruss, *The Ouija Board* (Moody Press, 1986).
 4. Logan, *op. cit.*
 6. Survey by Rev Peter Anderson cited in Tom Walker, *The Occult Web* (UCCF, 1987).
 7. *But Deliver Us From Evil* (Darton, Longman & Todd, 1974), p. 62, cited in Russ Parker, *The Occult* (IVP, 1989), p. 58.
 8. Logan, *op. cit.*, p. 130.
 9. *Satanism in America* (National Criminal Justice Task force on Occult Related Ritualistic Crimes), p. 15.
10. They were published in his book, *On the Threshold of the Unseen* (Dutton, 1918), cited in Gruss, *op. cit.*, p. 12.
11. Michael Perry, ed., *Deliverance* (SPCK, 1987), p. 49.
12. *Ibid.*, p. 45, 50.
13. *The Sun*, 13th Dec. 1990.
14. Kurt Koch, *Between Christ and Satan* (Evangelization Publishers, 1970).
15. Dr Stuart Checkley, *Doorways to Danger* (Evangelical Alliance, 1987).
16. *Man, Myth and Magic*, no. 73, p. 2060f, cited in McDowell & Stewart, *Understanding the Occult* (Here's Life, 1989).
17. *Proceedings of the American Society for Psychical Research*, p. 394, cited in McDowell & Stewart, *op. cit.*
18. 27th Dec. 1933, cited in Gruss, *op. cit.*
19. Paul Sann, *Fads, Follies and Delusions of the American People* (Crown, 1967), p. 143, cited in Gruss, *op. cit.*, p. 18.

20. *The Daily Telegraph*, 23rd & 25th Jul. 1988.
21. *Daily Mail*, 11th Sep. 1986.
22. Tyne Tees TV, cited in Logan, *op. cit.*, p. 131.
23. Shan, Clan Mother of the House of the Goddess, appearing on *Newsline* (Sky TV), 31st Oct. 1990.
24. *Barnsley Chronicle*, 1st June 1990.
25. Korem & Meier, *The Fakers* (Baker Book House, 1989), pp. 70–71, cited in McDowell & Stewart, *op. cit.*
26. Parker, *op. cit.*, p. 14.
27. *New York Times*, 26th & 28th Oct. 1979, cited in Gruss, *op. cit.*
28. Checkley, *op. cit.*
29. *Sunday Mirror*, 20th Aug. 1989.
30. *Daily Star*, 30th Nov. 1990.
31. Audrey Harper, *Deliverance Means Love* (Kingsway, 1992), pp. 43–44.
32. *Ibid.*, p. 45.
33. *The Sun*, 18th Feb. 1991.
34. *Idea* (Evangelical Alliance), Mar.–Apr. 1989.
35. *Newsline* (Sky TV), 31st Oct. 1994.
36. June, aged 16, *The Sun*, 13th Dec. 1990.
37. *The Woodspring Evening Post*, 5th Feb. 1990.
38. Laurie Mansbridge, 'Satanism', *Bella* magazine.

Chapter 5: Beyond the veil

1. *Sutton Coldfield Observer*, 27th Jan. 1989.
2. Michael Perry, ed., *Deliverance* (SPCK, 1987), p. 46.
3. Hilary Abramson, 'Altered States', *The Sacramento Bee Magazine*, 25th Oct. 1987.
4. Cole, Graham, Higton & Lewish, *What is the New Age?* (Hodder & Stoughton, 1990), p. 113.
5. *Ibid.*, p. 116.
6. Kurt Koch, *Between Christ and Satan* (Evangelization Publishers, 1970), p. 129.
7. Ralph Gasson, *The Challenging Counterfeit* (Logos International, 1966), p. 45, cited in Russ Parker, *The Occult* (IVP, 1989), p. 60.
8. Jess Stearn, *Adventures into the Psychic* (Signet, 1982), p. 163, cited in Ankerberg & Weldon, *The Facts on the Occult* (Harvest House, 1991), p. 12.
9. *Christianity Today*, 15th Dec. 1978, cited in Ankerberg & Weldon, *op. cit.*, p. 34.
10. Samuel M. Warren, ed., *A Compendium of the Theological Writings of Emmanuel Swedenborg* (Swedenborg Foundation, 1977), p. 618, cited in Ankerberg & Weldon, *op. cit.*, p. 18.
11. From a booklet distributed by the NSAC, cited in Edmund C. Gruss, *Cults and the Occult* (Baker Book House, 1974), pp. 57f., quoted in McDowell & Stewart, *Understanding the Occult* (Here's Life, 1989).
12. Michael Perry, ed., *Deliverance* (SPCK, 1987), chap. 8.
13. Kenneth McAll, *Healing the Family Tree* (Sheldon, 1990), p. 72f.
14. Erika Bourguinon, *Religion Altered States of Consciousness and Social Change* (Ohio State University Press, 1973), cited in Ankerberg & Weldon,

op. cit., p. 29.

15. McDowell & Stewart, *op. cit.*, p. 166.
16. Peter Andersen, *Satan's Snare* (Evangelical Press, 1988), p. 24.
17. *Doorway to Danger* video (Evangelical Alliance).
18. *Doorways to Danger* (Evangelical Alliance, 1987).
19. Maureen Cornish, 'Ex-witch warns of occult threat', *The Sutton Coldfield Observer*, 27th Jan. 1989.
20. Andersen, *op. cit.*, p. 23.

Chapter 6: Alternative realities

1. Rudin & Rudin, *New Age: New Dark Age* (International Cult Education Program).
2. Ellis & Clarke, *The New Age and You* (Kingsway, 1992), p. 8.
3. David Spangler, *Reflections on the Christ* (Findhorn Founda-tion, 1978).
4. *Satanism in America* (National Criminal Justice Task Force).
5. *San Francisco Examiner*, 8th Dec. 1977, cited in Cole, Graham, Higton & Lewis, *What is the New Age?* (Hodder & Stoughton, 1990).
6. *The Spiritual Community Guide* (The Spiritual Community, 1972), p. 25, cited in Constance Cumbey, *Hidden Dangers of the Rainbow* (Huntingdom House, 1983), p. 60.
7. Harold J. Berry, *Transcendental Meditation* (1988).
8. Maharishi Mahesh Yogi, *The Meditations of the Maharishi*, pp. 17f., cited in Peter Anderson, *Satan's Snare* (Evangelical Press, 1988), p. 58.
9. Kevin Logan, *Paganism and the Occult* (Kingsway, 1988), pp. 137f.
10. *Ibid.*, p. 58
11. *Ibid.*, p. 139.
12. *Doorways to Danger* video (Evangelical Alliance).
13. A letter from a concerned carer.
14. Rachel Storm, 'The black magic games that turned into terror', *The Independent*, 17th Oct. 1988.
15. Dick Sutphen, 'Everyday Brainwashing', ORCRO magazine, Sep. 1990.

Chapter 7: Teenage dabblers

1. *Devil Worship: the rise of satanism* (Jeremiah Films, 1989).
2. *Ibid*.
3. Wiliam H. Swatos Jr., 'Adolescent Satanism: A Research Note on Exploratory Survey Data, *Sociological Analysis: A Journal in the Sociology of Religion*, vol. 34, no. 2, Dec. 1992.
4. 'Satanists classified by police', *Kansas City Times*, 26th Mar. 1988.
5. Audrey Harper, *Deliverance Means Love* (Kingsway, 1992), pp. 27f.
6. *The Examiner*, 10th Oct. 1989.
7. *Devil Worship: the rise of satanism* (Jeremiah Films, 1989).
8. Anton LaVey, *The Satanic Bible* (Avon Books, 1969).
9. *Ibid.*, p. 70.
10. Bureau of Criminal Investigation, Missing Persons Unit, vol. 3, no. 3.
11. Schwarz & Empey, *Satanism* (Zondervan, 1988).
12. Jerry Johnston, *The Edge of Evil* (Word, 1989), p. 158.
13. *The Western Daily Press*, 18th May 1989.
14. *Devil Worship: the rise of satanism* (Jeremiah Films, 1989).

15. *Ibid.*
16. Independent Radio News, 8th Jan. 1994.
17. *Fortean Times* 66.
18. *Edinburgh Evening News*, 5th Aug. 1992.
19. *The Woodspring Evening Post*, 5th Feb. 1990; *The Daily Mail*, 6th Feb. 1990.
20. *Devil Worship: the rise of satanism* (Jeremiah Films, 1989).
21. *Watch-Alert Newsletter*, 2nd Mar. 1990.
22. *Satanism in America* (National Criminal Justice Task Force), p. 19.
23. *Ibid.*
24. *Exposing Satan's Underground* (Geraldo Rivera Specials).
25. *The People*, 30th Oct. 1988.
26. *Exposing Satan's Underground* (Geraldo Rivera Specials).
27. *Satanism in America* (National Criminal Justice Task Force).
28. *Ibid.*, p. 37.
29. *Campus Life* 90.
30. *Exposing Satan's Underground* (Geraldo Rivera Specials).
31. *Satanism in America* (National Criminal Justice Task Force).
32. *Tampa Tribune*, 17th Feb. 1989; John Charles Cooper, *The Black Mask: Satanism in America Today* (Old Tappan, 1990), pp. 11–12.
33. *Alberquerque Journal*, 22nd Apr. 1986.
34. *Cult Awareness News*, Oct. 1989.
35. *Kansas City Times*, 26th Mar. 1988.
36. *Huston Chronicle*, 11th Sep. 1985; Jerry Johnston, *op. cit.*, p. 54.
37. *Florida Times-Union*, 10th Jun. 1988, cited in Pat Pulling, *The Devil's Web* (Huntingdon House, 1989), and Jerry Johnston, *op. cit.*, p. 13.
38. *Penthouse* magazine, USA, Jan. 1986.
39. Both from Steve Eddy, 'Crimes Rooted in Devil Worship Rising in the County', *The Orange County Register*, 28th Feb. 1988, cited in Bob and Gretchen Passantino, *When the Devil Dares Your Kids* (Eagle, 1991), p. 158.
40. *Salt Lake City Desert News*, 8th May 1986, cited in Jerry Johnston, *op. cit.*, p. 64.
41. Pat Pulling, *op. cit.*, pp. 45, 53.
42. *The Montgomery Journal*, 16th Nov. 1988; *Delaware News*, Apr. 1989.
43. *The Arizona Republic*, 27th Nov. 1988.
44. Kevin Logan, *Satanism and the Occult* (Kingsway, 1994).
45. *Ibid.*
46. US Justice Department; Allen Hueston, *Teenage Suicide: An Overview*.
47. Roger Boyes, 'German youths murdered boy in satanic ritual', *The Times*, 12th Jan. 1994; 'Satanists jailed', *Daily Telegraph*, 10th Feb. 1994.
48. Reuters, 28th Oct. 1987.
49. Guido Horst, 'The occult triumphs in the schools', *Der Spiegel*, 1st Jan. 1989.
50. *Ibid.*
51. *File 18 Newsletter*, Feb. 1990.
52. 'Outcry over Satan killings', *The European*, 7th–9th Dec. 1990.
53. *Jerusalem Post*, 8th July 1995.
54. *The Independent*, 30th Jul. 1992.

55. Tim Tate, *Children for the Devil* (Methuen, 1991), pp. 110f.
56. *The People*, 19th Jun. 1988.
57. Logan, *op. cit.*

Chapter 8: The sorcerer's apprentice
1. Vivienne Crowley, *Wicca, the Old Religion in the New Age*, pp. 150f.
2. David Burnett, *The Dawning of the Pagan Moon* (MARC, 1991), p. 199.
3. 30th Oct. 1987.
4. 20th Mar. 1989.
5. 31st Oct. 1990.
6. Richard Cavendish, *A History of Magic* (Arkana, 1990), p. 158.
7. *Newsline* (Sky TV), 31st Oct. 1990.
8. Cavendish, *op. cit.*, p. 118.
9. 'Witchcraft in Lancashire', *Prophecy Today*, vol. 3, no. 5.
10. Kevin Logan, *Paganism and the Occult* (Kingsway, 1988).
11. Burnett, *op. cit.*, p. 77.
12. Doreen Valiente, *An ABC of Witchcraft* (Robert Hale, 1972), p. xv.
13. Wade Baskin, *Satanism* (Citadel Press, 1972), p. 156.
14. Charles Godfrey Leland, *Aradia: The Gospel of the Witches*, cited in Valiente, *op. cit.*, p. 34. On p. 223 Valiente describes Leland as a practitioner of magic and witchcraft.
15. Carl Jung, *Four Archetypes* (Princeton University Press, 1969), cited in Winkie Pratney, *Devil Take the Youngest* (Huntingdon House, 1985).
16. Margaret Murray, *The Witch Cult in Western Europe* (Oxford University Press, 1921), p. 28, cited in Burnett, *op. cit.*, p. 102.
17. *The Sorceror's Handbook* (Crown, 1974), p. 361.
18. Burnett, *op. cit.*, p. 48.
19. Baskin, *op. cit.*, pp. 76–77.
20. *Paths of Magic*, quoted in Logan, *op. cit.*, p. 69.
21. *Kilroy*, 20th May 1988.
22. Anton LaVey, *The Satanic Bible* (Avon Books, 1969).
23. Felix Unger, *Demons in the World Today* (Tyndale, 1982), pp. 76f., cited in Daniel Grothaus, *Magic and Spells*. Grothaus is the founding direction of the Cult Crime Impact Network.
24. Samuel Weisner, *Real Magic* (1989), p. 116, cited in Burnett, *op. cit.*, p. 144.
25. Logan, *op. cit.*
26. Kathryn Paulsen, *The Complete Book of Magic and Witchcraft* (Signet, 1970), p. xi, cited in Daniel Grothaus, *op. cit.*
27. *Devil Worship: The rise of satanism* (Jeremiah Films).
28. *Newsline* (Sky TV), 15th Oct. 1990.
29. Val Simpson, 'Wicca's world', *The Guardian*, 1990.
30. *Winning with Witchcraft*, advertised in the widely read *Foulsham's Almanack*.
31. Stewart Farrar, *Evening Telegraph*, 21st Aug. 1993.
32. Mendez Castle of the Process Church of the Final Judgment (a British satanic cult), cited in Arthur Lyons, *Satan wants You* (Mysterious Press, 1988).
33. Russ Parker, *The Occult* (IVP, 1989), p. 17.
34. Peter Haining, *The Anatomy of Witchcraft* (Souvenir Press, 1972), cited in Tim Tate, *Children for the Devil* (Methuen, 1991), p. 137.

35. Baskin, *op. cit.*, p. 295.
36. *Ibid.*, p. 170.
37. Pat Pulling, *The Devil's Web* (Huntingdon House, 1989), p. 154.
38. *Ibid.*, p. 154.
39. *The Daily Mirror*, 2nd Dec. 1988; *The Sunday Sun*, 4th Dec. 1988.
40. For more details about the Order of the Nine Angles and *Fenrir*, see Logan, *op. cit.*, and Andrew Boyd, *Blasphemous Rumours* (HarperCollins, 1991), pp. 192f.
41. *Devil Worship: The Rise of Satanism* (Jeremiah Films).
42. Anton LaVey, *The Satanic Bible* (Avon Books, 1969), pp. 30–31.
43. *Devil Worship: The Rise of Satanism* (Jeremiah Films).
44. *Ibid.*
45. *Ibid.*
46. Paul Valentine (founder of the Church of Satanic Liberation), *Witchcraft and Satanism*, vol. 2 (Starlog Video & O'Quinn Productions, 1986).
47. Anton LaVey, *The Satanic Bible* (Avon Books, 1969), p. 94.
48. *Ibid.*, pp. 52, 57.
49. Soror H., on the beliefs of the Process Church of the Final Judgement (a British satanic cult), *Lamp of Thoth* magazine.

Chapter 9: Pied pipers

1. 'Some thoughts on preventing persecution of pagans', *The Pipes of Pan*, no. 3, 1988, p. 10.
2. Vol. 1, no. 1, 1984, p. 19.
3. *The Star*, 3rd Jun. 1988.
4. Bill & Sharon Shnoebelen, *We Were Witches*.
5. BBC, 20th Nov. 1987.
6. *Channel 4 News*.
7. *The Sunday Telegraph*, 20th Feb. 1994.
8. *The Sunday Mail*, 10th Jun. 1990.
9. *Central Weekend Television*, 13th May 1988.
10. Helen Sewell, *The Witch Report*.
11. *The Independent*, 20th Mar. 1989.
12. *Kilroy*, 20th May 1988.
13. From archive footage, *Channel 4 News*, Hallowe'en 1990.
14. *Devil Worship: The Rise of Satanism* (Jeremiah Films).
15. Laurie Mansbridge, 'Satanism', *Bella* magazine.
16. Felix Unger, *Demons in the World Today* (Tyndale, 1982), p. 77, cited in Daniel Grothaus, *Magic and Spells*. Grothaus is the founding direction of the Cult Crime Impact Network.
17. Mansbridge, *op. cit.*
18. HarperCollins, 1991.
19. *Idea*, Apr.–May 1995.
20. *The Daily Telegraph*, 17th May 1995.
21. Tim Tate, *Children for the Devil* (Methuen, 1991), p. 28.
22. *Ritualistic Abuse – Implications for Practice* (NSPCC, 16th Jun. 1989).
23. Report on the Helpline (Broadcasting Support Services).
24. Pp. 94f.
25. P. 96.

26. Tate, *op. cit.*, p. 99.
27. Richard Cavendish, *A History of Magic* (Arkana, 1990), p. 159. The Crowley quotation is from Francis King, *Encyclopaedia of the Unexplained*, p. 276.
28. Cavendish, *op. cit.*, p. 159.
29. Interviewed for *Dispatches* (Channel 4), 14th Feb. 1992.
30. *The Times*, 8th & 30th Jun. 1993.
31. Kevin Logan, *Satanism and the Occult* (Kingsway, 1994).
32. Anne, from *File 18 Newsletter*, vol. 5, no. 90–92, Apr. 1990.
33. *The Guardian* and *The Times*, 18th Jun. 1994.
34. See also Logan, *op. cit.*
35. Avon Books, 1993.

Chapter 10: Fade to black

1. Bob & Gretchen Passantino, *When the Devil Dares Your Kids* (Eagle, 1991), p. 12.
2. Tommy Sullivan, Jefferson Township, New Jersey.
3. Tom Strong, 'Satanism linked to son killing mother and himself', *The Detroit News*, 13th Jan. 1988, cited in Passantino & Passantino, *op. cit.*, p. 34.
4. Ed Kiersh, *Book of Shadows*.
5. Carlson & Larue, *Satanism in America* (Gaia, 1989).
6. *The Daily Mail*, 13th Mar. 1990.
7. *Satanism in America* (National Criminal Justice Task Force). Texas report endorsed by two chiefs of police, five sheriffs, a chief deputy, a chief investigator, two probation officers and a detective.
8. 'Dancing with the Devil', *TVF* (Channel 4, 1991).
9. Pat Pulling, *The Devil's Web* (Huntingdon House, 1989).
10. Trish Heimer, Vice President, Record Industry of America Association, quoted in 'Dancing with the Devil', *TVF* (Channel 4, 1991).
11. Arthury Lyons, *Satan Wants you* (Mysterious Press, 1988), p. 171, cited in Passantino & Passantino, *op. cit.*, p. 155.
12. Quoted in *20/20* magazine, Feb. 1990.
13. Bob & Gretchen Passantino, *op. cit.*, p. 119.
14. 'Dancing with the Devil', *TVF* (Channel 4, 1991).
15. *Devil Worship: The Rise of Satanism* (Jeremiah Films).
16. 'Crisis in Valhalla', *The Independent*, 9th Jun. 1994.
17. Kevin Logan, *Satanism and the Occult* (Kingsway, 1994).
18. 'To unleash the beast in man', *Werewolf Order*, no. 7, Spring 1990.
19. *20/20* magazine, Feb. 1990.
20. *The People*, 24th Jul. 1988.
21. *20/20* magazine, Feb. 1990.
22. *The Press Enterprise*, California, 7th May 1986.
23. *Journal of the Tennessee Medical Association*, vol. 78, no. 12, Dec. 1985.
24. Pulling, *op. cit.*
25. *Rising to the Challenge* (PMRC).
26. Pulling, *op. cit.*, p. 116.
27. *Cult Awareness News*, Apr. 1989.
28. *Journal of the Tennessee Medical Association*.
29. *Old Tappan*, New Jersey (Fleming H. Revell Co., 1990), cited in Bob &

Gretchen Passantino, *op. cit.*, p. 107.
30. 'Dancing with the Devil', *TVF* (Channel 4, 1991).

Chapter 11: Dangerous obsessions
1. Susan Page, 'Role Playing', *The State Journal*, quoted by the National Coalition on Television Violence, Jan. 1985.
2. *Dungeon Master's Guide*, a basic rule book, p. 31.
3. *Dungeons and Dragons Handbook*, p. 7.
4. Quoted in Pat Pulling, *The Devil's Web* (Huntingdon House, 1989).
5. *Satanism in America* (National Criminal Justice Task Force on Occult Related Ritualistic Crime, USA), p. 16.
6. 'Brink of death priest tells', *The Sunday Mail*, 19th May 1985.
7. Quoted in Peter Anderson, *Satan's Snare* (Evangelical Press, 1988).
8. *The State Journal*.
9. The parents of Michael, aged 16, who shot himself in the head. National Coalition on Television Violence, Jan. 1985.
10. *Witchcraft or Satanism???* (BADD).
11. 'Deadly role for deserter who believed he had evil power', Michael Fleet, *The Daily Telegraph*, 19th May 1993.
12. *The Observer*, 14th Aug. 1994.
13. *The Odessa American*, 29th Sep. 1985.
14. Pulling, *op. cit.*, p. 88.
15. *A Law Enforcement Primer on Fantasy Role Playing Games* (BADD).
16. From BADD's files.
17. *The Philadelphia Inquirer*, 9th Jun. 1988.
18. *The Odessa American*, 29th Sep. 1985.
19. Both quotations from the National Coalition on Television Violence, 17th Jan. 1985.
20. 18th May 1987.
21. Apr. 1987.

Chapter 12: Images of death
1. *Daily Mail*, 25th Nov. 1993.
2. *Ibid.*
3. *The Sunday Times*, 28th Nov. 1993.
4. *The Daily Mirror*, 18th Dec. 1993.
5. *Ibid.*
6. *The Observer*, 28th Nov. 1993.
7. *Ibid.*
8. *The Sunday Times*, 28th Nov. 1993.
9. Kevin Logan, *Satanism and the Occult* (Kingsway, 1994), p. 22.
10. *Mail on Sunday*, 30th Aug. 1987.
11. *The Daily Mirror*, 1st May 1990.
12. *The Daily Mail*, 2nd May 1989.
13. Leader column, 2nd May 1989.
14. *The Daily Mail*, 25th Jun. 1988.
15. Tom Davies, *The Man of Lawlessness* (Hodder & Stoughton, 1989), p. 79.
16. *Ibid.*, p. 81.
17. *Today*, 23rd Mar. 1989.

18. *File 18 Newsletter*, Feb. 1990.
19. Battle Cry Publications, Jun. 1984.
20. *The Examiner*, 19th Jun. 1984.
21. *Journal of the American Medical Association*, Mar. 1985. *Time* magazine four years later put that figure far higher, at 200,000 acts of violence.
22. Liebert & Sprafkin, *The Early Window* (Pergamon, 1988), pp. 6, 17.
23. *Cultural Trends*, 1994.
24. *Christian Broadcasting News*, Winter 1994.
25. *The Guardian*, 4th Jan. 1994.
26. *The Daily Telegraph*, 5th Oct. 1994.
27. Liebert & Sprafkin, *op. cit.*, p. 135.
28. *Newsweek*, 13th Dec. 1993.
29. Cited in 'Keyboard junkies', *The Independent on Sunday*, 17th Nov. 1991.
30. *The Complete A–Z of Super NES Games* (Paragon, 1993).
31. *The Daily Telegraph*, 10th Feb. 1994.

Chapter 13: To parents and teachers . . .
1. *Cult Awareness News*, Kansas City, Missouri, Apr. 1989.
2. Peter Wilson, director of Young Minds, a child psychotherapy charity, cited in Melanie Phillips, 'How we make demons', *The Observer*, 28th Nov. 1993.
3. *Ibid.*
4. 'Lucifer Over Lancashire', *Open Space* (BBC, 3rd Mar. 1987).
5. Bob & Gretchen Passantino, *When the Devil Dares Your Kids* (Eagle, 1991), p. 17.
6. Geraldo Rivera Special. Sellers murdered his mother, his stepfather and a shop assistant.
7. Adapted from the Dundee Ritual Abuse Conference, 22nd Sep. 1989; *Satanism in America* (National Criminal Justice Task Force); *Satanism: A Ritual of Deception* (PsycHealth Institute).
8. Bob & Gretchen Passantino, *op. cit.*, p. 163.
9. *Mind Control* (Cult Awareness Network, Chicago).
10. *Satanism in America* (National Criminal Justice Task Force). This report was chaired by Joe Evans, a Texas sheriff.
11. *Idea*, Apr.–May 1995.
12. *Doorways to Danger* video (Evangelical Alliance).
13. *The Eagle Forum*, Colorado, vol. 10, no. 3.
14. Geraldo Rivera Special.
15. *Ibid.*
16. *Satanism: A Ritual of Deception* (PsycHealth Institute).
17. Adapted from *Danger, Children at Play* (Evangelical Alliance).
18. Kenneth McAll, *Healing the Family Tree* (Sheldon Press, 1990).
19. *Ibid.*, p. 71.
20. Rev. David Carr on *Central Weekend Television*, 13th May 1988.
21. Pat Pulling, *The Devil's Web* (Huntingdon House, 1989), p. 136.

Chapter 14: Breaking out
1. Adapted from Audrey Harper, *Deliverance Means Love* (Kingsway, 1992).
2. *Ibid.*, pp. 170, 174.